'"Transformation" is a word that is often ̣ ̣ ̣ ̣ ̣ ̣ ̣ ̣ ̣ about and has consequently lost much of its power. But if you really do want to properly, unflashily and authentically transform Adult Social Care then start here, with Bryony.'

– Phil Holmes, Vice President of the Association of Directors of Adult Social Services

'"Us, not us and them." Bryony captures the central problem that no amount of system or 'strength-based' change will solve. Our language underpins the othering we practice – Bryony shows us how to face this.'

– Martin Routledge, Convenor Social Care Future

'Bryony's book is just what everyone in the social care space needs right now; a brilliant, must read about how we reframe the narrative from one of "them and us" to a humanised one of "all of us".'

– Elly Chapple, BA HRM and Psychology of Human Communication, Founder #FlipTheNarrative

'This is a truly outstanding book by an author who over recent years has become wholly integral to the development of rights-based practice with adults, recognising that the language we use is evidence of the values that we take into every situation. Whether it's dispelling labels or advocating love, understanding the power of language, and using that towards the advancement of better social care ensures that this book is a vital companion to all those interested in social care.'

– Rob Mitchell MBE, Principal Social Worker

'Labels stick! Bryony's book is a brilliant exploration of the power of words and of the importance of gloriously ordinary language.'

– Tricia Nicoll, Founder of Gloriously Ordinary Lives

Rewriting Social Care

of related interest

Social Work, Cats and Rocket Science
Stories of Making a Difference in Social Work with Adults
Elaine James, Rob Mitchell and Hannah Morgan,
with Mark Harvey and Ian Burgess
Forewords by Lyn Romeo and Mark Neary
ISBN 978 1 78592 519 1
eISBN 978 1 78450 985 9

The Social Work, Cats and Rocket Science
Guide to Rights-Based Practice
An A–Z, from Advocacy to Zones of Influence
Edited by Elaine James and Rob Mitchell
Forewords by Sara Ryan and School of Rock and Media
ISBN 978 1 80501 231 3
eISBN 978 1 80501 232 0

Love, Learning Disabilities and Pockets of Brilliance
How Practitioners Can Make a Difference to the
Lives of Children, Families and Adults
Sara Ryan
Forewords by Michael Edwards and by Rob Mitchell and Elaine James
ISBN 978 1 78775 191 0
eISBN 978 1 78775 192 7

(Re)writing SOCIAL CARE

Challenging and Changing Practice and Language for a Better, Brighter Future

Bryony Shannon

Jessica Kingsley Publishers
London and Philadelphia

First published in Great Britain in 2025 by Jessica Kingsley Publishers
An imprint of John Murray Press

1

Copyright © Bryony Shannon 2025

The right of Bryony Shannon to be identified as the Author of the Work has been
asserted by them in accordance with the Copyright, Designs and Patents Act 1988.

A CIP catalogue record for this title is available from the
British Library and the Library of Congress

ISBN 978 1 80501 177 4
eISBN 978 1 80501 178 1

Printed and bound by CPI Group (UK) Ltd, Croydon, CR0 4YY

Jessica Kingsley Publishers' policy is to use papers that are natural,
renewable and recyclable products and made from wood grown in
sustainable forests. The logging and manufacturing processes are expected
to conform to the environmental regulations of the country of origin.

Jessica Kingsley Publishers
Carmelite House
50 Victoria Embankment
London EC4Y 0DZ

www.jkp.com

John Murray Press
Part of Hodder & Stoughton Ltd
An Hachette Company

The authorised representative in the EEA is Hachette Ireland, 8
Castlecourt Centre, Dublin 15, D15 XTP3, Ireland (email: info@hbgi.ie)

Contents

Part Three: Changing Our Practice:
From Transactions to Relationships

Part Four: Changing Our Story:
From What's Wrong, to What's Strong

Preface

I've always written to make sense of my world. A daily diary for almost 15 years from the age of seven. Notes between friends at school (pre mobile phones and social media) analysing the complexities of teenage life. Letters home from travels around Australia in a pre-university gap year. Endless to-do lists.

When I got a job as an information and communications officer in a local authority adult social care department, I started writing to make sense of adult social care. Summarizing statutory guidance, policy documents, research reports, and news stories to produce a monthly 'Developments in Adult Social Care' bulletin. Drafting and editing procedures, guides, newsletters, web pages, factsheets, and 'standard letters'.

When I got that job back in 2006, much of my writing involved trying first to make sense of the complexity, jargon, and acronyms of social care myself, then presenting information in a concise and accessible form to support other people to understand it too.

Over the years though, I became increasingly uncomfortable with many of the words and phrases I was reading, hearing, and indeed using myself to describe the purpose and practice of adult social care, and to communicate with and about people. Uneasy with the story this language was telling, and the attitudes and behaviour it reflected and reinforced. Frustrated with the picture being painted, and the decisions made as a result.

I started my 'Rewriting social care' blog in 2019 to understand more about this narrative. After years of trying to clarify and explain social care in plain language, I wanted to explore why so many words and phrases make me go, hmmm... I wanted to reflect on what the language we use reveals and perpetuates, and explore how we can shift the narrative to tell a very different story.

Little did I realize how compelling this would be. How much I'd learn, and expose, through studying the language that's so ingrained and influential in public attitudes, political debate, press coverage, and practice – and by highlighting the missing words.

I also didn't anticipate how many amazing people I'd meet and connections I'd make as a result of my writing.

So, to the people who encouraged me to write my blog in the first place, thank you.

To everyone who has read my words, liked, commented on, and shared my social media posts, and contacted me to talk more, thank you.

And to the people who continue to inspire and influence me with your own writing and your own stories, thank you.

I hope my words help to shift the narrative and play a little part in creating a more human, humane future for us all.

Introduction:
Why Language Matters

'Language is the most powerful tool we have. Let's use it well.'
(SURVIVING SAFEGUARDING, 2018)

Can you think of a time when you've felt labelled? Or put in a category you didn't feel part of, or felt ashamed to be included in?

Or when you've felt unfairly blamed?

Or you've read or heard something you really didn't understand? How did, or does, it make you feel?

I've asked a few groups of social workers around the country these questions.

Here are some of the words they used to describe how being labelled, blamed, or excluded made them feel.

Angry. Frustrated. Disempowered. Dehumanized. Stupid. Sad.
A number. Upset. Not valued. Worthless. Judged. Lonely. Embarrassed
Helpless. Ashamed. Alone. Traumatized. Powerless. Unheard. Unloved.
Not wanting to be me.

Social work, and social care more generally, *should* be about dignity and respect. Identity and inclusion. Valuing people and flourishing lives. But when we don't pay attention to the language we use with and about people, our words can so easily harm rather than heal.

The way we communicate directly with people matters, and the way we communicate about people, and about our purpose and practice matters too. The words and phrases we use within, and about, social care are powerful. They paint pictures in our minds. These images, and the ideas they generate and reinforce, influence the way we all think, feel, and behave. They reflect, and shape, our view of ourselves, each other, and the way we work together. Speak volumes about the past and affect all our futures. But I genuinely believe that because the language of social care is so deeply entrenched, we don't think enough about the true meaning or impact of the words we use, the story they tell, and the future they shape.

This is a book about language. About how the words we hear, read, and choose to use expose and perpetuate attitudes and behaviours. About words that are too dominant, and words that should dominate.

It's also a book about change. Changing how we communicate with and about people. Changing how we understand and articulate the purpose of social care. Changing how we practice. And ultimately changing the story of social care.

And mainly it's a book about being human. About recognizing each other as equal, valued human beings, and about creating a more human, humane future for us all.

Part One focuses on the language we use about people, and about people's relationship with social care, illustrating what the labels we attach represent and how we must move from thinking of 'them and us' to 'all of us'.

Part Two explores how we define the purpose of social care, and ways to refocus our 'why' from 'getting a service' to living gloriously ordinary lives.

I firmly believe we must change our language to change our practice, and we must change our practice to change our language. So, in Part Three I'll consider what our language reveals about our practice and how both need to change to shift from a transactional to a relational approach.

And in the final part, I'll explore the dominant story of social care and illustrate how important it is to tell a different story if we want to achieve lasting change.

(Please note that some quotations used in this book are not attributed to a specific person or organization. They are still direct quotes – either heard or found online – and are included to illustrate a point, rather than to be attributed to a particular source.)

But I want to start where I began my blog, by summarizing why I think language matters.

Sticks and stones

Reading my SW files a few years ago and seeing me described as manipulative by a teacher I'd trusted shattered me. That teacher has since passed (while I was still at the school) and I'd grieved her for years. Was tough to take and people think it's just words. It's not. I was 14.

(CARELEAVER123, 2022)

'Sticks and stones may break my bones, but words can never hurt me.' So the old saying goes. In reality though, the damage done by careless use of language can last much longer than the time it takes a broken bone to heal. Too often our language shows an absence of kindness, and, even worse, a lack of interest in what really matters, and what will really help.

Wendy Mitchell wrote and spoke many times about the impact of people's language on her: how when her doctor delivered her diagnosis of dementia when she was 58 years old, he said, 'There's nothing we can do'. How the first question her manager asked when Wendy shared her diagnosis was, 'How long have you got?' How 'if someone tells you day after day that you're a "sufferer", you end up believing it'. She emphasized how language can make or break someone and suggested that 'language is the cheapest thing to change' (Mitchell, W., 2018; Mitchell, W., n.d.).

The words we use, and the way that we use them, can change lives. This can be for the better, when used with empathy and compassion, but too often for the worse, as we wield words like weapons, and inflict lasting pain.

The very same language we adopt as part of our professional identity, and to feel included, so often denies other people their own identity. And our jargon and acronyms so easily exclude. We refer to CHC, CQC, DoLS, ICBs, MCA, MSP, NRPF. We attend DST, MDT, MARAC, MAPPA, and VARM meetings. We work with AMHPs, ASYEs, OTs, and PSWs, in teams with acronyms as names.

Our language should heal, not harm.

Build bridges, not walls.

Them and us

This labelling and classification of people remains a constant drag that means we never get beyond consideration of 'them' and 'us'.

(RYAN, S., 2021)

As well as the direct impact words can have on all of us, language also influences the way we think about, and behave towards, each other. Throughout history, words have been used to deliberately divide and dehumanize. Eugenicists in the late 19th and early 20th century described disabled people as 'feeble minded' and 'social rubbish', while the Nazi regime labelled disabled people as 'useless eaters' and 'lives unworthy of life' – narratives used to justify horrific atrocities. And more recently, dissent and violence have undoubtedly been fuelled through the calculated framing of people migrating to the UK. 'Illegal.' 'Marauders.' 'An invasion on our southern coast.'

When we pay attention to the terms we use to communicate about people, we expose the attitudes and assumptions that shape our practice.

Indeed, we don't talk much about people. We talk of 'customers', 'service users', 'clients', 'patients'.

'Those.'

Often, we don't identify people as human beings at all. They are 'cases'. 'Referrals.' Reference numbers from our 'case management' systems.

Terms like 'deficient', 'deviant', 'disorder', and 'divergent' imply that some people are different from what is expected, from what is 'normal'. They overlook how we are *all* different, and ignore how alike we all are.

Labels like 'vulnerable' frame people as weak and needy, while references to 'demand', 'burden', and 'respite' imply that people are an inconvenience, are getting in the way.

And we use strange jargon to talk about where these 'other' people live, their friends and family, what 'they' do.

This different, distant group don't move house or live in homes like we do. They are 'placed in' 'settings', 'schemes', 'accommodation', 'units', 'beds'.

They don't have a wash, brush their teeth, and get dressed like us. They have 'personal care'. They are 'fed' and 'toileted'.

We have family and friends, lovers, soulmates. They have 'carers', 'peers', 'nearest relatives', 'next of kin'.

We go to work, meet friends, exercise, go shopping. They 'access employment', 'maintain relationships', 'access the community', and 'engage in meaningful activities'.

We fall over. They 'have a fall'.

We get cross, angry, upset. They 'display challenging behaviour'.

We have vague plans, and things we might get round to doing one day. They have 'outcomes' to achieve.

We wouldn't use this language in our kitchen with our family, or at the cafe or pub with our mates (Nicoll, 2024). If social care is all about people living gloriously ordinary lives, why do we use language that suggests little is ordinary, never mind glorious?

This language influences our perception of people and exposes the assumptions that drive our practice.

We frame people as passive recipients of 'care', 'service users', 'the cared for', 'those with care and support needs'. There's no sense of reciprocity in this narrative, of people's gifts and potential, the need to be needed, the right to choice and control. As such, people are seen, treated, and expected to behave as 'people who need help', not active citizens with experience, skills, ideas, and knowledge to contribute. With rights to be upheld.

As well as implying superiority, our language suggests ownership: 'our customers', 'my cases'.

All this framing helps to define our roles and justify our paternalistic approach: 'professional', 'assessor', 'care manager', 'case coordinator', 'carer'.

'Looking after.' 'Protecting.' 'Caring for.'

In addition to labelling people, we label how people behave – particularly when people don't act how we believe they should. We use phrases like 'difficult', 'challenging', 'refuses to engage', 'non-compliant', 'hard to reach' all too readily. This language implies the person is the problem. It overlooks what's happened to them, what's happening around them, what they are communicating, and why. It justifies the use of medication, restrictions, restraint. And it blames people instead of acknowledging our own influence and impact. Our failure to listen to what really matters to people. To fully involve people in conversations and decisions about their lives. To use language people understand.

Our failure to understand people.

Maybe it's us who are refusing to engage? Maybe it's our behaviour that challenges? Maybe we're the ones who are the hardest to reach? Maybe that's deliberate?

We refer to 'the frontline', 'duty', 'officers'. The language of battles. Us versus them. Words that imply we're on opposing sides. Often it feels as if we are.

All these words and phrases erase personhood and identity. They create distance, imply difference. Not like 'us'. Not so important. Not so human. Not so visible.

And once you're not so visible, your life becomes that bit less valued. And once you're seen as less valuable, you become a whole lot more vulnerable.

Once you're written out of the story, you're effectively written off.

People were 'patients' or sometimes 'service users'. This language protected me from the reality of what I was doing to people caught in the system... I learnt that dehumanizing people through my use of the language of the professional made it easier for me to cope. (James, Mitchell, & Morgan, 2019)

Easier to cope. Easier to ignore.

The social care sorting office

When we pay attention to language, we notice what it exposes. If we look at the words we use about our practice, they reveal the way our system is set up to continuously move people around.

Our sorting office approach.

Despite endless references to how 'person-centred' we are, our language reveals how processes are at the centre of our practice, not people.

'Cases' 'transition' to adult social care from children's services. We 'screen', 'triage', 'signpost', 'allocate', and 'refer'. We 'discharge to assess'. We determine 'pathways' and 'journeys', which often result in a 'placement' or a 'transfer of care'.

We've industrialized 'care' and automated our processes, labelling and processing people like parcels in a sorting office. And as such, we've removed all traces of humanity to such an extent that we think it's okay to refer to people as numbers and cases. Indeed, our sorting office approach relies on us maintaining distance. Real lives are complicated and messy – tangled webs of aspirations, expectations, memories, dreams, hopes, fears, opportunities, barriers. Real lives don't fit into our neat categories – especially not good lives. If we focus only on problems and attach the corresponding labels, it's so much easier to fit people into the boxes on our forms, channel them down our one-size-fits-all, linear conveyor belts, and apply our standard service solutions.

It's much quicker to apply quick-fix solutions than to really explore what a good life looks like to someone and how we can work with them to achieve it. 'Personal care needs' are quickly met with the purchase of a standard 'four calls a day', but you can't buy friendships, hobbies, jobs, love. All those things that enhance our lives rather than just maintain our existence – all those things that make us unique, make us who we are – don't come in off-the-shelf packages. But if we don't recognize people as unique human beings we don't need to think about their lives. And if we dehumanize people enough – if we forget they are mums, dads, daughters, sons, sisters, brothers, friends, us – we don't even feel uncomfortable imposing solutions we'd never want for our own family or friends.

For ourselves.

Smoke and mirrors

I've been constantly fascinated by the ability of social care to reinvent its language but never its values.

(NEARY, 2018)

Language evolves. The *Oxford English Dictionary* publishes four updates a year, with new words and phrases added and definitions revised. The language of social care evolves too. We talk of 'personalization', 'co-pro-duction', 'strengths-based approaches', and 'asset-based community development'. But all too often, while we've introduced different termi-nology, we haven't changed our behaviours or our bureaucracies at all.

A new vocabulary imposed from above without an associated shift in power and practice can be misinterpreted internally and greeted with suspicion externally – particularly if the new language is seen as a thinly veiled attempt to divert people from our doors and relinquish our responsibilities. And indeed, many of our 'buzz words' are code for exactly that: 'prevention', 'independent', 'community'.

Missing words

The language we use in and about social care matters.
The words we don't use enough matter too.
Love. Home. Belonging. Joy. Hope. Rights. Trust. Sorry.
People.
We.
Us.
The absence of these words in relation to people's lives and our practice reveals just as much as the words that dominate.

* * *

We can continue to produce glossaries, jargon busters, factsheets, and guides to demystify our jargon and translate our processes into 'plain language'. We can employ 'navigators' and advocates to help people understand the complexities of social care and negotiate their way through. But in doing so, we're just perpetuating the system.

We *can* make some simple switches to the way we talk. Replace 'those' with 'people'. Refer to 'working with people', not 'dealing with cases'. Say 'support' instead of 'care' or 'services'. Use 'chose not to' instead of 'refused'. Ask 'why?' instead of using words that blame.

Little changes can make a big difference. These subtle shifts in language can help us refocus and rehumanize our practice.

But.

We'll have to keep referring to people as numbers, referrals, beds, 'Mum' if we keep forgetting to ask their names. If we continue to pass people round like parcels, we might as well call them cases. We can't talk of connection when we're still signposting people away. We can't focus on what matters and what's strong, when we start with 'What's the matter?' and 'What's wrong?' We can't refer to people's homes if where they live feels like a 'setting' or a 'placement', not somewhere they belong.

Language matters, and I think words are just as important as actions, but we also need action – not just alternative words.

We need to dismantle our social care sorting office with its associated barriers, assumptions, battlegrounds, and quick-fix solutions, and return our focus to people, not processes. Lives, not services. Us, not them and us.

We need to stop assuming the role of the expert in people's lives, and reclaim our role as experts in listening, making connections, upholding human rights, and building lasting relationships.

We need to welcome people rather than pushing them away. Trust our instincts, our judgement, and the people we're working with. Make decisions with people, not for them, and focus on capabilities and possibilities rather than problems and risks.

We need to change our practice as well as our language.

We need to rewrite social care.

* * *

Why do we still use this language?

As well as reflecting on why language matters, it's also important to consider why we continue to use this vocabulary.

Why we still think it's okay.

So, here are ten reasons I believe lie behind our use of this 'professional' language.

Reasons – not excuses.

There is no excuse.

It's everywhere

Dehumanizing, stigmatizing, and othering language is everywhere in social work and social care. It forms the content of our job descriptions and job adverts ('You will be required to work with complex cases', 'You will be working with vulnerable service users') and the structure of our departments ('Complex Needs Team', 'Challenging Behaviour Unit').

It's written into policies, procedures, and practice guidance ('Death of a service user policy', 'Working with uncooperative and hard to engage families').

It's built into our 'case management systems' – including in that term itself.

It's embedded in the national data collections and statutory reporting requirements ('Client level data', 'Cohorts of service users').

It features in media coverage of social care ('Care for UK's most vulnerable faces "collapse"') and in government press releases ('NHS to expand services to keep vulnerable out of hospital').

The ubiquity of this language offers some legitimacy to its use.

When something is so prolific, so ingrained, we easily accept it without challenge.

Without thought.

We learn it

Social work degrees are advertised as 'allowing you to make a positive difference in vulnerable and disadvantaged people's lives' and 'helping you build the knowledge and skills to help shape the lives of vulnerable people'.

University departments 'work closely with service users when recruiting students' and 'collaborate with a wide range of service users' to develop course content.

Entry requirements include relevant social care experience, which could include 'personal experience as a service user'.

You'll prepare for the 'challenging role of a social worker' through simulations including 'engaging a service user'. Placements include 'working with people with complex needs'.

We teach this language.

We are taught these words.

We like it

This 'professional' language offers us an identity. Using these words demonstrates we're in the gang. We're genuine members of the profession. We belong.

It's affirming and validating, albeit at the expense of 'others', who definitely don't belong.

These words also offer us and our teams and organizations credibility. They give purpose to our roles.

'Protecting our most vulnerable.' 'Caring for the elderly.' 'Supporting the disabled.' 'Looking after those with learning disabilities.' 'Safeguarding vulnerable groups.' 'Keeping those with dementia safe and sound.' 'Helping the frail out of hospital.' 'Maintaining the disabled, elderly, and those otherwise in need of care within the community.'

Protecting. Looking after. Caring for. Safeguarding. Assisting weak, helpless 'others'.

That's our job. Isn't it?

Using this language demonstrates our expertise. But this notion that we're the experts doesn't sit well in a relational approach, where lived experience should be valued just as highly as learned experience. Where people are recognized as the experts in their own lives. Where listening, curiosity, being alongside, and learning together are key. Where it's often much better to say, 'I don't know – let's find out together' than 'I know, I'll tell you what you need to do'.

It's efficient

Our social care sorting offices prioritize efficiency over empathy and efficacy. We count how many, how much, how long. We work in 'fast-paced', 'busy' teams. We have targets for the number of 'assessments' or 'reviews' completed in a week. Support is 'commissioned' and 'delivered' with just enough time for 'tasks', not conversations and compassion.

And when we have deadlines and targets to meet, it's quicker to make assumptions and to categorize than it is to ask, how are you? What would you like to talk about today? What's important to you right now?

It's quicker to use acronyms, labels, and reliable stock phrases on our forms.

Labelling people means we can process them more quickly through our system, and slot them more easily into our standard service solutions.

It's also quicker to say 'my cases' than 'the people I'm working with'. 'Customers' rather than 'the people we serve' 'Our service users' rather than 'the people we support'. 'Chair 7' rather than 'the person sitting in chair 7'; 'Mum' rather than asking and remembering people's names.

And anyway, you know who I mean when I refer to 'the vulnerable', don't you?

You know.

Them.

Those.

Not us.

It's effective

We apply labels like 'vulnerable', 'complex', and 'high risk' to people to make sure they gain entry to our system, to demonstrate eligibility for services and support. These labels help us screen, 'RAG rate', prioritize, and triage. They help us justify decisions and costs to panels. Their inclusion in reports and funding bids helps us evidence 'demand', 'need', and the 'worthiness' of our proposals.

Without these labels, no one passes go.

While some terms open doors to support, we use those same terms – and others – to quickly slam doors shut. We label people as 'too vulnerable', 'too complex', 'too high risk' as a way of saying, 'go away; you can't come in'.

To shift responsibility elsewhere.

This language offers a sense of control. It ensures we can frame people's experiences, behaviour, and identity through our own lens. It helps us assert our power and authority over 'users', kept submissive by our approach.

Sometimes we feel powerless within 'the system'.

We feel as if we're drowning.

These familiar words help anchor us.

Keep us safe.

It justifies our actions

This language is deployed to legitimize. During the Covid-19 pandemic, decisions were made to 'protect our most vulnerable'. And more recently, councils declaring or facing bankruptcy have noted that all new spending will cease, except for 'protecting vulnerable people', 'looking after vulnerable residents', 'safeguarding the most vulnerable'. This is validating actions while simultaneously blaming precarious budget situations on 'the increased complexity of vulnerable adults, children, and families needing support', 'an ageing population', and 'growing demand for core services like social care for vulnerable children and adults'.

Dehumanizing people helps reduce empathy. Seeing 'cases' rather than people makes it easier to do to and for, not with. To assess. Judge. Place. Exclude.

This language helps us to defend our practice, systems, and institutions, to justify our prejudices and priorities.

The blaming labels we apply to people allow us to place the 'problem' firmly with them.

Nothing to do with us.

And classifying people's behaviour as 'challenging' or 'aggressive' makes it easier to gloss over the causes, and to rationalize restrictions and restraint.

Our dehumanizing language helps us justify actions that are inhumane.

But in removing the humanity from other people, we diminish our own humanity.

And excusing current practice by deflecting and defending means there's never any challenge.

Never any change.

It helps us cope

Distancing people by applying labels that remove their humanity can make it easier to cope. In the same way we turn off the news when everything feels overwhelmingly awful and hopeless, ensuring this element of separation is our survival mechanism. It shields us from the pain and trauma of people's lives. It protects us from acknowledging that their reality could just as easily be ours.

This detachment also means we don't have to show our own emotions or be vulnerable ourselves.

We're not challenged

Maybe we're not aware of the impact or implications of our words, or maybe we're using them with deliberate intent or disregard. Either way, our continued use of labels and jargon suggests we're spending time with people who aren't challenging our language.

Maybe we're comfortably surrounding ourselves with people who are using it too. Maybe the people we're communicating with and about are too daunted to question or object. Maybe we're just not working alongside the people who would call out this vocabulary in an instant if they were granted a seat at our table.

We don't challenge

It's not easy to admit we don't understand language people are using, especially when we feel everyone else 'gets' the jargon and acronyms that remain alien and meaningless to us. And it can be hard to question the language someone else is using, even if we feel it's damaging.

So sometimes it's less scary to stay quiet and not ask what certain words mean, or why certain phrases are used so casually and so callously.

Sometimes it's easier just to use them too.

Prejudice

Though we'll undoubtedly be reluctant to admit it, or even appalled at the thought, much of this language results from, and exposes, prejudice and ableist beliefs.

I've heard and read claims like, 'I don't like the term "service user" but I don't know what to use instead' so many times.

The fact we can't possibly consider substituting the word 'person' for service user/client/customer/patient/case, or use 'us' instead of 'them', speaks volumes about how distant and detached we've become.

Flipping the narrative

Systems built for humans are not necessarily humane systems. They can be disempowering and humiliating. They can overlook lives instead of witnessing them... While hope and healing lie in relationships, too often our human systems are cool, distant and transactional. Murmurs of apology can be heard everywhere, admissions that these are just the rules and roles and hopefully others can appreciate that. Systems like that are hard on those who seek help, and hard on those who deliver it.

(TULLOCH & SCHULMAN, 2020)

Principles of social justice, human rights, collective responsibility, and respect for diversities are central to social work. And yet so much of our language is oppressive, designed to exclude rather than include. Eroding rather than upholding people's rights and identity.

In a session facilitated by Tricia Nicoll at the Social Care Future gathering in October 2023, there was a conversation about flipping the idea of 'professional language', so it becomes 'professional' to use kind, respectful, and plain language, and unprofessional to use, or not to challenge, words that dehumanize, other, and blame. One of Tricia's tests for Gloriously Ordinary Lives is a test about language. She asks us to ask ourselves whether we would use this language in our kitchen with our family, or at the cafe or pub with our mates (Nicoll, 2024).

If the words we use with and about the people we support and serve aren't words we'd use with and about the people we love, they're probably words that get in the way of gloriously ordinary lives.

There's always a more human, humane word.

There's always a more human, humane word.

Correction (Mistakes are part of being human!)

The final line on this page should read:

There's always a more human, humane *world*.

PART ONE

CHANGING OUR MINDS

Us Not Them and Us

It isn't patient, or service user, or client or customer. It's people. That's the first thing to 'fix'.

(MITCHELL, R., 2021)

This part focuses on the language we use to communicate about people, and people's relationship with social care. It explains how our language exposes 'them and us' divisions; how the words and phrases that dominate our narrative distance and dehumanize, and how this helps to justify and perpetuate a paternalistic approach to practice.

And it explores a different language that flips this narrative from 'them and us' to all of us. Not new labels – we don't need more of those – but a shift from thinking about and describing people as 'vulnerable', 'special', 'needy', 'consumers', 'users', and 'cases' (them), to recognizing *everyone* as valuable, ordinary, needed citizens. People. Us.

On one level, these are basic choices about words to avoid. It literally is that simple.

And yet it's also so much more than that.

It's a total mindset shift to genuinely see *all* people as equal.

All people as human.

Human

Dehumanizing always starts with language.

(BROWN, 2017)

I talk and write a lot about seeing people as human beings, being human, and about how much of the way we currently work in the 'human services' is pretty inhumane. So, let's start by delving a little deeper to illustrate how our language dehumanizes people, and the absence of humanity in our 'systems'.

Human: A label we all share

As Elly Chapple rightly says, 'human' is 'a label we all share' (Chapple, 2024). And yet many of the other labels we so liberally apply imply that older people and disabled people are lesser human beings.

The Frameworks Institute suggest that 'when people believe that being human is tied to the existence of certain physical, mental, and affective abilities, anyone who lacks those abilities is seen as less human' (O'Shea *et al.*, 2023), and Mark Neary observes that 'language is the first step to turning people into non human objects' (Neary, 2018).

There's a long history of such language in relation to older and disabled people.

Less human

The inference of people being lesser, lacking, inferior, defective is pervasive and deep-rooted.

Terms like 'idiot', 'cripple', 'invalid', and 'imbecile' are centuries old. 'Handicapped' was first used in 1884. The Idiots Act became law in 1886, replaced in 1913 by The Mental Deficiency Act with its 'definition of defectives'. In the late 19th and early 20th century, disabled people were described by eugenicists as 'feeble minded' and 'social rubbish', and as 'useless eaters' and 'lives unworthy of life' by the Nazi regime.

Fast forward to today, and while our language may have changed, it still exposes the perception of older and disabled people as lesser humans.

Older people are labelled as 'frail', 'deteriorating', 'declining', 'infirm'.

People living with dementia are described as 'not all there', 'fading away', 'empty shells', 'dying again and again and again'.

Disabled people are viewed as 'less able', 'less healthy', 'physically challenged', 'suffering'.

The language of 'deficiency', 'disorder', 'divergence', 'difficulty' is rife in relation to learning disability and neurodiversity, along with sweeping generalizations that autistic people 'find communication and social interaction difficult', 'don't feel emotions', 'lack empathy'.

All these words and phrases suggest that older and disabled people lack the characteristics and abilities of 'normal', 'healthy' human beings.

Of being human.

Our everyday language is also peppered with ableist phrases like 'turning a blind eye', 'falling on deaf ears', 'having a senior moment', 'going insane', 'feeling paralysed', 'idiotic', 'dumb', 'senile', 'demented' – associating ageing and disability with problematic, negative behaviour.

We can talk all we like about diversity and inclusion, but they are empty words when, rather than recognizing that ageing and disability are part of diverse human life, our language reveals an underlying belief that some people are 'normal', and some people are 'different'.

And when we view inclusion as 'fitting in'.

Superhuman

In contrast to the subhuman narrative, there's the portrayal of older and disabled people as superhuman.

'Japan's "super-agers" reveal secrets to extremely long life.' '102-year-old completes Great North Run.' 'Disabled superhuman smashes fastest 10km scuba diving record.'

These stories tell of 'remarkable', 'admirable', and 'inspirational' people 'overcoming disability' and 'defying their age'. 'Unsung heroes who battled disability to achieve their dreams.' 'An inspirational story of disability conquered.' 'Elderly man defies age with downhill skiing.' 'Meet two inspirational people that help others despite their own learning disabilities.'

This implies that impairments are barriers disabled people must overcome themselves, with courage and determination. As well as helping to perpetuate the perception of disabled people as 'shirkers' and 'skivers' in contrast to these 'strivers', this narrative also removes all focus from addressing ableist attitudes, microaggressions, and disabling barriers in society.

Adjectives like 'courageous', 'brave', and 'inspirational' are also frequently applied to disabled people doing everyday things. This led Stella Young to coin the phrase 'inspiration porn' to highlight the objectification of disabled people for the benefit of non-disabled people.

In an article titled 'We're not here for your inspiration', she wrote that 'using these images as feel-good tools, as "inspiration", is based on an assumption that the people in them have terrible lives, and that it takes some extra kind of pluck or courage to live them'. She goes on to say, 'my everyday life in which I do exactly the same things as everyone else should not inspire people, and yet I am constantly congratulated by strangers for simply existing' (Young, 2012).

'The assumption is made that disabled lives are lesser than others, therefore any hint of success or living a "normal" existence must be exceptional' (Renke, 2021).

The same, but different

'The elderly.' 'The disabled.' 'The cared for.' 'Those with care and support needs.' Oh, we do love to assign people to dehumanizing boxes, defining people not as human beings, but by a single characteristic or circumstance.

Not only do these groupings imply that everyone in each category is alike, but they also suggest that bit of distance.

Separate.

Other.

The same as each other, but different. Not like us.

Not human

Older people collectively referred to as a 'silver tsunami' and a 'demographic time bomb'. Disabled people described as 'the wheelchair'. People in hospital labelled by their location ('bed 6', 'chair 9'), or as being in the way.

'Bed blockers help fuel the A&E crisis by taking up space from other patients.'

The implication that older and disabled people are objects, and that their presence is problematic or unwanted, is pervasive and reinforced by repeated references to people as 'demand' and as a 'burden'.

Common terms like 'feeding', 'toileting', and 'sitting services' all suggest animals, not humans.

And we keep talking about 'cases' and 'referrals', not people.

Inhumane

The underlying belief that older people and disabled people are lesser humans, whether explicit in our thinking or buried in our consciousness, casts a long shadow over our practice.

Less human equates to less valued.

Less valuable.

As Mark Neary observes, 'the minute someone is seen as non-human, the door is opened to all sorts of unspeakable violence towards them' (Neary, 2018).

This unspeakable violence includes violations of bodies and minds. Identity and personhood. Freedom and autonomy. Hope and imagination.

When people are viewed as units of need, cases, objects, our organizations are designed to process and transact, not relate. And as organizations grow, the potential for relationships diminishes.

Our current ways of working are industrial sized and shaped, not human sized and shaped – dehumanizing people working inside these institutions too.

The framing of older and disabled people as weak, vulnerable, not all there, less able, is used to justify paternalistic and restrictive practice that excludes people from decisions about their lives. Excludes people from a life.

Looking after.

Locking up.

Looking away.

Assigning people to boxes with their associated assumptions and judgements leads to one-size-fits-all responses and solutions.

Achieving our efficiencies as we erode unique identities.

And viewing people as 'other' stifles conversations and aspirations, with little consideration of the vital importance of love, joy, freedom, meaning, and purpose.

Reflecting on spending time with people living in a care home, Madeleine Bunting writes that she was 'overwhelmed by the sheer scale of human need bursting out of that neat building' (Bunting, 2020). The visible ache of desire for connection.

A desperate need to feel human.

Individual

Perhaps in an attempt to redress this categorization and dehumanization, we also refer to people as 'individuals'.

Ironically, often the way we use the term 'individual' makes it sound like another othering label, and indeed one dictionary definition of an 'individual' is 'a person of a particular type, especially a strange one' (Oxford Learner's Dictionaries, n.d.).

An individual is also defined as 'a person considered separately rather than part of a group' (Oxford Learner's Dictionaries, n.d.). This is echoed in our practice focus on people as individual 'cases', rather than people being and becoming 'who they are in relationship to others' (Cottam, 2021).

Too often we ignore the importance of connection and relationships; of interdependence and reciprocity; of belonging.

We also ascribe specific, desirable characteristics to 'individuals' – a generic mould we expect people to fit in to.

We determine human value in terms of contribution and consumption.

The Frameworks Institute paper describes two key assumptions of this mindset – that people are valuable to society 'because of their economic productivity' and 'if they are self-sufficient'. The authors suggest that this 'overemphasis on economic value makes it difficult for people to think about people's social value more broadly, simply as humans' (O'Shea et al., 2023).

And Hilary Cottam suggests that 'our systems – social and economic – are designed around who we imagine humans to be. Today that imagined human is the solitary, calculating and insatiable homo economicus… the individual who realizes himself through a ruthless quest to maximize individual material gain' (Cottam, 2021).

These assumptions fuel our focus on 'independence' in terms of self-sufficiency, and the notion that people who require additional support to live their lives are not only 'lesser', but also represent a drain on valuable reserves.

'Baked into the disability support system are eugenic principles that characterize disabled people as less than human and therefore unworthy of society's scarce resources' (Bartnik & Broad, 2021).

Rehumanizing

This dehumanization of people has perpetuated our systems and institutions and has in turn distanced detached desensitized and dehumanized us sufficiently to prevent us from questioning or challenging this narrative or practice.

As Maya Angelou reflects:

> We have to undo these lessons which have been learned by all of us. And not just taught to us – but we've learned them. And so it will be no small matter. But we can undo it. We can learn to see each other and see ourselves in each other and recognize that human beings are more alike than we are unalike. (Schnall, 2009)

We can have all the transformation leads, teams, plans, and funds we like, but we're never going to achieve real, meaningful, lasting change until we learn to see each other and see ourselves in each other and recognize that human beings are more alike than we are unalike.

And, as Brené Brown observes:

> Because so many time-worn systems of power have placed certain people outside the realm of what we see as human, much of our work now is more a matter of 'rehumanizing.' That starts in the same place dehumanizing starts – with words and images. (Brown, 2017)

Us, not them and us.
Human.
A label we *all* share.

From Vulnerable
to Valuable

*Met with a 10 boy last week for socially distanced walk and talk.
Wanted to make sure he wasn't hungry. He explained to me that
he could go into school if he wanted as was on the 'valuable' list. My
heart swelled. I didn't correct him.*♥

(VIKI, 2020)

We must stop labelling people as vulnerable.
Here are ten reasons why.

It's meaningless

When we refer to 'vulnerable people', most of the time we don't
explain who we mean, why we're suggesting people are vulnerable, or
what they're vulnerable to. It's a nebulous label, and as such it's pretty
meaningless.

Back in June 2020, the then Health and Social Care Secretary Matt
Hancock said that 'from the earliest days of this crisis, we recognize
that people in social care were uniquely vulnerable' (Department of
Health and Social Care, 2020b). Putting aside the exasperating reference to 'in social care', what did 'uniquely vulnerable' in the context of
the pandemic actually mean?

A quick Google search at the time revealed the following people
and places had all been described as 'uniquely vulnerable' to Covid-19:

People living in urban slums. Women and girls. Los Angeles.
Rural communities. Refugees and asylum seekers. The US economy.

Farm workers. Small businesses. Hammersmith. Disabled people. 9/11 heroes. People living with schizophrenia. Black Americans. People experiencing homelessness. Windsor. Pregnant women. Support staff in schools. People in prisons. Babies. The US.

When we (the government, local authorities, the media, charities, banks, supermarkets, the public) make blanket references to 'vulnerable people', do we actually know who we mean?

It's othering

The vulnerable label distances and divides.

We may not be explicit in who we mean when we apply the label – but we don't mean 'us'. We're talking about different, separate, others. *Those* who are vulnerable.

Frequently, we combine the term with additional labels to further distance. 'Vulnerable service users.' 'Vulnerable customers.' 'Vulnerable cases'.

Often, it's used interchangeably with other objectifying labels like 'the disabled' or 'the elderly'.

This categorization means that any sense of identity and personhood is lost as people are grouped together and classified as 'the vulnerable'.

It's dehumanizing

- 'We must continue to protect vulnerable during Covid-19 pandemic.'
- 'Work needed to help vulnerable access care.'
- 'Council providing three-minute care visits to vulnerable, finds ombudsman.'

As these headlines demonstrate, not only do we 'other' people through our use of the term vulnerable, but we also dehumanize them.

It seems copy editors in particular have taken to dropping any sense of humanity. So now we don't even refer to 'vulnerable people', or 'vulnerable groups' – just 'vulnerable'.

It's possessive

Often, we add the possessive 'our' alongside the vulnerable label, extending the protective, paternalistic power dynamic and further legitimizing decisions made for and about people, not by or with them. 'Our vulnerable service users.' 'Our vulnerable customers.' 'Our vulnerable residents.'
We're in charge.
We know best.

It's excluding

Our welfare system is based on demonstrating enough vulnerability to qualify for help. Our services are for 'the vulnerable'. We care for 'our most vulnerable'. If you don't tick the right boxes, you're either not vulnerable enough – or the wrong kind of vulnerable – to be eligible. Too vulnerable and your options are restricted because your needs are 'too complex'.

How many people are we failing by not recognizing and responding to their vulnerability?

How many people are we excluding from support?

And in turn, how many people are we excluding from society by applying the 'vulnerable' label and 'protecting' people from a full and flourishing life?

It's stigmatizing

Weak. Frail. Fragile. Ailing. Sickly. Helpless. These are all synonyms for 'vulnerable'.

It's become a term with negative connotations, a label to distance yourself from. It's not a word many people either do – or want to – associate themselves with. As a result, how many of us don't ask for the assistance we have a right to because we don't want to admit our vulnerability?

And yet as human beings, we're all vulnerable. Being open and honest about our vulnerabilities allows us to connect with each other as equals. To build trusted relationships. To let people in to see who we really are, not what we're pretending to be.

Not only does our use of the term vulnerable stigmatize people; it also stigmatizes vulnerability.

It's paternalistic

If we label you as vulnerable, we're removing any sense of agency from you. The term suggests helplessness and perpetuates a protective approach, which further removes choice and control. As soon as the vulnerable label is applied, any sense of power is removed from you, and you're screened, sorted, prioritized, and processed down a predetermined pathway.

Local authorities describe their role as *caring for* vulnerable residents'. Social workers *protect* some of society's most deprived and vulnerable people'. Care workers *care for* our most vulnerable'. Unpaid carers *look after* vulnerable relatives'.

Use of the term legitimizes and even celebrates 'doing to' – illustrated during the pandemic with the focus on the 'brave heroes' who 'looked after', 'protected', and 'cared for' 'the vulnerable'.

It's blaming

> *The broad definition of a 'vulnerable adult'…is a person: 'who is or may be in need of community care services by reason of mental or other disability, age or illness; and who is or may be unable to take care of him or herself, or unable to protect him or herself against significant harm or exploitation.*
>
> (DEPARTMENT OF HEALTH AND SOCIAL CARE, 2000)

Vulnerable adults are 'unable to take care of themselves' and 'unable to protect themselves from abuse'. Adults are vulnerable due to age, disability, or mental health problems. Vulnerability is inherent, due to individual characteristics.

Broken people. Broken families. Broken communities. Broken lives.

The Care Act 2014 made a deliberate attempt to move away from this blaming narrative, with a shift in terminology from 'vulnerable adult' to 'adult at risk' to acknowledge that people are not intrinsically vulnerable, that we are all vulnerable at times, and that vulnerability is the result of external factors. Situations and circumstances. Politics, policies, prejudice, and power dynamics.

'If I put you in a room with a lion, you would be vulnerable' (Severwright, 2021).

Despite this shift, we haven't moved far.

The deficit-based, medical model is alive and kicking.

By labelling people as vulnerable, we're suggesting there's something wrong with them. Blaming people rather than recognizing the external factors that make people vulnerable.

We're not only failing to see people as unique individuals with pasts, futures, gifts, and goals – human beings with human rights – we're also failing to acknowledge or attempt to change the attitudes, situations, and circumstances that create vulnerability.

During the pandemic, we saw a further sinister step. Not just blaming people for being vulnerable, but in turn blaming 'the vulnerable' for 'restrictive' measures. A quick Twitter search in the summer of 2020 revealed tweets like 'Vulnerable people can just stay inside! Why should the rest of us wear masks??!!', and 'Vulnerable people need to stay at home and keep safe. Let the rest of us live.'

And in December 2020 when the Prime Minister announced new measures to restrict the spread of the virus, *The Daily Telegraph* claimed 'Christmas is sacrificed to protect the vulnerable' (Carpani & Kelly-Linden, 2020).

It's dangerous

The vulnerable label is dangerous.

It suggests difference. Them, not us. Others. Those.

Its blanket use suggests that some people are not quite so human. Not quite so valuable.

Its blanket use leads to blanket responses.

Who can forget the chilling words scrawled on a government whiteboard in March 2020? 'Who do we not save?'

In an article titled 'The fight against Covid-19: Whose life counts?' published in April 2020, Sanchita Hosali wrote:

> Medically, very difficult decisions will need to be made, about who will get treatment and who will not... When these decisions are made not on the basis of medical judgement, but rather on the basis of ingrained, discriminatory attitudes about whose life has more value, that is when we have a societal problem. (Hosali, 2020)

Our use of the term also suggests an inevitability to abuse or to death, precluding too many questions, too much scrutiny.

When a vulnerable person is murdered, or abused, or dies from Covid in a care home or avoidably in hospital because of the failure of medical professionals, the term already implies that it was at least in part because it was harder to protect them. (Crowther, 2021b)

On 23 April 2020, Dr Hans Kluge, Regional Director of the World Health Organization Europe, suggested that 'even among very old people who are frail and live with multiple chronic conditions – many have a good chance of recovery if they are well-cared for' (World Health Organization, 2020).

The day before, in a government Covid-19 briefing, England's Chief Medical Officer Chris Whitty had stated he was 'sure we will see a high mortality rate in care homes sadly because this is a very vulnerable group' (ITV News, 2020).

Herd immunity.

The Clinical Frailty Scale.

Blanket 'do not resuscitate' orders.

Hospital discharge guidance.

Delays in testing.

Lack of adequate personal protective equipment.

Staff shortages/agency staff working across multiple sites/lack of sick pay.

Visiting restrictions.

Congregate living.

A very vulnerable group.

It makes people more vulnerable

For all the reasons outlined above, I firmly believe that labelling people as vulnerable makes people more vulnerable.

'Simply put, if we describe a group of people in a certain way it can influence the actions or decisions we take towards them' (Taylor, 2020).

The label is othering and dehumanizing. Possessive and paternalistic. Excluding and stigmatizing. Blaming and dangerous.

We are all vulnerable in different – and similar – ways. Our vulnerability makes us human but does not – and should not – define us. The blanket labelling of people as vulnerable erodes identity, removes choice, limits autonomy, and legitimizes doing to, not with.

In labelling and grouping people like this, we're not just failing to see each other as unique human beings with human rights – we're also failing to acknowledge or attempt to change the attitudes, situations, and circumstances that create vulnerability.

* * *

Challenging the use of the term 'vulnerable' is not about denying vulnerability. Far from it. But we must end its discriminating, dehumanizing, and patronizing use. Stop the lazy, blanket, and ultimately dangerous application of the term as a label, without reason or context. Recognize and challenge the attitudes, decisions, and actions that increase and reinforce vulnerability.

As Paul Taylor states, 'No group of people is inherently vulnerable. If people are experiencing vulnerability in a particular situation that vulnerability is often produced by other people, institutions or circumstances' (Taylor, 2019).

We don't need any more euphemistic labels, or indeed any alternative terms. I'm not suggesting we start describing people as 'valuable' rather than vulnerable, which would no doubt see the term subjected to the same 'the valuable', 'most valuable', 'more valuable', 'not valuable enough' interpretation.

But if we drop the vulnerable label and focus instead on the equal value we all have as human beings, and our equal rights to a fulfilling life, then it's much harder to advocate for, or agree with, our existing approach, and much easier to shift our attention to removing barriers and making sure we *all* have access to the support we need to live the lives we choose to lead.

We are all vulnerable.
We are all valuable.
We are all human.

From Special to Ordinary

*O*ften our language implies some people are different from the rest of 'us'.

Words like 'disorder', 'deficit', and 'divergence' suggest deviance from what, and who, is ordinary.

One such term is 'special'.

Special means 'different from normal' (Collins, n.d.), like a special friend is different from other friends, or a special meal is different from most meals, or a special occasion is different from the everyday.

Except that's not what we mean, is it?

Because when the term special is used in relation to disabled people, it means different from 'us'.

Other.

Not 'normal'.

Special needs

'Special' is frequently used in a derogatory way, as in, 'He's a bit special'. And the phrase 'special needs' ('my child has special needs', 'people with special needs', 'she's special needs') is often adopted by people who feel uncomfortable saying 'disabled'.

But this euphemistic use of the term implies disabled is a negative or insulting word and should be avoided, rather than an acknowledgement of the way people with physical and mental impairments are restricted and excluded by the world around them.

'Special needs' suggests there's a 'problem' with the person, and they need to be looked after, treated, or fixed.

And that other people ('us') need to go 'above and beyond' to meet 'extra', 'special' needs, almost as a favour.

Go on then, maybe, if I must.

The blanket use of the term 'special needs' doesn't clarify the adjustments or support people require, or the barriers people face. It just groups people together. The same as each other. Different from 'us'.

'Disabled people don't have "special" needs. What is special about the need to use the loo, go to the park, have clothes that fit?' (SEIN, 2024).

We all have the same needs. The basic physiological and safety needs we all need to meet to survive, and the things we need to ensure we thrive. Love. Belonging. Connection. Dignity and respect. Freedom. Acceptance. Inclusion. Participation. Purpose.

Ordinary, everyday, human needs. And human rights.

Jenny Morris observes that a welfare system based on needs rather than rights means 'eligibility for benefits and services is still determined by assessment of how much our bodies are affected by impairment and/or illness, rather than the disabling barriers we experience' (Morris, 2013).

On a deficit-based assessment of what's wrong with people.

And a welfare system based on needs not rights means that power lies in the hands of whoever is determining that needs are 'special' and therefore 'eligible'.

Special care, support, or protection

Being vulnerable is defined as in need of special care, support, or protection because of age, disability, risk of abuse or neglect.

(OFFICE FOR HEALTH IMPROVEMENT AND
DISPARITIES, 2022) (EMPHASIS ADDED)

'Special care.' 'Special education.' 'Special schools.' 'Special transport.' 'Special housing.'

Special equals separate. Different from 'normal', from the 'mainstream'.

Special equals separated.

There's a smattering of the patronizing, paternalistic, charity model approach in this language. And more than a dash of blame.

Take, for example, the Children and Families Act 2014, which states:

A child or young person has special educational needs if he or she has a learning difficulty or disability which calls for special educational provision to be made for him or her. A child of compulsory school age or a young person has a learning difficulty or disability if he or she (a) has a significantly greater difficulty in learning than the majority of others of the same age, or (b) has a disability which prevents or hinders him or her from making use of facilities of a kind generally provided for others of the same age in mainstream schools or mainstream post-16 institutions. (HM Government, 2014)

This legal definition implies it is the young people's fault that 'special educational provision' needs to be made for them. It suggests they have a problem with learning and making use of 'mainstream facilities', rather than recognizing that the problem lies with one-size-fits-all 'mainstream facilities'. It doesn't Rather acknowledging the attitudes, policies, and environments that create barriers to participation and inclusion – to ordinary lives – and focusing on removing them.

Ordinary

Our goal is to see mentally handicapped people in the mainstream of life, living in ordinary houses in ordinary streets, with the same range of choices as any citizen, and mixing as equals with the other, and mostly not handicapped, members of their own community.

(THE KING'S FUND, 1980)

So began The King's Fund report titled 'An ordinary life', published in February 1980 and reprinted in July 1982 with the acknowledgement that 'there has been widespread and still growing interest in the ideas it contains; and the title itself has for many people become a shorthand way of symbolizing the philosophy which should guide the provision of services for people with mental handicaps'.

Our language may have changed in that time, but the philosophy of disabled people living ordinary lives remains, and Neil Crowther notes 'just how much it is echoed in the Social Care Future vision' of everyone 'living in the place we call home, with the people and things that we love, in communities where we look out for one another, doing the things that matter to us' (Crowther, 2024).

As Tricia Nicoll observed when giving evidence to the House of Lords Adult Social Care Committee, 'Everybody now coming out of a pandemic can really understand the idea of just wanting life to be a bit ordinary. Most of us just want a really ordinary life' (House of Lords Adult Social Care Committee, 2022).

It's only when the ordinary becomes extraordinary by virtue of accident, illness, injury, that we realize how precious the 'ordinary' is. Going out with your mates. Picking up a bit of shopping for your mum. This very ordinary stuff is the stuff of life. (Farquharson, 2019)

Gloriously ordinary

I started to use the idea of something being gloriously ordinary when my kids got to be in their mid-teens... It felt like up until then, we had done pretty well in the world of ordinary – local school, local friends, the girl had piano lessons from a local teacher and the boy went to Saturday cinema... As parents, we were really clear that they were going to have the same day to day life, opportunities and experiences as other young people of their age. As they got into teenage years it seemed that the gap widened and the system was much keener for the 'special' alternative – the expectation that the boy would do his Duke of Edinburgh through the youth club for people with learning disabilities, or that the girl should go to the 'special' swimming session... I found myself repeatedly telling people that I wanted things to be ordinary – 'gloriously ordinary' and that seemed to resonate with people.

(NICOLL, 2023)

In defining what she means by 'gloriously ordinary', Tricia Nicoll explains it's a combination of the 'mundane' and the 'heart sing'. The mix of the day-to-day essentials, and the stuff that really makes life worth living. And of course, the things that some of us see as mundane give other people great pleasure, and equally what is glorious to some of us might be the stuff of nightmares for others.

We're *all* different, not just some of us. Yet fundamentally we are also all the same.

We all want, and need, life to be ordinary. Gloriously ordinary.

❊ ❊ ❊

The use of the term 'special' stigmatizes and separates.

It's loaded, and dangerous, eroding the identity and devaluing the human needs, human rights, and humanity of too many people.

If we're genuinely committed to participation and inclusion, to respecting difference and ensuring equality of opportunity, it's time to change this narrative.

It's time to recognize disabled people as ordinary, equal human beings – and to focus on making sure everyone can live gloriously ordinary lives.

From Needy to Needed

*I*ndividuals with needs.' 'Adults with needs.' 'People with needs.' That's all of us, right?

But in the language of social care serviceland, 'adults with needs' is shorthand for 'adults with care and support needs'.

This language describes people by what they require support with, not who they are, were, or want to be.

It places people in a box that says, 'I need help'. It says, 'you're needy', not 'you're needed'.

'You need me', not 'we need each other'.

And as well as defining people's identity, it also shapes our response.

Passive recipients

The Care Act guidance is clear that 'local authorities should ensure that individuals are not seen as passive recipients of support services, but are able to design care and support based around achievement of their goals' (Department of Health and Social Care, 2023).

Despite this, our language reveals how people are still seen as passive recipients of services: 'clients', 'customers', 'patients', 'service users'.

And for all our talk of inclusion, deficit-based assessments and 'care packages' that focus only on 'care needs' limit opportunities for people to participate and contribute. Jan Sutton writes that:

> disabled people have had to learn to 'sell' our inabilities, our 'can't do's', in order to get the basic level of support that we need to survive... We all know that our aspirations, our skills, our experience are not to be included. If we want to get the support that we need to function, we've got to play the game. (Sutton, 2014)

Dependent

Disability is synonymous with 'dependency', and dependency is synonymous with vulnerability and helplessness.

Dictionary definitions expose the stigma attached to the term. 'You talk about someone's dependency when they have a deep emotional, physical, or financial need for a particular person or thing, especially one that you consider excessive or undesirable' (Collins, n.d.). 'A situation in which you need something or someone and are unable to continue *normally* without them' (Cambridge Dictionary, n.d.) (emphasis added).

Not only does a requirement for assistance imply 'lesser', 'incapable', 'subordinate' human beings, as Jenny Morris explains it's also 'translated into a need for "care" in the sense of a need to be looked after'. She writes:

> Once personal assistance is seen as 'care', then the 'carer', whether professional or a relative, becomes the person in charge, the person in control. The disabled person is seen as being dependent on the carer, and incapable even of taking charge of the personal assistance s/he requires. (Morris, 1993)

So often we use phrases like 'people who have care and support needs *and their carers*'. 'Disabled people *and their carers.*' 'Older people *and their carers.*'

In contrast to this dominant narrative, many disabled people argue that dependency is created not by people's impairments but by an ableist and disabling society. That disabled people are 'dependent' because they are denied access to 'mainstream' opportunities and are forced to seek assistance they have little or no control over. That our system of 'welfare' requires that disabled people deny strengths and successes and focus on what they can't do. That it fails to ensure people have enough money to live with dignity and respect and makes people increasingly reliant on families and charities for support.

And that our institutional approach perpetuates dependency, doing to and for people, and making decisions about people without them.

'Carers' and 'the cared for'

The narrative in relation to 'unpaid carers' highlights and reinforces this dependent relationship. 'Do you look after someone who depends on you because of an illness or disability?' 'Do you look after someone who is dependent on you?'

Simon Brisenden suggests that this enforced dependency on a relative or partner is 'the most exploitative of all forms of so-called care in our society today for it exploits both the carer and the person receiving care. It ruins relationships between people and results in thwarted life opportunities on both sides of the caring equation' (Morris, 1993).

As well as the impact on caring relationships, the notion of 'carers' doesn't sit comfortably alongside the concept of self-directed support. Frances Hasler writes how in the 1980s, as members of the disabled people's movement were campaigning for the right to independent living, the concept of rights for carers was also growing. She notes how 'the carers' movement', representing female family carers, was based on the construction of disabled people as 'dependent', casting them as 'a "burden" shouldered by female caregivers', and excluding their voices from the debate (Hasler, 2004).

In contrast to the identity (welcomed or not) offered by the 'carer' label, its application often leads to the removal of identity of the 'family member, partner, or friend who needs help.' They become 'the cared for person', defined in terms of their relationship to someone else rather than as a person in their own right – or just 'the cared for' – not even identified as a human being.

Here are a few examples I've spotted online (emphasis added):

- 'Accessing the right support for *the cared for*.'
- 'Available support may depend on whether *the cared for* is an adult or a child.'
- 'If you require a joint assessment with *your cared for*, our social care teams will be happy to support this.'

While the 'carer' has an active role, 'the cared for' person is just that – cared for. Passive. Invisible.

And there's no sense of people caring for and about each other in this narrative. No suggestion of reciprocity, of mutual support. No recognition that 'carers' may also be drawing on support themselves. You either tick the 'carer' box or the 'cared for' box.

Independent

The language of 'needs' and 'dependency' is stigmatizing and other-ing. It implies people are a 'problem', a 'burden', and a drain on scarce resources. It perpetuates notions of helplessness and justifies pater-nalistic 'care'. It removes any sense of people's agency, participation, and contribution, of people being needed. And it focuses our attention on 'fixing' people to 'maintain their independence', not on removing barriers to 'independent living'.

However, as I'll explore further in Part Two, references to 'inde-pendence' and 'independent living' are too frequently (mis)interpreted as people living without support, or people living on their own.

While 'dependent' implies a one-way relationship and perpetuates 'them and us' divisions, 'independent' implies no relationship at all – 'I' not 'we'. And while 'I' is preferable to being 'part of the "we" whose mealtimes, diet, bedtime and so on are dictated to you because you're "one of them", "the disabled", "the client", "the patient"' (Morris, 1993), in practice 'independence' often resembles 'being in your pyjamas by 5pm and being on your own with an alert button between 7pm and 9am' (Neary, n.d.).

Interdependent

So, I feel it's more helpful to shift away from this narrative of depend-ency and independence, and to focus instead on interdependence. To recognize that no one is completely independent. That we all depend on each other.

We need each other to survive. To meet our physiological and safety needs. And to thrive we need genuine connections: family, friendships. We need to hold and be held, to be part of a bigger whole, to belong. We need to love, and to be loved in return.

We flourish through our interdependence. We're better together. Our connections and relationships *give us* our independence, and our individual rights and freedoms depend on our social cohesion.

When we view people as needy and dependent, our response is to 'protect' and 'look after'. However, if we flip this thinking, and view people as interdependent and needed, our focus shifts to relationships and reciprocity. To the importance of connections and communities and how both can be sustained. To what must be in place to ensure inclusion and participation.

To ensure equal, ordinary lives.

When we view people as needy and dependent, we think 'them' and 'problem'.

But when we focus instead on interdependence, well, that equates to all of us – and benefits us all.

...and Marvellous was suddenly wrenched out of old age like a seed potato wrenched out of the familiar comfort of dark. She had little time to think about Death, pushed aside as it were, by activity, youth and noise. Things were required of her again and this time by people and not by dreams. And Marvellous blossomed, having quite forgotten what an exciting and necessary jolt being needed gave. (Winman, 2017)

From Consumers to Citizens

The use of the term 'customers' in councils grew through the later decades of the 20th century, becoming more common than 'client' to describe the association between people and services.

In this consumer story, transactions trump relationships and, as Cormac Russell observes, 'independence becomes prized over interdependence' (Russell, 2020).

So, let's explore the terms 'client' and 'customer', what they symbolize, and why we need to flip this narrative to see, communicate about, and work alongside people as citizens, not consumers.

Client

The dictionary definition of client is 'a customer or someone who receives services' (Cambridge Dictionary, n.d.), 'One that is under the protection of another: dependent' (Merriam-Webster, n.d.).

The term symbolizes an unequal and paternalistic power dynamic.

In a *British Journal of Social Work* article titled 'What's in a name: "client", "patient", "customer", "consumer", "expert by experience", "service user" – what's next?', Dr Hugh McLaughlin notes that while 'in the late 1970s, the social work relationship was epitomized by the term "client"', there was concern then 'that the notion of a "client" represented an objectification of the social work relationship whereby it was assumed power laid with the professional to identify what the passive client needed' (McLaughlin, 2009).

Around the same time, 'neoliberals emphasized the financial cost of welfare systems and argued for the creation of privatized markets that might deliver a reduced welfare state' (Cottam, 2018). The 1980s, under the Thatcher government, saw an increasing shift towards the market, with a focus on efficiency and the privatization of public services.

And so our thinking shifted to see people as independent consumers: self-reliant 'individuals' in a never-ending, competitive cycle of working more, earning more, spending more.

Identity gained, and status measured, through production and consumption.

Customer

In this new world order, people's relationship with social workers and with public sector organizations generally was rebranded to that of 'customer' – a transactional rather than relational connection.

While 'a client is a person or company that receives a service from a professional person or organization in return for payment, a customer is someone who buys something, especially from a shop' (Collins, n.d.).

Social workers became 'care managers' – 'commissioning' and 'brokering' 'packages of care' from private 'providers'. Focusing on 'the individual as the source of risk and required change, without considering wider societal constructs and structural inequalities which shaped and sustained the individual's distress' (James, Mitchell, & Morgan, 2019).

And 'care' became commodified, with the 'work' of caring increasingly relocated from families and communities to institutions and serviceland.

'These changes were momentous. They cemented the central role of the market in the provision of care' (Humphries, 2022).

'The industrialization of social care was well and truly born' (James, Mitchell, & Morgan, 2019).

The implementation of the NHS and Community Care Act 1990 embedded these changes, and the 'care management' approach is still very evident today.

But the notion of people as 'customers' of social care is wrong in so many ways.

Think 'customer' and you automatically think transaction. Buying and selling. Customers consume. Money changes hands. But fundamentally in social care, our 'business' is good lives, and good lives are built – not bought.

'People do not shop for human services and they certainly don't shop for a life' (Duffy, 2015).

You can't purchase friendships, relationships, purpose, or love.

You can't buy ambition, happiness, or hope.

'Ultimately, we cannot be customers of relationships' (Fox, 2018). The term customer implies choice. As customers we choose whether to buy and how much we're prepared to pay. We browse a range of products, compare prices, get quotes, read reviews. We make snap decisions or take our time. If we're not happy we cancel our order, return our purchase, and get a refund.

The shift towards the market approach to social care was designed to assure such choice. However, often the people we label 'customers' don't choose to come to us, but they've exhausted all other options, tried everything else, and social care is their last resort.

And once they approach us, we're the ones who choose what type of support to offer and whether we can even 'help' at all. We present a limited range of services as solutions. Our choice is imposed on 'our customers'.

Customers give shops or business their custom. And custom also means a personalized approach – custom-made or custom-built – the opportunity to design your own. But customized usually means exclusive and therefore expensive and unattainable. Most of the time as customers, we may have choice, but we don't have a say in design. And despite all our talk of 'personalization' and 'co-production' this is often the case in social care too.

Custom also means a traditional way of doing things. The larger the organization, the less responsive it is to individual circumstances and preferences. While the local cafe may be able to respond to requests for no onions or extra sauce, the high-street chain can't alter the make-up of their pre-packed sandwiches.

So, while we may aspire to a personalized approach, the scale and bureaucracy of local authorities means all too often, as with tailored clothing or made-to-measure furniture, such an approach remains out of reach for the majority.

Much time and effort are spent on 'mapping' the 'customer journey', but ultimately the 'pathway' is our design, and the result is linear: 'front-door' – screening – assessment – eligibility determination – plan – approval – service – review.

Despite this one-size-fits-all road map, the reality of our system is a complex tangle of processes and referrals requiring procedures, factsheets, navigators, and advocates to interpret it. And the reality of people's lives is a complex tangle too. Most people's lives don't run in straight lines, and everybody's life is different. Process maps only work in social care when we focus on problems, label people by need or diagnosis, fit them into the associated box, and prescribe the corresponding service.

Customers may go on journeys, but people live lives.

Those who defend the use of the term 'customer' do so in part because of its association with customer service – the 'customer experience'. Good customer service is about good relationships. Responding quickly. Being helpful. Building trust and respect. Listening to feedback and continually learning, developing, and improving. If we believe that by referring to people as customers, we'll somehow magically assume those same values and behaviours, we might as well give up now.

Ultimately the term 'customer' is yet another distancing and dehumanizing label. By describing people as customers, we gather them into a group 'over there', not like us. And not just any group, but a group whose identity is defined solely by people's relationship to us as consumers of our services.

'Our customers.'

Citizen

In order to survive and thrive, we must step into the Citizen Story. We must see ourselves as Citizens – people who actively shape the world around us, who cultivate meaningful connections to their community and institutions, who can imagine a different and better life, who care and take responsibility, and who create opportunities for others to do the same. Crucially, our institutions must also see people as Citizens, and treat us as such.

(ALEXANDER, 2022)

Within society in general, the cracks in the consumer story are increasingly apparent, and the need to find a different narrative is becoming increasingly urgent. Jon Alexander writes:

We cannot face a crisis of inequality from within a story that tells us competing for status is human nature. We cannot face a crisis of loneliness and mental ill-health from within a story that tells us we are independent, isolated individuals who must stand alone. (Alexander, 2022)

Within the world of social care, we need to acknowledge the cracks in this narrative of self-sufficiency and the consumption of services.

We need to recognize that there's no space for people in our current sorting office system.

We need to reject our part in the business of processing 'cases' and walk away from our role as brokers of hours and beds. Instead of facilitating transactions between customers and providers, we need to see people and families as a key part of the solution, not the problem. And see our role as enablers and connectors, weaving webs of relationships and support.

Instead of 'dealing with' a generic group of customers, distinguished only by the service they consume, we must be liberated from the constraints of our current system.

Shift our focus from transactions to relationships.

See people not as individual consumers of services but as citizens who contribute to, and belong in, communities. Who have choice and control. Rights and responsibilities.

See each other as equals, all bringing our own experience and expertise, and working together to build better lives for us all.

Service User

*I*n his article about 'the terms we use to describe the relationship between those who assess and commission services and those who are the recipient of those services', Hugh McLaughlin observes that with the election of New Labour in 1997 came a focus on 'modernization' and an emphasis on partnerships, 'with the consumer or customer seen as someone who should be involved in these partnerships'. He suggests that 'the drive for a "service user" mandate comes from both the consumerist tradition of the 1990s and the democratic tradition of developing participation to ensure the suitability of services' (McLaughlin, 2009).

The 1998 Department of Health *Modernizing Social Services* white paper included the provision of 'user-centred services' in its list of priorities (Department of Health, 1998) and by then the 'service user movement' was already well established in relation to mental health services.

And so references to people as 'service users' grew, along with an emphasis on 'service user involvement'. But a term that may have been intended to affirm people's identity and participation has become a label that does little for either.

We describe people as service users whether they're using a service or not. It's become a generic term to define people we might and do support. The National Health Service (NHS) has patients. Adult social care has service users. But by describing people as service users, we're defining them solely through their relationship to services and denying them a unique identity. We're seeing a single element of a person rather than the whole person in the context of their whole life: who they are, were, and want to be. We're ignoring the experiences, characteristics, relationships, and ambitions that make them human.

We use the term to group people together – defined by the service they may or may not use. There's an implication that everyone in the group is the same. Same label. Same needs. Same old service solutions.

Often the phrase is shortened to 'user'. Like 'customers', 'users' suggests people are passive recipients. Users of generic services designed, developed, and provided to them, rather than people identifying, shaping, and controlling their own support. The term also has obvious associations with drugs and exploitation. Whether it describes an addictive or abusive relationship, it's not a healthy one, and inevitably there's a destructive power imbalance in which one party is controlled by another.

And all too frequently we add possessive pronouns like 'my' or 'our' when referring to service users – reinforcing the sense of ownership and control.

Identifying people as service users allows us to define our response in terms of services. It excuses the way we process people and pass them around. It makes it easier for us to deny their humanity, and to avoid our own humanity.

Our detached attitude is, to a significant extent, a symptom of our current ways of working. Indeed, our sorting office approach relies on us keeping our distance. Maintaining our professional boundaries and keeping 'our service users' firmly 'over there' helps us keep the show on the road.

Alex Fox claims that within the current power imbalances of our traditional public services, 'detachment is the only manageable relationship one worker can have with numerous service users'. He suggests our current approach brings together 'two people in crisis: the personal crisis of the support seeker and the ongoing professional crisis of the hard-pressed public service worker', and that 'impersonality protects each from the other's crisis' (Fox, 2018).

But while this othering, this separation, this indifference may help us cope, it's dangerous. Really dangerous.

When we stop identifying people as fellow humans, we're failing to respect them. Failing to fight for their rights. Failing to believe in them. Failing them.

Reading Sara Ryan's book *Justice for Laughing Boy*, I was horrified by the following cold, stark reference to Connor Sparrowhawk's death in Southern Health board papers: 'A Serious Incident Requiring Investigation (SIRI) occurred in one of the Trust's learning disability in-patient facilities leading to the unexpected death of a service user. The post-mortem indicates the user died of natural causes...' (Ryan, S., 2018).

I then found out that the Care Quality Commission has a regulation on the 'notification of death of service user' (Care Quality Commission,

2023), and countless other NHS trusts and care providers have their own 'death of a service user' policies.

What does it say about our 'care' system when even in death we still refer to people as service users?

When we continue to deny people an individual identity?

When we refuse to refer to people by their name?

From Cases to People

*W*e talk about cases all the time. We screen, allocate, assess, manage, transfer, and close cases. We carry caseloads. We have active cases and passive cases. We 'deal with' complex/challenging/difficult cases. We record case notes and maintain case records in our case management systems. We hold case conferences and carry out serious case reviews. We learn from case studies, case file audits, and case law.

In our everyday lives, if we talk about cases, we're probably packing for a holiday. Maybe we're reading a crime novel where there's a case to be investigated, or watching the news where there are prime suspects in a case. We might even be defending our case in an argument or courtroom.

The term case has multiple meanings, but many of them relate either to baggage, or to something we investigate, judge, or learn from. When we talk about cases in social care, we're usually either talking about people with cases (problems to be dealt with) or people as cases (i.e. baggage).

Problems to be dealt with: People with cases

In social care, people have cases, not lives. We've become detectives investigating these cases. Case records and case notes are our clues. We piece together scraps of information from our case management systems about the cases we've been allocated. Decisions about futures are taken by managers who judge and authorize based on words on their screens about the past.

Standard phrases. Common terms. Boxes ticked. Job done.

We like our case studies too. The Care Act guidance contains over 30 scenarios faced by fictional folk, including Deirdre, Brian, Jacinta, Kate, Mr A, Miss Y, Mrs D, Ms P, 'an older man', 'two brothers', and 'a resident'. Most of these case studies start with a diagnosis, a 'condition', or a label. 'Beryl was diagnosed with stomach cancer.' 'Sally is 40 and has a physical disability.' 'Lynette who has learning disabilities.' 'Mrs Pascal, who is frail and elderly...' 'Adbul is a deafblind man.' 'Isabelle is 15 years old with complex needs' (Department of Health and Social Care, 2023).

Case studies (such a detached and clinical term) tell of real and imaginary scenarios to illustrate a principle or explain an approach – evidence to inform our practice. But ironically, while the literature overflows with case studies, all too often we're failing to listen to the real stories of the people we're working with every day.

Suitcases, labels, conveyor belts, and journeys: People as cases

Our social care departments have much in common with airports. Both have queues, gates, and labels. There is screening and scanning. Interactions are fleeting and increasingly automated. The clock is always ticking. There's always a 'journey'.

We have become the baggage handlers. People are our cases.

Our equivalent to the check-in desk is our 'front door', where we ask formulaic questions about cases. If cases clear this initial stage, we apply labels to describe them and where they're going next. The next stage usually involves further screening where, like the staff checking hand luggage at the departure gate, we line cases up and assess them when we're ready – inducing anxiety as we decide whether they meet our entry criteria.

Then – if we let them in – we swallow them up into our system. Like the numerous conveyor belts in airports, there are multiple pathways and processes and, as with suitcases, the destination is usually assigned from the start. And like suitcases, social care cases may be mishandled or damaged as they pass through our hands, or sent to the wrong place, or lost completely in our system.

Much of the language we use in relation to cases reflects this processing of people.

We 'screen', 'prioritize', 'allocate', and 'handle' cases. We 'carry' caseloads. We 'refer', 'place', and 'transfer' cases and have 'case transfer protocols' to describe when we can shift responsibility to other teams or organizations. We 'manage' cases – helped (and often hindered) by our 'case management systems'.

And we recruit social workers as baggage handlers to process cases through our system.

This, from a recent recruitment campaign for children's social workers, sums it up: 'Are you a social worker looking to move into screening and referring cases?'

Are you?

* * *

Of all the words that make me go hmmm' (and there are lots!), 'case' is up there at the top of the list. Describing people's lives as cases is bad enough – but people as cases?

In no way would I ever defend the use of client, customer, or service user – but at least they imply a human (just about). A case is an inanimate object. Talk of 'my case' and not only are you assuming ownership, but the person you're possessing has become not quite human in your eyes. Something to process, to 'deal with', rather than someone who just needs a bit, or a lot, of support to get on with living their life. And the danger of this dehumanizing, othering attitude – conscious or unconscious as it may be – is that objects don't have wishes, feelings, hopes, and rights.

So why do we do it? Why do we describe people and their lives as cases?

Maybe it's to do with professional status? Doctors and lawyers have cases so why shouldn't we?

Maybe it makes it easier to manage our 'workload' if we label people's lives as cases we can solve, write about, learn from, and close?

Maybe it makes it easier to justify 'screening', 'handling', and 'placing' people if we call them cases and distance ourselves sufficiently to pretend it's okay to move them like baggage around our system?

Telling a different story

Those of us who work in social care don't join the 'workforce' to process cases through a system. We do so because we believe in human rights, social justice, families, friendships, love. We believe in people. We want to make a difference. We care.

So, in our better, brighter future we talk about, and work with, people, not cases. We're no longer detectives piecing together clues from notes and records on our system. We've rejected our role as baggage handlers attaching labels and carrying cases through our gates and on and off our conveyor belts.

Our new world revolves around building and maintaining connections and relationships, with people rather than processes at its core. Instead of dealing with cases, we work with people. We've dropped our jargon and labels and regained our humanity and humility. We listen hard, understand what matters, and focus on finding ways to be useful. We're kind. We're people, with our own experience, skills, values, and ambitions, helping other people with their own experience, skills, values, and ambitions to get on with living the life they choose.

Forget those anonymous case studies. We're telling a different story, and it's a story we're proud to tell.

From Labels to Gifts

Too often in the language of power we hear citizens being turned into patients, residents, service users, consumers or recipients; in other words, we turn the active into the passive, we don't see the multiple gifts that each of us brings, instead we convert each other into an impossibly long list of needs waiting to be met.

(DUFFY, 2023)

Labels are for parcels. Jars. Suitcases. They describe a destination, explain what's inside. They are attached. They stick.

But in social care, our labels are for people. Service user. Case. Customer. Client. Referral. Self-funder. Full-fee payer. Carer. Cared-for. Expert by experience. Nearest relative. Challenging. Difficult. Complex. Vulnerable. Frail. Learning disability. Eligible. Not eligible. Non-compliant. Avoidable admission. Bed blocker. Frequent flyer. Optimized. Activated.

We attach labels, and they stick.

Labels open doors

The search for an accurate diagnosis takes over your life, ultimately knowing that if you have a name for what is wrong, this will give you the passport to the support and services that you need.

(FOX, 2018)

People usually require a label (vulnerable, at risk...) to enter our social care world. And once they're in, our labels define their 'journey'. We rely on these labels. We use them to structure our services and name our teams. Without them we're not quite sure which pathway to direct people down, or where to refer them next.

Labels help us process people quickly. Move 'cases' round our system. Sometimes we add a priority label – sending people off down a predetermined pathway, or on to the next stage in a workflow, with a rating, a flag, a red/amber/green, or a high/medium/low attached. And people and families seeking support learn to adopt our labels too – fully aware that certain terms guarantee entry to 'the system'.

In her book *Radical Help*, Hilary Cottam mentions Olive. She suggests that Olive originally gained the label 'housebound' from a visiting social worker 'whose job it is to assess the allocation of services'. The social worker applied the label to ensure Olive received some support rather than none, and 'Olive felt she must describe herself this way to keep the help she genuinely needed' (Cottam, 2018).

'If you don't use "their language" on those meetings it makes it more difficult to get support. I regularly use/d language I hate because it has a sort of hyper-functionality' (Runswick-Cole, 2019).

Labels close minds

While labels may open doors, they also close minds.

Often, we see, and apply, labels before we've met people. And in doing so we attach all our associations and assumptions and have our standard service solutions at the ready. Then we attach more labels, describing people as cases or referrals, or as the next stage in our workflow: a safeguarding, a DoLS, NFA...

Labels are generic. They allow and perpetuate our one-size-fits-all approach.

When people are given multiple labels, we refer them to multiple teams or organizations. And each team or organization sees the part of the person with a label that matches the name above their door: the need, the problem, the risk, the diagnosis, the condition. Each service screens and assesses according to their entry criteria, and people give the same answers to the same questions over and over again. Each team or organization fixes, treats, manages, or maintains a part.

Few, if any, see the whole.

And if we struggle to find the right label(s), inevitably we can't quite fit people into an obvious box, so we attach some alternative labels.

Complex. Difficult. Inappropriate referral.

Labels shape identity

What you can't know unless you have #disability is how all the paper-work chips away at your soul. Every box you tick, every sentence about your 'impairment' and 'needs' becomes part of the narrative of your identity...

(LOOMES-QUINN, 2018)

While we may talk about personalized, 'strengths-based' approaches, the generic labels emphasizing what people can't do, what they need, and what's wrong remain the ones we apply and the ones that guarantee support.

Labels also shape the identity of the people who attach them. Assessor. Case coordinator. Care manager. These 'professional' labels all suggest 'doing to' – reinforcing a power dynamic and leaving no doubt about who really makes the decisions. Who is really in control.

Labels dehumanize

All of these words, all of the nos, all of the labels – the boxes I was put in – became a part of what I believed about myself, what I believed I was capable of, what I believed I could and couldn't do. I became those labels, those words, those NOs. I became small and weak and frail as I withdrew inward, into the shell of my former self.

(BELTON, 2018)

As well as shaping identity, labels deny identity.

They identify people not by any of the elements that make them unique (and human), but by a single factor that makes them the same (and just a little less than human).

These labels also add that bit of distance. Suggest that bit of difference.

Many years ago, following my suggestion that we describe people as – well – people, a colleague told me that first she'd been told to refer to service users not clients, and now I was asking her to say people instead of service users, and in a few years' time we'd probably find some other term to use instead of people. At the time I was a bit stunned by this. But reflecting on it now, I think it's an indication of that innate desire to separate, group, and distance. The assessor and the assessed. The provider and the consumer. The carer and the cared for.

'Us' and 'them'.

Labels blame

You over there. You're not just different, separate, not quite human. You're wrong. You've failed. It's your fault. Nothing to do with us. Not responding. Not engaging. Not behaving. Not vulnerable enough. Too vulnerable. Not ticking the right box. Ticking too many boxes. Not fitting neatly into any service. Not doing what we want you to do. Non-compliant. Hard to reach. Difficult. Challenging. Complex.

How quickly we apportion blame in the labels we use.

How quickly we walk away.

Nothing to do with us.

Seeing the person, not the label

The search for the perfect 'label' has spanned both decades and continents. There have been numerous surveys and much debate about the 'preferred terms for labelling individuals'.

'What do we call "them"?'

But we don't need to add new labels; we need to remove them. And we can only do that by radically rewriting social care.

Like sorting offices and baggage handling systems, we rely on labels – precisely because we operate a similar system of screening, sorting, prioritizing, and processing. We use labels to decide on eligibility, determine pathways, and prescribe services. We use labels to distance ourselves from the reality of people's lives, to help us justify the way we 'deal with' people like parcels and suitcases. And we use labels to blame, to shield us from the reality of our collective failures.

Too often we apply labels because we're too far removed – physically, emotionally, usually both – from people in the context of their families and their communities and their whole lives.

'Because that's what we're talking about. People. Relationships. Families. Normal stuff. Any other label distances and sets up a "different from the rest of us" dynamic that is not useful' (Neary, 2015).

Gifts

Our dominant approach to welfare is the 'professional gift model', where 'the taxpayer gives money to the government, the government gives money to the professional who turns that money into services that are offered to the needy person as a gift – that is, something that cannot be defined, shaped or controlled by the individual' (Duffy, 2010).

The 'gift' of services. A 'package' of care.

But what if we flip this narrative, drop the labels, and focus instead on people's gifts and potential? On seeing and valuing who people are and want to be. What people can do, could be, want to do next. And on giving our own gifts of time, compassion, dignity, respect, honesty, humility, humanity.

Applying a label is easy. Recognizing and nurturing gifts and potential requires a whole different way of thinking and working, where conversations are led by people seeking support and based around what matters most to them. Where our role is listening – with no assumptions – and understanding, building trust, making connections, joining the dots. Where our aim is for people to flourish, not just survive. Where support is a springboard, not a safety net.

This moves us beyond focusing on basic physiological and safety needs – the bottom tiers of Maslow's hierarchy – to recognizing, valuing, and focusing on the importance of belonging, esteem, and self-actualization.

It moves us from focusing only on what 'professionals' give, to starting with what people, families, and communities have, and investing our time and resources in nurturing, developing, and connecting what is present and abundant.

Today in Stirling an 87-year-old man with dementia was reading a book to a 93-year-old neighbour because she can't see the words anymore. There's no 'service' that could replicate the relationship, connection & care created here. *Everyone* has something to give to their neighbour. (Ellis Gray, 2023)

Labels are for parcels, jars, suitcases. Not people.

Them, Us, and Covid-19

I published my first blog post in August 2019, and just over six months later we were 'locked down'. I wrote several posts during the lockdowns, with a number explicitly focusing on the language of the pandemic.

As all our lives changed, so did our language. New terms like Covid-19, self-isolate, and social distancing were added to the dictionary. Others took on new meaning (lockdown, shielding, zoom...), and yet more saw a surge in use – virus, pandemic, keyworker, hero, vulnerable...

Words we'd rarely or never heard or used before dominated the headlines, crowded our screens, and peppered our conversations.

And we pretty much accepted and adopted this new vocabulary without question.

But I had a question.

What influence did the language of the Covid-19 pandemic have on our response?

Back in March 2020, cohesion and solidarity dominated our narrative and shaped our behaviour. On 22 March – Mother's Day – Prime Minister Boris Johnson wrote that 'this disease is forcing us apart – at least physically. But this epidemic is also the crucible in which we are already forging new bonds of togetherness and altruism and sharing' (Prime Minister's Office, 10 Downing Street and The Rt Hon Boris Johnson MP, 2020b).

Announcing the first lockdown the following day, he concluded that 'each and every one of us is now obliged to join together... We will beat the coronavirus and we will beat it together' (Prime Minister's Office, 10 Downing Street and The Rt Hon Boris Johnson MP, 2020c).

The 'One world: together at home' concert raised millions. Hashtags like #TogetherApart, #BetterTogether and #TogetherWeCan trended on Twitter. We clapped together on Thursday evenings. We came together on our streets and in our communities to support each other. We followed the rules and stayed at home: together – apart. And research suggests our collective compliance was largely due to 'the belief that we are all in it together' (Jackson, 2020).

This was about 'we', not 'me'. 'Us', not 'them'.

Or was it?

By the time the news broke that the Prime Minister had Covid-19 in late March 2020, the cracks in this narrative were already clear. Claims from politicians and pop stars alike that the virus 'does not discriminate', 'is no respecter of individuals, whoever they are', and is 'the great leveller', which has 'made us all equal in many ways' (Sky News, 2020; Grant, 2020; White, 2020) were met with anger at the time (Maitlis, 2020) and as the weeks and months went by, and the true impact of the virus and the response became increasingly and horrifyingly apparent, the cracks in this narrative became chasms.

Winners and losers

The vocabulary of war was dominant. Early on, the Prime Minister described acting 'like any wartime government' and referred to Covid-19 as a deadly enemy (Prime Minister's Office, 10 Downing Street and The Rt Hon Boris Johnson MP, 2020a).

A 'war room' was set up in the Cabinet Office. In his 'address to the nation' on 23 March, Boris Johnson mentioned 'beating the virus' and 'fighting the disease', claiming 'in this fight we can be in no doubt that each and every one of us is directly enlisted' (Prime Minister's Office, 10 Downing Street and The Rt Hon Boris Johnson MP, 2020c).

This rhetoric continued to be adopted by his colleagues and echoed in the media.

When Boris Johnson was admitted to hospital, journalists invariably described him 'battling' the virus. His deputy Dominic Raab asserted his confidence that 'he will pull through, because if there's one thing I know about this Prime Minister, he's a fighter' (Roberts *et al.*, 2020). And Donald Trump referred to the Prime Minister's 'own personal fight with the virus', adding that he was 'hopeful and sure that he is going to be fine. He's a strong man, strong person' (Trump, 2020).

On an individual level, framing Covid-19 and our response in military terms was distressing for people who personally and professionally cared for and about people who died with the disease, as it suggested that all involved didn't fight hard enough, or weren't strong enough, to win the battle.

On a broader level, the aggressive language of war hid the compassion involved in the care and treatment of people with the virus, not to mention the science, medicine, and research involved in the response. It suggested an attack from a hidden aggressor, conveniently deflecting attention from preventative and preparatory steps not taken. And it indicated violence and retribution, when in reality most people were not 'taking up arms' but were quietly and peacefully playing their part by staying at home and carrying on with their lives as best they could, in a universal, collaborative act of love.

Heroes and 'the vulnerable'

In war, there are heroes. And the hero narrative was strong during the early stages of the pandemic. People who had always played a vital yet barely acknowledged role in our communities became 'keyworkers', 'essential workers', 'critical workers', 'heroes'.

While this recognition was absolutely deserved and no doubt appreciated, weekly clapping and shiny new 'CARE' badges hardly made up for the years in the shadows: the minimal wages, the zero hours contracts, the lack of recognition or respect, the 'low-skilled' label, the threat of deportation, the discrimination, the abuse.

These 'heroes' didn't enlist to fight or sign up for war. The reason that health and social care workers were 'brave', 'courageous', 'battling', and dying was because they didn't have the protective equipment, workplace environments, and working conditions to keep them safe.

In contrast to the heroes, there were 'the vulnerable', not recognized as individual human beings – just 'those over 70' and 'those who have an underlying health condition'. An anonymous, homogeneous, helpless group, at greater clinical risk from the virus, who must be protected and shielded. Looked after. Cared for. Done to.

The 'vulnerable' label identified a different, separate, other group of people. So much so that many people understandably didn't identify themselves in the dehumanizing category, and many not included believed they weren't at risk. The message was for 'them', not 'us'.

The narrative divided us into the protectors and the protected. The saviours and the saved. But in reality, these lines were blurred. We were all heroes in our own ways, and we were all vulnerable. We could all care about each other. And we all needed – and deserved – to be cared about.

We all mattered.

Healthy people and 'those with underlying health conditions'

We all mattered. But there was a sinister implication in the unfolding story of the pandemic that some lives – and deaths – mattered more.

One message was clear from early news reports. 'Us' healthy people wouldn't get the virus, or if we did, we'd only have mild symptoms. The people most at risk were 'those with underlying health conditions'.

Them.

As details of the first people to die in the UK emerged, the 'with an underlying health condition' tag was inevitably attached. However, as more and more people died, the headlines focused with horror on people dying 'with no underlying conditions':

- 'They were healthy: 13 of the 260 who died in UK's blackest day so far in coronavirus crisis had no underlying health conditions.'
- 'Coronavirus warning: More than a dozen who died yesterday had NO prior health conditions.'
- 'ALMOST one in every ten coronavirus deaths in England and Wales were in "healthy" people, figures released today have revealed.'

There's a dark message here that some people were more dispensable. 'They' would have died anyway. The death of a 'healthy' person is therefore more shocking, and more tragic.

> Read the many media reports and a common line comes out: 'Most people recover, and fatalities are largely only among those with underlying health conditions.' It is a sentiment I have heard constantly in recent days, supposedly as a form of reassurance. (Ryan, F., 2020)

The 'most people' and 'those with underlying health conditions' phrases became deeply ingrained. Indeed, the standard letter sent to parents when a child in school tested positive stated 'please be reassured that for most people, coronavirus (Covid-19) will be a mild illness' and suggested 'if you are able, move any vulnerable individuals (such as the elderly and those with underlying health conditions) out of your home'.[1] The

---

[1] I can't find the original source of this letter. I first saw the phrases in a letter I received as a parent, but google either phrase and you'll see numerous examples of the same text.

message was about others, with no sense that 'you' as a parent or carer could be one of 'those' 'vulnerable individuals'.

In late April 2020, we paused to remember the 'keyworkers' who had died during the pandemic. Journalists concentrated their attention on 'the healthy' who were dying, particularly the 'healthcare heroes'. And the government continued to focus its daily updates on 'those hospitalized in the UK who tested positive for coronavirus' who have 'sadly died' (Department of Health and Social Care, 2020a).

But there was a shocking lack of acknowledgement of the number of people who were dying in care homes, especially as talk increasingly turned to peaks and plateaus and to easing restrictions and relaxing the rules.

At that time, the World Health Organization estimated that people who died in care homes represented half of all deaths across Europe, but in the UK, they were being written out of the story of the pandemic.

'In the week to 17 April 2020 almost a quarter of recorded deaths from the virus happened in care homes, [and] from 10–24 April 2020, care homes reported 4,343 deaths from coronavirus', but deaths of people in care homes weren't included in daily official figures of Covid-19 deaths until 29 April 2020 (The Guardian, 2020).

And no data on the deaths of people with a learning disability was published until early June 2020. In November 2020, Public Health England reported estimates that as many as 692 per 100,000 people registered as having a learning disability died with Covid-19 between 21 March and 5 June, a death rate 6.3 times higher than the general population (Public Health England, 2020).

Them and us, not us

Then there are the 'deaths'. These are presented coldly as mortality rates... This approach is literally dehumanizing people. People's lives deserve to be so much more valued than being whittled down into a number at a press conference.

(ROBINS, 2020A)

Increasingly the narrative was about numbers, not people. 'Cases.' 'Daily deaths.' 'Covid fatalities.' Trends and curves. Grim statistics that highlighted but also hid the human cost of the disease. The individual lives lost, and the lives changed forever.

The metaphors and labels employed suggested an inevitability about the virus and its consequences – distracting us from the truth about the government's response. It very soon became clear that we were not 'all in this together', and that some of us were at significantly greater risk either directly or indirectly from Covid-19. This gave some insight into the virus but said much more about our attitudes, values, politics, and power.

It could be argued that the language used during the pandemic saved lives, galvanizing people to work together – and indeed to stay apart. But the language, particularly the use of the term 'vulnerable', undoubtedly also negatively influenced policy, attitudes, and behaviour. It stifled debate and deflected attention from the systems, structures, and prejudices that cause and perpetuate vulnerability. It justified paternalistic 'fixing' and denied people a voice and a choice. And it accentuated the 'them and us' divide.

I can't help thinking that if, instead of 'protect the NHS' and 'protect the vulnerable' (them), the core message had been to 'protect each other' (us), we'd have experienced fewer divisions and maybe – just maybe – saved lives.

PART TWO

CHANGING OUR PURPOSE

A Life Not a Service

People want support to have a life not a service. –Clenton Farquharson
(NATIONAL DEVELOPMENT TEAM FOR INCLUSION, 2017)

The very first line in the Care Act guidance – point 1.1 – states 'the core purpose of adult care and support is to help people to achieve the outcomes that matter to them in their life' (Department of Health and Social Care, 2023). This prominent statement *should* steer and shape our practice. But it seems this explicit message has been lost in translation, and as such the purpose of our roles is determined by a very different view of the overall purpose of social care, and of the people we support and serve.

When we see people as vulnerable, weak, and needy, we see social care as a safety net, and our roles in terms of maintenance. We adopt the medical model approach of treating and fixing. The charity model approach of rescuing. Looking after. Caring for. 'Doing to'.

When we view people as customers, we view social care in terms of 'service delivery', and our default response is to 'do for'. We assess for, commission, and broker services supplied to passive recipients. 'Providers' and 'service users'.

And when we think about people as 'demand' and social care in terms of finite services, our purpose becomes to ration. To screen and redirect.

Processes dominate our practice to such an extent that as well as describing *what* we do (screen, triage, assess, review), they've also become our 'why'.

Our purpose has become the enactment of our processes.

Job adverts refer to social workers 'screening and risk-assessing cases', 'assessing service users', and 'reviewing placements'. We have 'assessment officers' and 'review teams'. 'Performance' is measured by the number of assessments and reviews we complete. The number of 'cases' we close.

Through all the lenses I mentioned above, the people we serve are 'a problem'. And through all these lenses, the solution to the problem is a service.

So ultimately, the purpose of social care has become the delivery of services, and the purpose of social work has become assessing people for services.

Purpose also means 'a person's sense of resolve or determination'; our 'sense of purpose'.

In serving this institutional machine, our own sense of purpose has been crushed.

Lost.

Instead of embracing our values, passion, and initiative, our current system sucks us in to its structures, processes, and hierarchies, and spits out robots reliant on forms and procedures to complete tasks and achieve targets.

Our bureaucracies have dehumanized us, and in turn we've dehumanized the people we serve.

We've forgotten that we *all* need a strong sense of purpose and meaning to live well. A need to feel useful. Necessary. Needed.

Our processes serve our institutional purpose, but usually ignore the purpose of the people we're employed to serve. We focus on the help people need to get up and dressed, but not their reason to get out of bed.

Social care has become a destination ('getting care', 'going into care', 'placed in care'), not a vehicle to support people to be who they want to be, and to do the things that matter most to them.

However, if we reimagine the purpose of social care, and indeed public services more generally, we can liberate both the 'assessors' and the 'assessed' from these bureaucratic and dehumanizing confines.

If we see social care in terms of supporting people to live good lives – gloriously ordinary lives – our purpose becomes to understand what that good life looks like, and to work alongside people to achieve it.

If we see people as human beings with gifts and potential, our purpose becomes supporting people to find, retain, or regain their own sense of purpose. Supporting people to flourish and to thrive.

And in turn, what matters to them becomes what matters to us.

And we remember that our purpose is *people*, not process.

Independent

'The purpose of social care is to enable people to live an independent life.'

In 2006 the United Nations Convention on the Rights of Persons with Disabilities (CRPD) recognized the equal right of all disabled people to live independently and be included in communities, with choices equal to non-disabled people.

There's no mention of 'independent living' in the Care Act 2014 though – a missed opportunity to explicitly incorporate the CRPD right into domestic law. And the associated statutory guidance dismisses the term as 'relatively abstract', suggesting the focus on wellbeing and the 'outcomes that truly matter to people' is clearer.

Maybe this focus is clearer. But the guidance does state that 'the concept of "independent living" is a core part of the wellbeing principle' and that 'supporting people to live as independently as possible, for as long as possible, is a guiding principle of the Care Act' (Department of Health and Social Care, 2023). As such, references to 'independence' feature prominently in statements about the purpose of adult social care.

But when we pay attention to the way we use the term, it's obvious we're not all thinking or talking about the same thing.

In practice, independence is often understood in terms of the dictionary definition of 'not relying on other people or needing help or money from anyone else'. As people 'taking care of themselves' (Collins, n.d.).

We 'promote independence to build self-reliance and to minimize the need for high end care'. We 'maximize the independence of individuals so that they are able to do more for themselves'. We 'want you to stay well and independent for as long as possible, so our support isn't needed'.

'When I say I want independence my social worker tells me she will end my social care package then I will have independence' (Sharp, 2024).

This narrative implies that drawing on support equates to loss of independence.

It's far removed from the concept of independence equating to choice and control, where 'independence is not linked to the physical or intellectual capacity to care for oneself without assistance; independence is created by having assistance when and how one requires it' (Morris, 2014).

As Michael Oliver explains:

> In advancing the idea of independence, professionals and disabled people have not been talking about the same thing. Professionals tend to define independence in terms of self-care activities such as washing, dressing, toileting, cooking and eating without assistance. Disabled people however, define independence differently, seeing it as the ability to be in control of and make decisions about one's life, rather than doing things alone or without help. (Oliver, 1990)

Getting back to normal

The concept of independence as self-sufficiency is perhaps most obvious in relation to 'reablement'. 'The reablement approach supports people to do things for themselves'.

The dictionary definition of reablement is 'the job or activity of helping people return to *normal life* again after a period of being ill or in hospital' (Cambridge Dictionary, n.d.) (emphasis added).

And reablement is described on the NHS website as 'temporary care to *help you get back to normal* and stay independent' (NHS, n.d.) (emphasis added).

Colin Goble writes:

> From this perspective, which remains the dominant one in our society, disabled people are dependent because their bodies, senses or minds are somehow 'defective' and don't allow them to function independently. In short, they are 'not normal', and a return to normality, or some approximation of it, becomes the goal of rehabilitation practice. (Goble, 2004)

He observes how our 'professional interventions' use 'scales and tools' to measure people's 'performance against "normative" standards', and how we develop programmes to reduce the gap between where people are on the scale and what is considered 'normal'.

As such, Jenny Morris writes (quoting Simon Brisenden):

> Disabled people are victims of an ideology of independence. It teaches us that unless we can do everything for ourselves we cannot take our place in society. We must be able to cook, wash, dress ourselves, make the bed, write, speak and so forth, before we can become proper people, before we are 'independent'. (Morris, 2014)

Reducing 'care package' costs

The Reclaiming Our Futures Alliance of disabled people suggests that:

> the language of independent living has been appropriated by Government and public bodies to justify the cuts they are making... It is common practice for essential support to be removed from Disabled people through social care assessments under the justification of 'helping' them to 'improve their independence'. (Reclaiming Our Futures Alliance, 2019)

It's hard to disagree when adult social care strategies mention ambitions to 'increase service user independence to reduce the financial value of care packages' and maximize independence 'to reduce the need for costly interventions' and 'minimize costs to the taxpayer'.

This is the promotion of independence to 'manage demand', not to ensure wellbeing and the outcomes that truly matter to people.

Living independently 'in your own home'

We generally imply that living in 'your own home' equates to independence, and that any support you draw on in 'your own home' will 'allow you to remain independent'.

'Home care, or domiciliary care, is support provided in the person's own home to allow them to stay independent for as long as possible.' 'Small devices can detect and monitor your movements passively and can help you live independently in your own home.' 'Supported living allows people with disabilities or mental health to maintain independence within the community.'

This equates independence with living 'in the community' as opposed to an institution, but not with people's rights to liberty, autonomy, dignity, privacy, participation, and inclusion.

How many of the people supported to 'live independently' in their own home can control who comes through their front door, and when? Can eat what they feel like eating, and when they feel hungry? Can choose what time to go to bed and who shares their bed?

And, whether we interpret independence in terms of self-determination or self-reliance, too often 'living independently' equals secluded lives – a reality far removed from the CRPD Article 19 directive that disabled people should have access to the 'assistance necessary to support living and inclusion in the community, and to prevent isolation or segregation from the community' (United Nations, 2006).

We may make sure people have 'equipment to help with daily living' or 'four calls a day' for 'personal care needs', but it's unlikely life feels good if your only conversations are with Alexa or with a paid worker you've never seen before and may never see again, if the only time you're touched or held involves 'washing and dressing', 'feeding', and 'moving and handling'.

It's hard to realize or remember who you really are and why you matter if you have no one in your life to affirm your identity and value, and nothing to do to give you any sense of meaning or purpose.

For as long as possible

'Social care aims to help older and disabled people to stay as independent as possible for as long as possible.' The 'as long as possible' qualifier from the Care Act guidance is frequently repeated in references to the aims of social care.

This implies that at some point living in your 'own home' will not be possible, and that a 'placement' in residential care is inevitable, regardless of whether it's what you choose – a narrative far removed from the Article 19 requirement that disabled people 'have the opportunity to choose their place of residence and where and with whom they live on an equal basis with others and are not obliged to live in a particular living arrangement' (United Nations, 2006).

❋ ❋ ❋

Once again, just to bang on about this one more time, this right is about *choice*, not a particular kind of accommodation or 'independent living skills' or living alone or without support. It's about disabled people having the same choices as non-disabled people about where you live and who you live with, and having access to the services you need to enable you to live there and be included in the community. It's a right that has at its core a desire to tackle institutionalization and the segregation and isolation of disabled people. (Series, 2015)

Given the varying interpretations and how harmful they can be, I believe we need to think carefully about how helpful the language of independence is in relation to the overall purpose of social care.

I'm not advocating we abandon the principles of independent living articulated in Article 19. However, I don't think we need to talk about independence to ensure that the principles of autonomy and inclusion are at the heart of what we do. We just need to talk about people leading the lives they *choose* to lead – then work together to make that a reality for everyone.

From Institutions
to Communities

*B*ack in 1946, Sir William Beveridge – architect of the Welfare State:

> voiced his concern that he had both missed and limited the power
> of the citizen and of communities... He was increasingly aware that
> communities rather than distant, cold and hierarchical institutions,
> are often much better at identifying needs and designing solutions.
> [But] Beveridge had designed people and their relationships out of
> the welfare state. He realized too late that he had made a mistake.
> (Cottam, 2018)

Despite Beveridge's acknowledgement of the importance and power of
communities, institutions continue to dominate our approach. Rather
than recognizing the strengths and opportunities in communities, too
often neighbourhoods and networks are written off as part of the problem (think 'sink estates', 'no-go areas', 'hard to reach' communities),
and services and 'settings' remain our default solution.

Instead of ensuring that people can participate, and draw on
'community-based support', we've created a system that isolates and
removes people from communities in the name of 'care'.

However, more and more of us are now accepting what Beveridge
realized all those years ago. We know that if we're going to ensure that
everyone can live the life they choose to lead, we must dismantle our
institutional approaches and focus instead on working in and alongside
communities, sustaining human networks of support.

But this dismantling takes much more than closing large establish-
ments. As Alex Fox observes, 'throughout these changes and improvement programmes, and their "task and finish groups", the asylum

remains unseen: its assumptions, its relationships, its power dynamics and its abhorrence of love' (Fox, 2018).

Paying attention to how we communicate about 'community' helps to shine a light on these ingrained attitudes. So, let's look at the current narrative, explore what it exposes, and consider where we need to focus our attention if we're really going to put communities at the heart of social care.

Institutions

If you can't get up at 3am and microwave yourself a burrito, you're living in an institution.

(OPEN FUTURE LEARNING, 2023)

If we're going to shift away from the dominance of institutions, first we need to be clear about what we mean by the term.

The Equality and Human Rights Commission defines an institution as 'residential accommodation where:

- residents are isolated from the broader community
- residents live together with people other than those with whom they have chosen to live
- residents do not have control over their day-to-day lives and over decisions that affect them, or
- the interests of the organization itself tend to take precedence over the residents' individualized needs or wishes.' (Equality and Human Rights Commission, 2021)

While we generally associate institutions with 'care settings', the isolation and lack of choice and control mentioned in this definition can be just as much a feature of life for people 'living in the community'.

'Institutions are made as much of thoughts, beliefs and organizational practices as of bricks and mortar' (Goble, 2004).

As Neil Crowther writes:

We tend to think of institutions and institutionalization as about being in a place. But institutionalization is really about the dismantling of the self, through the dismantling of its scaffolding: not respecting or upholding routines and rituals, familiar people and things, one's own bed, the clothes one wears, the food one eats, the places one can go, the television one watches or the music one listens to. This may be more likely in congregate care facilities, but it can also happen outside of them where risk averse policy and practice, or life and limb care pays no attention to personhood, identity and autonomy. (Crowther, 2020a)

'The community'

'Community' is like a magic word in serviceland.

Toby Lowe suggests that the term 'has a strange power to it. It conveys a sense of togetherness and positivity. It speaks both of solidarity and homeliness'. But, he observes, 'you will, almost never, hear people say what they mean by "community"' (Lowe, 2021).

Dictionaries define 'community' as 'the people living in one particular area or people who are considered as a unit because of their common interests, social group, or nationality' (Cambridge Dictionary, n.d.). 'A group of people who are similar in some way'. A 'sense of having something in common' (Collins, n.d.).

Community means people who share something. Indeed, the word derives from the Latin for common. A common geography, history, experience, culture, characteristic, identity, interest, profession...

There are numerous wonderfully diverse and eclectic communities. And yet we talk about 'the community', not communities.

And in the same way we think of institutions in terms of buildings, we refer to 'the community' in terms of a place.

There's no sense of people or relationships.

Of the *feeling* of community.

Of being welcome.

Of belonging.

Accessing the community

In one of his many brilliant and powerful blog posts, Mark Neary writes:

> I wish they would drop this 'accessing the community' stuff. Steven is the community. 'Accessing' it means that he is on the outside of it, waiting to be given admittance. That reveals a strong attitude – 'this is ours and you are not part of it unless we allow you to be'. (Neary, 2014)

A comment in response to Mark's post reads:

> My daughter doesn't want to 'access the community'. She likes going out, when she can choose where and when... She loves company, and chatting to people, but wants little to do with day centres or over-organized activities. The other night, she hid her shoes, because to her accessing the community sometimes means doing things that other people want her to do.

The phrase 'accessing the community' shrieks difference.

We go out.

'They' access the community.

It suggests 'the community' is somewhere you go, not something you're already part of.

Somewhere you 'access' as an 'activity' or an 'outing', depending on your schedule, when (and if) you're 'allowed'.

Somewhere you fit into. You're fitted into.

Not somewhere you belong.

Living in the community

I hope Nigel will be so embedded in his community that there will always be people who'll look out for him, love him and care for him after I'm no longer here. That's what every parent wants.

(SALMAN, 2019B)

Baroness Sheila Hollins' son Nigel, who has a learning disability, 'lives independently in a flat near his family with support from a personal assistant' and 'people see Nigel in the shops, cafe or train station. He has a life in the community'. She stresses that returning people from inpatient units to communities 'will never work until people understand it's not about a building and a staff team, or rotas and procedures, but about putting somebody like Nigel at the centre of the plans'. Professionals should understand that what people need to live their life is to belong in communities (Salman, 2019b).

How many older people and disabled people 'living in the community' are really *living*, with genuine choice and control over their lives?

How many people 'living in the community' are really known, needed, and included in communities? Belonging, not just fitting in?

Community living skills

College courses for young autistic people and people with a learning disability are designed to 'equip [learners] with the essential skills for living which will enable them to remain within their local community' and 'take part in community life'. Care providers offer 'services that help people develop their capacity to live in the community' and 'enable them to gain the skills for living in the community'. 'Reablement teams' aim to 'work with people to help them acquire or regain the skills and confidence to live successfully in the community'. And the Care Act guidance mentions helping people to 'develop or regain the skills of independent living and active involvement in their local community' (Department of Health and Social Care, 2023).

All this suggests, once again, that some people are not already seen as part of communities, and will only become part of 'the community' if they complete the course or accept the service (which 'can be accessed via a referral from the service user's care coordinator' and 'requires a risk assessment and a health and social care needs assessment') and gain the skills to be allowed in.

So much for inclusion.

So much for human rights.

Prevention

The Care Act guidance states that 'local approaches to prevention should be built on the resources of the local community'. That assessments should seek to understand how people's 'needs may be prevented, reduced or delayed by others within the community, rather than by more formal services', and help 'a person with lower needs to access support in their local community' (Department of Health and Social Care, 2023).

Despite the guidance stressing that 'prevention should be seen as an ongoing consideration', there's often a strong emphasis on prevention being something that happens 'before' social care, when people have 'low-level' or 'ineligible' needs. The way we talk about 'community' is similar. Angela Catley notes that 'the sense that social care is something (tasks?) that happens when "community" "prevention" "resilience" 😕 and strong gatekeeping has failed. Rather than the support people get to live a full life...in their community, using their strengths etc 😊' (Community Catalysts, 2023b).

And Alex Fox observes that:

while ideas for prevention and early intervention are based on the belief that the boundaries can be redrawn, not erased, they themselves rest on familiar assumptions about the divide between community-based citizens and the subjects of service land, rather than removing that divide. (Fox, 2018)

If we're going to remove this divide, we need to tell a different story.

A story that places social care at the heart of communities, and communities at the heart of social care. That recognizes community as the relationships between people. As participation and inclusion.

That appreciates we *all* have much to give, and so much more to gain.

And that articulates the role of local authorities – as Fredric Seebohm envisaged back in 1968 as reaching 'far beyond the discovery and rescue of social casualties, [to] enable the greatest possible number of individuals to act reciprocally, giving and receiving service for the wellbeing of the community' (Harvey, 2020).

As Mark Harvey suggests, 'You wouldn't be surprised if you found that paragraph in the Care Act now.'

Fredric Seebohm's recommendation is echoed by Social Care Future's articulation of social care as helping to 'weave the web of relationships and support in our local communities that we can draw on to live our lives in the way that we want to, whatever our age or stage in life'. This vision 'recognizes people who draw on social care being both givers and receivers of support to and from their community. It is about people caring about and supporting one another, rather than invoking ideas of "vulnerable people" being "cared for"' (Crowther & Quinton, 2021).

So, let's stop talking about 'the community' as if it's a place for us to signpost people to 'before social care', train people to have the skills to enter, and 'allow' people to 'access' from the confines of service-land. Instead, let's talk about communities where we look out for one another, and all play our part in creating communities where everyone belongs.

Safe

There are 416 references to 'safe'/'safety'/'safeguarding' in the Care Act 2014 statutory guidance. The term dominates our narrative. But what do we really mean by 'safe'? And is the extent of our ambitions really just that people are 'safe'?

In this chapter, I'll explore this language and how it defines our purpose, practice, and perception of people. Then, in the next chapter, I'll consider reimagining the purpose of social care, from 'keeping people safe' to supporting people to flourish.

From safety net to springboard.

Safe

The statutory guidance is clear that 'professionals should work with the adult to establish what being safe means to them and how that can be best achieved' (Department of Health and Social Care, 2023).

When I think about what being safe means to me, this is what comes to mind:

- Closing my own front door behind me and feeling that I'm home.
- Having enough of a rough idea about what's happening in the next few days and weeks, but not so much of a plan that I feel pressured or constrained.
- The certainty of nature and seasons, especially spring, as hope emerges from the ground in green shoots, and promise unfurls with new leaves on the trees.
- Being held, and feeling held, by people who love me.

These are all things that help me to feel safe. They enable me to be me. Provide security. Roots. The ground beneath my feet.

So, to me, 'safe' means belonging. Friendship. Love. Noticing and feeling noticed. Acceptance. Connection, and just enough control.

In the dictionary definition, 'if you are safe, you have not been harmed, or you are not in danger of being harmed' (Collins, n.d.). And this is where we locate our purpose and our practice. 'Keeping people safe.' 'Safeguarding vulnerable adults.' 'Protecting those at risk of harm.' Indeed, the Care Act guidance is clear that 'in any activity which a local authority undertakes, it should consider how to ensure that the person is and remains protected from abuse or neglect'.

However, the guidance is also clear that 'it is not possible to promote wellbeing without establishing *a basic foundation* where people are safe', and that 'people have complex lives and being safe is only one of the things they want for themselves' (Department of Health and Social Care, 2023) (emphasis added).

'Being safe is not a freedom in its own right – it is what allows us to get on with the rest of our lives' (Equality and Human Rights Commission, 2009). Too often we focus on 'safety' as a destination, not as a 'basic foundation' – an essential element of people's wellbeing but one that matters little without other elements. As Lord Justice Munby famously observed, 'What good is it making someone safer if it merely makes them miserable?' (*Local Authority X v MM & Anor (No. 1) [2007] EWHC 2003 (Fam)*, 2007).

And too often we ignore the fact that it's the other elements of people's wellbeing that ensure their safety. We perpetuate the belief that our policies, assessments, plans, services, and institutions keep people safe, and overlook the extent to which connections, relationships, meaning, and purpose keep people safe.

As Rob Mitchell reflects in relation to the Munby quote, 'I remember realizing early on in my career that the most vulnerable people to abuse are the ones who didn't have anyone who loved them' (Mitchell, R., 2023).

And as Maff Potts reminds us, 'The more people in a community who know each other by their first name the safer that community is' (Potts, 2021b).

Things that do not involve any risk

The dictionary also defines the term safe as 'things that do not involve any risk'. (Collins, n.d.).

And we take this literally, with a perpetual focus on 'assessing risk', 'managing risk', and 'reducing risk'. But it's impossible to live – to have a life – without risk, so whose risks are we really concerned about here? Who exactly are we protecting?

Here's a social work trap. How many times do we get this: 'Can you provide assurance to me/the board/this meeting that P is absolutely safe?' Our answer must surely always be 'No, I cannot do that. No one can. And the reason you are asking me is to make you safe, not the person.' (Mitchell, R., 2022)

Safe places

A safe place is one where it is unlikely that any harm, damage, or unpleasant things will happen to the people or things that are there.

(COLLINS, N.D.)

In our own lives, we might define our home or our community as our safe place. The place we feel welcome and known, where we feel we belong.

But in serviceland, 'safe places' or 'places of safety' are institutions. 'Residential accommodation provided by a local social services authority.' 'A hospital.' 'A police station.' 'An independent hospital or care home for people who are mentally disordered.'[1] They are places that people are 'admitted to' and, 'discharged to'. 'Conveyed to', 'transported between'. 'Kept in'. 'Ddetained in'.

Places with procedures, uniforms, wards, 'assessment rooms', and 'staff rest areas'.

Places where people become 'patients' and 'service users'.

Alex Fox suggests that 'one of the signs you are living in an invisible asylum is that you are in a place of "safety", as defined by others who have a professional (but not necessarily personal) responsibility for keeping you "safe".' He acknowledges the benefits of a society with such a 'safety net', but stresses 'it is important to recognize that support of this kind will never be unproblematically benign. It is support which at times keeps people safe from death, but at other times keeps people "safe" from life"' (Fox, 2018).

---

1   These are the places defined as 'places of safety' in Section 135 (6) of the Mental Health Act 1983.

And reflecting on his dad's experience in a hospital where 'somewhere in the transition between two wards, his dentures went missing and could not be found', Neil Crowther writes:

> That afternoon I spoke to the social worker. I think she felt she was being sympathetic, but when I told her about the dentures going missing she replied that 'It happens all the time...and hearing aids too'. She then went on to advise that my dad was 'in a place of safety'. I suggested she might reconsider whether someone is safe in a place where patients routinely lose the means to eat or to hear but she was on auto-pilot. (Crowther, 2020b)

In our 'auto-pilot' mode, the places we call 'safe' are often places where people are disconnected from their identity and from the people, places, and things that matter most to them. From the people, places, and things that make them feel safe.

Safeguarding

The Care Act 2014 introduced 'adult safeguarding' as a statutory duty, and the related statutory guidance 'endorses the Making Safeguarding Personal approach [which] represents a fundamental shift in social work practice in relation to safeguarding, with *a focus on the person not the process*' (Department of Health and Social Care, 2023) (emphasis added).

'Safeguarding' is another magic word in serviceland, the key to the door of a whole new world – or at least a whole new 'workflow'. And as if the term 'safeguarding' wasn't jargon enough, there's also a whole new language ('concern', 'allegation', 'adult at risk', 'Section 42 enquiry'...) and a huge heap of acronyms: SAB, SAM, SAR, SCR, DHR, MASH, MARAC, MAPPA, MSP, PiPoT, and many more.

We recruit social workers to 'triage and assess safeguarding concerns'; to 'undertake safeguarding investigations and develop and implement protection plans'; to 'contribute to the operational delivery of the multi-agency safeguarding policy and procedures'; to 'participate in safeguarding adults strategy meetings'; to 'prepare safeguarding reports for safeguarding case conferences'; to 'pro-actively work towards the timely resolution, recording and closure of safeguarding enquiries in line with agreed timescales and team performance frameworks'.

We still focus on the process, not the person.

Those who cannot protect themselves

'Vulnerable person.' 'Adult at risk.' 'Safeguarding cases.' 'Those who cannot protect themselves.'

As well as denying and eroding unique identities, our labels imply deficits and helplessness.

Contrast this with community-based alternatives. With the Camerados approach of asking someone who is struggling to help you. With the peer-led People Focused Group (PFG) in Doncaster, where instead of asking what's wrong or what people 'need', they ask, 'What would you like to contribute to your community? What skills and gifts would you like to share?' When I asked PFG Director Glyn Butcher what this approach means to people. Glyn said, 'It gives people a sense of purpose. It gives people a sense of identity. It says that I'm worth something. It says that I'm valuable. It says that it's okay to be me.'[2]

A secure footing

The full sentence from the Care Act guidance I quoted earlier is that 'it is not possible to promote wellbeing without establishing a basic foundation where people are safe *and their care and support is on a secure footing*' (Department of Health and Social Care, 2023) (emphasis added).

Care and support on a secure footing? Can *anyone* say that?

Highlighting the fragility of the care and support system on Twitter recently, one person who draws on support said that they thought it was 'almost unquantifiable' how much difference it would make if people knew that 'things aren't constantly moments from full collapse'. They described the current system as 'wildly unsafe both physically and psychologically'.

The statutory safety net of social care has too many holes to adequately assure safety, let alone to promote wellbeing and guarantee that people thrive.

Confining our thinking and ambitions to 'keeping people safe' and 'protecting our most vulnerable' traps us in a world where we hold all the power and responsibility. Where we focus on 'looking after', 'protecting', and 'caring for' 'others'. Where we judge what is 'appropriate', 'unwise' and 'safe'. Where we spend our time raising concerns, assessing

---

2   Glyn Butcher, People Focused Group Director, in a conversation with me recorded for the Social Care Future Community of Support on 29 February 2024.

risk, completing forms, writing policies, following procedures, making referrals, sitting in meetings, and 'learning lessons', while families, friends, neighbours, and community groups are busy weaving the webs of relationships and support that affirm identities, ensure belonging, and enable people to live fulfilling lives. They create genuinely safe spaces, like Camerados' public living rooms, with 'people who listen, who treat everyone the same, who don't judge or try to fix you' (Camerados, n.d.) and PFG's Wellness Centre where, as Glyn Butcher explains, 'We're not here to save people. We're here to help people flourish in whatever they choose to be.'[3]

If we reimagine the purpose of care and support as supporting people to flourish, to live gloriously ordinary lives, we flip our focus from what is or might go wrong, to what is possible and what is strong. Focus 'not simply on people's freedom from harm...but on what is required to accord them the freedom to flourish as human beings, ensuring they have genuine autonomy to shape a life worth living' (Equality and Human Rights Commission, 2009).

There are 416 references to 'safe'/'safety'/'safeguarding' in the Care Act 2014 statutory guidance, and 244 references to abuse.

There is one reference to 'love', and one to 'belonging'. There's no mention of 'flourishing' or 'thriving'.

It's time to flip this narrative.

'A ship in harbor is safe, but that's not what ships are built for' (John A. Shedd).[4]

---

3   Glyn Butcher, People Focused Group Director, in a conversation with me recorded for the Social Care Future Community of Support on 29 February 2024.
4   This quote is widely attributed to John A. Shedd, original source unknown.

From Safety Net to Springboard

The goal of a reimagined system of care and support is to enable all humans to flourish. Care can sometimes be reduced to tasks, focusing on our physical needs of eating, drinking and going to the toilet. Sometimes safety from harm overrides all other considerations. This sets the bar too low.

(ARCHBISHOPS' COMMISSION ON REIMAGINING CARE, 2023)

Safety net

Our current 'care system' is a safety net, not a springboard, where we define our purpose in terms of 'keeping people safe', not supporting people to flourish, and where too often our practice focuses on keeping people alive, not ensuring people thrive.

By its very definition, a safety net is there to save us when times are hard, things are tough, life is precarious. To catch us when we fall.

Describing the purpose of social care in this way perpetuates our medical model approach of fixing people, and our charity model approach of rescuing 'those who are vulnerable'. It frames people who require assistance to live their lives as helpless and in need. And it locks us into thinking of social care as a crisis response service.

Too often, people's basic human desire for love and connection is largely ignored in plans and 'packages' that focus on meeting 'personal care needs' and keeping people alive – not offering or sustaining reasons to live.

As Hilary Cottam observes, 'Our welfare state might still catch us when we fall, but it cannot help us take flight' (Cottam, 2018).

A safety net riddled with holes

The dominant social care rhetoric focuses on what is missing: hospitals having to 'keep patients' on wards for longer 'because there aren't enough care beds and homecare packages available'; 'chronic staffing shortages'; 'record social work vacancies;' the 'lack of providers'; the 'gaps in social care funding'; the 'vulnerable older and disabled people [falling] through a safety net riddled with holes'.

It's a narrative that highlights the absolute crisis facing the system. But in our obsessive focus on what's missing and what's wrong, we're overlooking what we have, and what is strong.

Abundance

When we view 'care' in terms of 'packages', 'hours', 'settings', and 'beds', resources are finite, and our narrative is inevitably one of scarcity.

But maybe, just maybe, 'the gap is actually in the definition and not in "provision"' (Catley, 2023a).

In our current definition, 'care' is a service and – as John McKnight observes – 'the central assumption is that service is a unilateral process, I, the professional, produce. You, the client, consume'. But if we shift to viewing care in terms of relationships, then we recognize and value people as 'assets', not 'demand', and 'you need me' becomes 'we need each other' (Cahn, 2000).

Instead of highlighting what is absent, we notice, build on, and invest in what is present.

This recognition and appreciation of abundance moves us naturally to thinking in terms of people and communities rather than services and institutions. Instead of focusing our attention on how we sustain a 'care sector', we consider how we ensure a sustainable care and support infrastructure. The 'web of relationships and support in our local communities that we can draw on to live our lives in the way that we want to, with meaning, purpose and connection, whatever our age or stage of life' (Crowther & Quinton, 2021).

Flourishing

Hilary Cottam writes that 'this idea that the work of caring for one another is core to our humanity and human wellbeing was well understood by our ancestors'. She references 'eudaimonia' – Aristotle's concept of 'flourishing'. That 'we need support to grow and develop and we need a sense of meaning' and 'for Aristotle, this meaning comes through collective participation...tending to one another and the wider infrastructure that shapes our world is what enables us to flourish' (Cottam, 2021).

We thrive through participation and being needed, having purpose and meaning, caring and feeling cared about. We flourish through interdependence.

However, 'in the West this understanding of human flourishing has gradually unravelled', as the 'ruthless quest to maximize individual material gain' means 'work' and 'care' are separated, and the 'messy business' of caring is 'outsourced, placed elsewhere, out of sight' (Cottam, 2021).

'Hidden', 'economically inactive' carers 'suffering under the burden of looking after loved ones'. 'Giving up work to care'.

And industrialized, institutional 'care', 'delivered' by the clock, where human 'messiness' is tidied neatly into 'visits', 'schedules', and 'settings', and where underpaid workers maintain isolated individuals.

You're unlikely to flourish in a world where caring – and requiring some assistance to live your life – means you're exhausted by uncertainty, juggling, and fighting for recognition, understanding, and support.

You're unlikely to thrive in a system that denies your human need for love, connection, meaning, and purpose, and even denies that you are human.

'When you're not perceived by other people and your social needs are so deprived, so povertous, there's nobody, it's just you, you don't actually know that you exist' –Alexis Quinn (BBC Newsnight, 2024).

To ensure we *all* flourish, we must stop segregating people and people's lives and focus instead on creating the conditions we all need to thrive.

Springboard

Just as trees stand tall in their individual beauty by entwining their roots with one another, so we as individuals, communities and nations only fully reach our potential within ecosystems of care and support.

(COTTAM, 2021)

In our safety net approach, 'care' is a service. A destination. An ending.

A springboard, in contrast, is about beginnings, opportunities, possibilities.

The Equality and Human Rights Commission report, 'From safety net to springboard', published in 2009, describes a vision of:

> an infrastructure of care and support which acts as a springboard by promoting and sustaining the capabilities of individuals and their families to maximize control over their own lives, to participate and contribute socially and economically, and through doing so improve their wellbeing and prosperity and that of the wider community and economy. (Equality and Human Rights Commission, 2009)

In this approach:

> Social care is not an end in itself but the means to a better life. [It is] about supporting active citizenship. It is built on the bonds of mutual interest and inter-dependency that define our common humanity, acknowledging that most of us will give and receive care and support during our lives. (Archbishops' Commission on Reimagining Care, 2023)

In this approach, care is a relationship, not a task or a transaction, and support is sourced – *and resourced* – in communities.

In this approach, we focus not on 'what's the matter', but on what matters to people and what makes people matter.

We focus not on 'what do you need', but on being needed.

We focus not on what's missing and what is or could go wrong, but on what is present, what is possible, what is strong.

Prevention

'Prevention', along with 'integration' and 'innovation' is one of the most used and abused terms within public service reform.

(FOX, 2018)

We have prevention officers, prevention workers, prevention teams, prevention services, prevention strategies, and prevention policies. But what exactly do we mean by prevention in relation to social care, and what is it that we're trying to prevent?

Stopping something from happening

Back in 1961, Lydia Rapoport wrote that 'the concept of prevention, borrowed largely from the public health model, is often used in a distorted and confusing manner in the social work framework' (Rapoport, 1961). And though the term is used ubiquitously 60 years on, 'there remains a lack of common understanding and consistency in approach to prevention, which is perhaps unsurprising given the absence of a single definition and the wide range of interventions and objectives' (Social Care Institute for Excellence, 2021a).

The dictionary definition of prevention is 'the act of stopping something from happening or of stopping someone from doing something' (Cambridge Dictionary, n.d.).

The 2018 'Prevention is better than cure' policy paper states that 'prevention is about helping people stay healthy, happy and independent for as long as possible. This means reducing the chances of problems from arising in the first place and, when they do, supporting people to manage them as effectively as possible' (Department of Health and Social Care, 2018).

But this document, and many others, focus heavily on preventing ill-health, disease, and 'people becoming patients'.

No one disputes that preventing problems and crises occurring is better than picking up the pieces and fixing things when they do. Prevention *is* better than cure. But this narrative means that prevention is still largely seen as being the realm of health and public health.

Preventing the need for care and support

People who use services don't want to be divided into the fixable and the not-fixable. –Sue Bott

(FOX, 2012)

The duties relating to prevention in social care were introduced in the Care Act 2014. The Act requires local authorities to prevent, reduce, or delay the need for care and support, and the associated statutory guidance makes it clear that 'wellbeing cannot be achieved simply through crisis management; it must include a focus on delaying and preventing care and support needs, and supporting people to live as independently as possible for as long as possible' (Department of Health and Social Care, 2023).

There are references throughout the guidance to preventing 'the development of needs for care and support', 'needs emerging across health and care', 'carers from developing needs for support', 'an escalation in needs for care and support', 'a person's needs from progressing', and 'future needs' (Department of Health and Social Care, 2023).

However, the way the guidance refers to 'those with care and support needs', and 'those people who may benefit from preventative support', perpetuates that sense of 'them and us'.

'It sounds like you are dividing disabled people up into two groups of problems: those who can be prevented and those, like me, who can't' –disability rights activist (Fox, 2018).

And the narrative around prevention often includes terms like 'independence' and 'resilience' – perpetuating the sense that 'self-sufficiency' and managing on your own is the goal.

Reducing the demand on services

Like the Care Act 2014 and the associated guidance, the *People at the Heart of Care* white paper includes references to preventing 'people developing needs for care and support' and 'future care needs' (Department of Health and Social Care, 2022).

The white paper also explicitly refers to preventing 'longer-term demand' and 'people from requiring social care in the first instance', and this framing of – and case for – prevention is common. A quick trawl of councils' prevention strategies reveals lines like 'unless we reduce demand and prevent need escalating, service provision in its current form will become unsustainable' and 'we need to use preventative approaches to reduce the demand on services and reduce costs'.

As well as linking the 'prevention agenda' to cost savings, this narrative perpetuates the framing of social care as a service. A destination. Something to be avoided.

Delivering prevention

To prevent needs emerging across health and care, integrated services should draw on a mixture of qualified health, care and support staff, working collaboratively to deliver prevention.
(DEPARTMENT OF HEALTH AND SOCIAL CARE, 2023)

There are multiple references in the Care Act 2014 and the statutory guidance to the 'provision of services, facilities or resources' to prevent, reduce or delay people's needs for care and support. It's ironic given the legislative shift from 'providing services' to 'meeting needs' that prevention is still described in terms of a service to be 'delivered'. And as such we have a menu of 'low-level interventions' to pick from. Social prescribing services. Befriending schemes. Falls prevention classes. Reablement support. Still commissioning and delivering a service to passive recipients. Doing to and for 'customers', not with and by citizens.

The door to serviceland

In the 🌍 of #socialcare why is all talk of strengths, community, connection, contribution – firmly linked to 'prevention' (keeping peeps away from the 🏠 to serviceland?) Once peeps are through that door it's all needs, needs, needs...strengths & contribution no longer important 😕'
(CATLEY, 2023a)

Despite the Care Act guidance emphasizing that 'prevention should be seen as an ongoing consideration and not a single activity or intervention', in practice there's a strong emphasis on prevention being something that happens 'before' social care, and once people have passed through the door to serviceland, they are 'beyond prevention'.

'Prevention teams' and 'prevention workers' often sit separately from social work teams, embedded within, and knowledgeable about, local communities and sources of support. They build relationships, connections, and community capacity, and then refer people on to 'assessment and care management' teams if their needs are 'too complex'.

If we return to the definition of prevention being about 'helping people stay healthy, happy, and independent for as long as possible', there's an implication that if you have 'eligible needs', the focus on health, happiness, and independence is out the window. And although the Care Act 2014 suggests that care and support plans should include 'advice and information about...what can be done to prevent or delay the development of needs for care and support or of needs for support in the future' (Care Act 2014, c. 23), plans still focus on services keeping people alive, not supporting them to thrive.

Flipping the narrative

'Prevention' and 'early intervention' are both terrible pieces of language. Let's start talking about the role social care can play, when organized well, in generating and helping us all to maintain our health and wellbeing.

(CROWTHER, 2022B)

The way we view and communicate about prevention perpetuates a focus on systems and service delivery, not people. On reducing demand and cutting costs. Needs and eligibility. Assessment and division.

So, what if we flip this narrative? If we must talk about prevention, let's stop talking about preventing needs, reducing demand, or delivering prevention services. Let's focus instead on preventing people from living in places that don't feel like home to them. From missing out on opportunities to build new relationships and keep existing ones. From losing connection with their neighbourhoods and communities. From living lives without hope or any sense of purpose. From feeling as if they're not listened to, heard, or understood. From feeling left out or left behind. From losing choice and control over their lives. From having their rights denied. From getting a service rather than a life, and from being denied the chance to live the life they choose to lead. And let's prevent people from being treated like a widget or a cog in the system, a case on the conveyor belt of social care. Prevent hand-offs and people having to tell their story multiple times. Prevent a focus on one-size-fits-all processes and pathways rather than on people and personalization. Prevent people waiting. Prevent people being labelled, blamed, and excluded through the words and phrases we use. Prevent stigma and othering. Prevent people being left out of conversations and decisions at all levels. And prevent a focus on outputs rather than outcomes.

But even better, let's drop the term prevention completely, and focus instead on what we want to promote, to grow, to flourish. A sense of belonging. Friendships and relationships. Love. Liberty. Identity. Meaning and purpose. Equal rights and equality of opportunity. Active citizenship. Interdependence and reciprocity. Connected communities. Hope.

From Care to Support

*W*e use the terms 'care', 'social care', and 'care and support' inter-changeably. My preference, however, is always 'support'.
Here's why.

Care

Care is community.

Care is connection.

Care is collaboration.

Care is choice.

Care is listening, and learning.

Care is families, friendships, neighbours, and colleagues.

Care is random smiles from strangers on the street.

Care is laughter and kindness and tears and messy and complicated and heart-breaking and joyous.

Care is about all of us, not them and us.

Care is a verb. 'To think that something is important and to feel interested in it.' Synonyms include 'look out (for)' and 'empathize with' (Merriam-Webster, n.d.).

Yet in our exhaustive, exhausted use of the term 'care', how often do we actually stop to consider care in terms of caring about, not for? Looking out for, not looking after?

Because in our language – and our practice – care is a noun. 'The process of protecting someone.' 'Attention that is given to something or someone, so that they are looked after, protected, or dealt with in the right way' (Cambridge Dictionary, n.d.).

In our language – and our practice – care is described in a plan and delivered in a package.

Care has a start date and an end date. It comes in episodes. Time frames. Short-term. Temporary. Intermediate. Long term. End of life.

Care wears a uniform.

Care has records, notes, charts. Risk assessments. Rotas. Timesheets.

Care has a cost. A fee. An invoice. A payment date.

Care is a transaction. You pay. We care. By the hour. By the minute. By the clock.

Care is a task. It's done to, and for.

Care is a setting. Somewhere to 'place' 'the vulnerable'.

Care is a service. A system. A sector.

Care is a one-way street, provided and received, with no sense of any kind of reciprocity, or relationship, or choice.

Care is confining. Constraining. Controlling.

Care is for 'others'.

'The work or practice of looking after those unable to care for themselves, especially on account of age or illness' (Oxford Languages, n.d.).

We divide people up into 'carers' and 'the cared for'. Helpers and the helpless. The people who give, offer, provide, deliver 'care', and 'those' who receive it.

'The cared for' are 'looked after', 'protected'. The language, and practice, of paternalism and benevolence, of power and control, wielded under the guise of 'looking after vulnerable people'.

'Keeping people safe.'

'Us', 'looking after' 'them'.

We talk about care as a destination. As somewhere people go. Moving into care. Going into care. Discharged into care. Placed in care.

And we talk about care as an outcome.

Assessments for care.

Getting care.

The end.

Full-stop.

Support

The words 'support' and 'supporting' tested particularly well in the focus groups to describe the function of social care.

(CROWTHER & QUINTON, 2021)

Ultimately, care is about people. Us. But the narrative of care is about others. Them.

We need to flip this narrative. Shift from 'We care for vulnerable people' to 'We care about one another', or even 'We *are* about one another'.

Shift from 'looking after others', to looking out for each other.

Shift from a focus on 'personal care' for 'the vulnerable', to genuinely personalized support so *all* of us can live the lives we choose to lead.

Shift from care, to support.

While 'care' implies looking after, doing to – a provider and receiver, an unequal power dynamic – 'support' suggests reciprocity. Being alongside someone as an equal. Being supportive. Doing with, not doing to.

'If you support someone or their ideas or aims, you agree with them, and perhaps help them because you want them to succeed' (Collins, n.d.). You're on their side, upholding their rights, supporting them to be who they want to be and to do the things that matter most to them.

While care implies a task – planned, scheduled, provided – support is a relationship.

While care implies 'personal care', support also covers the 'other practical assistance' in the Care Act 2014 definition:

> Adult social care – includes all forms of personal care and other practical assistance for individuals who, by reason of age, illness, disability, pregnancy, childbirth, dependence on alcohol or drugs, or any other similar circumstances, are in need of such care or other assistance. (Care Act 2014, c. 23)

While care implies a service, support is the 'greater variety of approaches' and 'number of broader options' referenced in the Care Act guidance, reflecting that 'the intention behind the legislation is to encourage this diversity, rather than point to a service or solution that may be neither what is best nor what the person wants'. 'The mixture of practical, financial and emotional support for adults who need extra help to manage their lives' (Department of Health and Social Care, 2023).

While care implies passive receipt (cared for), support can and should be self-directed. Flexible. Chosen. Created.

While care implies one-size-fits-all planned, brokered, scheduled, packaged, delivered, invoiced, and reviewed, support is creative. Co-produced by and with the people who will draw on it.

While care implies 'professional', support includes families, friends, neighbours, communities.

While care implies treating, fixing, and maintaining (survival), support widens the lens to focus on the barriers that need to be removed and the conditions that need to be in place to ensure that people thrive.

While care implies a destination, an outcome, a full stop, support is clearly a vehicle to something else, something more. Support to be, and to do, and to become.

While care implies 'others', support is something we all draw on to live the life we choose to lead.

From Care and Support Needs to Human Needs[1]

We all have human needs & may have cause to draw on support to realise them. That *should* be the function of 'social care'. But they're too often substituted for 'care & support needs' & our human needs are displaced.

(CROWTHER, 2023B)

Needs

Needs: a catalogue of things that mark you out as not quite human. Nobody else on the planet has these things.

(NEARY, N.D.)

The dictionary definition of needs is 'the things you must have for a satisfactory life' (Cambridge Dictionary, n.d.). There are the basic things we all need to stay alive, like food, water, air, clothing, shelter, and sleep, and to feel safe and secure. And there are the things that give us reason to live. The need for belonging and connection. Family and friendships. Love and intimacy. Dignity and respect. Freedom. The need to be recognized, accepted, and valued. The need to have something to do, and to look forward to. To have meaning and purpose.

References to needs dominate our narrative and practice. There are 1690 references to needs in the care and support statutory guidance. The guidance refers to nutrition, hygiene, clothing, and 'toilet needs'. It mentions the 'need for information and advice' and 'need for

---

1   All quotations in this chapter are from the Care Act statutory guidance, unless otherwise stated.

independent advocacy'. 'Communication needs' and 'mental health needs'. The 'need for care in a care home', and 'need for a cross-border residential care placement'. The 'need for NHS continuing healthcare', and 'need for nursing care'.

But there's no mention of the need to belong, and scant references to connection. While 'family or other personal relationships' are referred to, there's no mention of love, and the only references to touch and intimacy relate to abuse or 'intimate care needs'. Dignity and respect get a nod in relation to wellbeing, but there's no reference to recognition or acceptance. There's no mention of fun, delight, or joy.

'Our social service system counts only certain needs – for safety, shelter, food, income and physical care. It has few ways of understanding people's needs for adventure, purpose, connection and growth' (Tulloch & Schulman, 2020).

Our use of the term 'needs' is more aligned with Mark Neary's definition than with the dictionary definition, and the way we use this one little word highlights so much of what must change.

Care and support needs

When we talk about needs, we mean 'care and support needs'. Needs that 'arise from or are related to a physical or mental impairment or illness' or 'as a consequence of providing necessary care to an adult'.

The statutory guidance describes care and support as 'the mixture of practical, financial and emotional support for adults who need extra help to manage their lives and be independent – including older people, people with a disability or long-term illness, people with mental health problems, and carers'.

Over 11 million people in England and Wales – 18.6% of the total population – are aged 65 years or older (Office for National Statistics, 2022); 9.8 million people in England are disabled (Office for National Statistics, 2023). 'More than 15 million people in England – 30 per cent of the population – have one or more long-term conditions' (Naylor *et al.*, 2012). One in four people will experience a mental health problem of some kind each year in England (Mind, n.d.). And recent research estimates the number of unpaid carers across the UK could be as high as 10.6 million (Carers UK, n.d.).

Millions of people.

Millions of *us*.

And yet our language suggests 'people with care and support needs' are separate. Other.

'*Those* with care and support needs.'

We identify 'care and support needs' as something older and disabled people have, that ideally should be prevented, reduced, or delayed. This paints 'care and support needs' as A Bad Thing, and something to avoid.

The language of 'need' defines people as recipients, dependent on others for support, needing to be 'looked after' and 'taken care of'. It ignores the agency people have (and should have) and the contributions people make (and should be supported to make).

The need to give back. The need to be needed.

And it continues to frame care and support as a destination, not a vehicle. We talk about the care and support people need, not the lives people want to lead and the role of care and support in enabling people to live equal, ordinary, flourishing lives.

Assessing needs

We assess whether a person may or does 'have needs for care and support'; 'what those needs are'; if the needs are 'urgent'; if they can be prevented, reduced, or delayed; if 'current level of need is likely to fluctuate'; what 'on-going needs for care and support are likely to be'; if the person has a 'primary health need'; whether 'the adult's needs arise from or are related to a physical or mental impairment or illness'; if 'as a result of the adult's needs the adult is unable to achieve two or more of the specified outcomes'; whether 'the individual's needs impact upon their wellbeing'; and 'whether, and to what extent, the needs meet the eligibility criteria'.

If the person has 'eligible needs', we determine if they are already 'in receipt of care and support which meets their needs', 'which of their needs they would like the local authority to meet', 'how the local authority may meet those needs', and 'whether the local authority is paying for some, all or none of the costs of meeting those needs'.

So many judgements. So many decisions. So much time. So many forms. So many panels. So much arguing. So much power. So much fear.

'Eligible needs' or 'needs that are not eligible'.

'Social care needs' or 'health needs'.

'Unmet needs' or 'met needs'.

In or out.

Hierarchy of needs

The statutory guidance offers assurance that 'there is no hierarchy of needs'.

And yet there is.

'Basic needs.' 'Low-level needs.' 'Higher needs.' 'Wider needs.' 'Complex needs.' 'Urgent needs.' 'Changing needs.' 'Fluctuating needs.' 'Developing needs.' 'Ongoing needs.' And on, and on.

Basic needs

We generally define basic needs as our physiological, 'survival' needs.

Too often this is where we start – and end – our assessment: stuck at the bottom of Maslow's hierarchy and ignoring all the layers above. And, in turn, the support we prescribe focuses on 'life and limb care' – on keeping people alive but not supporting people to thrive.

Low-level needs

We're not really interested in so-called 'low-level needs'. Practical, everyday stuff like help with housework, gardening, laundry, or home maintenance. Emotional stuff like isolation and loneliness. The term 'low-level' suggests these needs aren't particularly important and, as such, 'low-level needs' are often not prioritized in our crisis-response mode.

We offer a leaflet or a signpost to 'the community'. A firm 'not eligible' and an instruction to 'come back if things get worse'. And things inevitably do get worse, and unmet low-level needs evolve into 'wider needs', 'higher needs', 'more complex needs', 'urgent needs'. And the cycle continues, because the 'small stuff' is really the big stuff.

Dignity. Respect. Connection. Belonging.

Complex needs

The other phrase that we must never ever be drawn into is 'complex needs'. It's a shifter of responsibility, a justification for anything, a checkmate conversation killer, all rolled into one. Died a preventable death? Ah yes, but she had complex needs. Entering his 16th year in an ATU? Ah yes, but he has complex needs. LA won't fund a home care package? Ah yes, we cannot find a provider that can manage his complex needs. It's the get out clause of all get out clauses. It's the king of multi disciplinary one-upmanship.

(NEARY, 2017)

The phrase 'complex needs' is most definitely used as the get out clause Mark Neary describes, but it's also a 'get in' clause. People feel they must describe family and friends as having 'complex needs' to pass through the 'front door' to serviceland. First conversations aim 'to ensure that complex needs are identified early and that people are signposted appropriately'. 'Professional staff...focus on more complex cases.'

We've even built complexity into the term 'complex needs', with references in the guidance to 'multiple and complex needs', 'highly specialized and complex needs', 'less complex needs', 'more complex needs', 'particularly complex needs', and 'the most complex needs'.

People with 'complex needs' quickly become 'complex cases' or just plain 'complex'.

But like 'challenging' and 'vulnerable', 'complex' is an unhelpful and meaningless term. 'Isabelle is 15 years old with complex needs.' It's used as a blanket label, and stigmatizes, others, and blames people who don't fit neatly into the boxes, processes, and services that dominate our 'system'.

Future needs

Addressing people's needs for love, connection, esteem, and self-realization may seem secondary to answering their needs for safety and stability. But these are all concurrent needs. If people...don't believe in themselves and in the future, they will keep slipping through the cracks, immune to offers of help, caught in an expensive decline.

(TULLOCH & SCHULMAN, 2020)

'Early discussions in families or groups about potential changes in the future (for example: conversations about potential care arrangements or suitable accommodation should a family member become ill or disabled) should be 'encouraged'. 'Councils must provide information and advice about 'how a person might plan for their future care and support needs and how to pay for them'.

There are numerous references to future needs in the statutory guidance. But no explicit reference to the need for a future. The need for something to anticipate. The need for hope.

One 'case study' refers to a person's 'plans for the future'. 'Stephen [who 'sustained a brain injury in a fall'] is articulate and can converse well about his plans for the future which includes detailed plans to meet up with friends and return to work again.' But these plans

– Stephen's anticipated future – are swiftly dismissed when 'the social worker judges that because Stephen lacks insight into his personal relationships and future plans, he may well also have trouble estimating his true care and support needs'.

The future is where needs develop, capacity is lost, and care costs escalate.

The future is something to fear.

'John is 32 and has been referred by his mother for an assessment, who is concerned for John and his future.'

'Dave is 32 and has been referred by his mother for an assessment, who is concerned for Dave and his future.'

Human needs

When we focus on care and support needs, we think in terms of deficit. What's missing. What's wrong.

We think in terms of 'them'.

But if we flip this narrative and focus on human needs, well – that's about *all* of us.

Our need for dignity and respect. For control over our lives and the freedom to make our own choices and decisions. For connection and relationships. For love. To feel anchored, secure, and that we belong. Our need for meaning and purpose. To participate and contribute.

Our need to be who we are, and to become everything we are capable of becoming.

'What is different – the crucial pivot – is that the purpose is not to patch up another's needs but to foster their capabilities. Relational work sees the future self a person can be and builds towards that' (Cottam, 2018).

Rights

...the fundamental problem with social care is that it is predicated on need rather than rights...

(EQUALITY AND HUMAN RIGHTS COMMISSION, 2009)

'Quite simply we cannot hope to improve people's health and wellbeing if we are not ensuring that their human rights are respected' –Rosie Winterton (Department of Health, 2007).

110

'Care and support needs' divide people up into 'them' and 'us'. But human needs, and human rights, are about all of us.

> These rights – and the intentions behind them – are at the core of what good care and support should mean at a day to day level. Whilst they may sometimes appear abstract, they are really about such mundane things as eating a meal when you are hungry rather than when a service wants to provide it; having a bath in privacy and comfort; being able to play with your children or go to church or to the pub in the same way as everyone else. (Equality and Human Rights Commission, 2009)

The things we need to survive and to thrive are also the things we all have a basic human right to.

But while references to needs dominate our narrative and practice, the language of rights is far less pervasive.

There are 1690 references to needs in the care and support statutory guidance.

And 41 references to rights.

Wellbeing

> [I] believe it's possible to flip our practice within the existing legal framework. It's about starting our practice from a different place, ironically from where the Care Act also begins: wellbeing. That's where rights should come in.
>
> (HOLMES, 2023A)

Promoting wellbeing and respecting, protecting, and promoting human rights are inextricably linked. Human rights are based on principles of fairness, respect, equality, dignity, and autonomy, and these principles weave their way through the Care Act 2014 and the statutory guidance.

However, while the overarching wellbeing principle 'is intended to cover the key components of independent living, as expressed in the UN Convention on the Rights of People with Disabilities', the Act and the guidance avoid the use of the 'relatively abstract' term 'independent living', and largely avoid explicit references to rights.

While the UN Convention recognizes that 'persons with disabilities continue to face barriers in their participation as equal members of society and violations of their human rights in all parts of the world', and as such there is a need to 'promote and protect the human rights of all persons with disabilities', the Care Act has nine 'areas' of individual wellbeing which must be promoted.

Now is it just me, or does 'area of wellbeing' not quite have the same authority and power as 'right'?

Isn't 'participation in work, education, training, or recreation' 'relatively abstract' compared to 'the right of persons with disabilities to work, on an equal basis with others', 'the right of persons with disabilities to education', and 'the right of persons with disabilities to take part on an equal basis with others in cultural life'?

Isn't 'domestic, family and personal relationships' 'relatively abstract' compared to 'no person with disabilities, regardless of place of residence or living arrangements, shall be subjected to arbitrary or unlawful interference with his or her privacy, family, home or correspondence' and 'the right of all persons with disabilities who are of marriageable age to marry and to found a family...'?

Isn't 'suitability of living accommodation' 'relatively abstract' compared to 'the equal right of all persons with disabilities to live in the community, with choices equal to others [and] to choose their place of residence and where and with whom they live on an equal basis...'?

Human rights may be embedded implicitly throughout the Act and corresponding guidance – and wellbeing is (in theory) 'at the heart of care and support', but this is a book about language, and the language of 'needs' is so much more explicit.

Eligibility

The overall basis of our current 'system' is one of eligibility rather than entitlement, and the legislation and guidance embed a needs-led, not rights-based, approach.

As such, eligibility dominates practice. Checking. Screening. Questioning. Box ticking – or not ticking. Forms. Processes. Panels. Waiting. Worrying. Arguing. Justifying. Disputing. Appealing. Defending.

And despite the Care Act guidance emphasizing the shift from providing services to meeting needs, needs are still largely interpreted as needs for a service, not a life. A need for something finite, in limited supply – which further embeds the requirement to ration and gatekeep.

Just whose needs are we meeting?

[We tell] people they need to move to a care home when we actually mean...we don't have the time, connections or resources to work with you and your family to knit together the creative tapestry of support you will need if you are to stay at home. (Catley, 2023b)

Switching instead to a rights-based approach – to a focus on wellbeing, participation, and good lives – opens opportunities. It shifts the focus from services, providers, and institutions to the abundance of resources in communities and how they can be nurtured, connected, and shared.

Power and politics

A needs-led approach puts people seeking support in an inferior, disempowered position – asking for needs to be met, dependent on the judgement of 'professionals' to determine need and eligibility.

Help me. Please.

In contrast, a rights-based approach shifts power, with people maintaining their dignity, organizations more explicitly accountable to people, and social workers working alongside citizens to uphold and promote rights and social justice.

The unrelenting focus on needs also keeps our attention on the personal rather than the political.

Needs-based practice locates the 'problem' with the person, avoiding any focus on systemic failings and changes.

Rights-based practice is political. It requires advocacy and activism, and this is surely a time when our political action is needed to address the human rights violations and gaps in care and services that the coronavirus has made (even more) visible. (McPherson, 2020)

Social work: A human rights discipline

Social work is a human rights discipline. It's not just an element of it – it is the core principle. –Ruth Stark

(SCHRAER, 2013)

The global definition of social work states that 'principles of social justice, human rights, collective responsibility and respect for diversities are central to social work', and the British Association of Social Work code of ethics suggests that 'respect for human rights and a commitment to promoting social justice are at the core of social work practice throughout the world' (International Federation of Social Workers, 2014; British Association of Social Workers, 2021).

But care management has trapped social workers in a never-ending cycle of screen triage signpost assess, plan justify commission place review close. Defending budgets, policies, and processes rather than human rights. Fighting with, not for, people and families.

Process has replaced politics.

Assessments have replaced activism.

Responsibilities

Perhaps the most deep-rooted systemic barrier to older and disabled people enjoying their human rights on an equal basis with others is paternalism. Put simply, society's prejudice that people who require some financial or practical support cannot safely take responsibility for their own lives is codified into our laws, institutions, professional qualifications, culture, practice, and public discourse.

(CROWTHER, 2022A)

The language of needs embeds and perpetuates the belief that people 'with care and support needs' are 'needy', 'vulnerable', 'helpless' and therefore must be 'looked after' and 'protected'.

In contrast, the language of rights recognizes *everyone* as equal citizens, with shared human rights, *and* shared responsibilities.

It shifts the focus to purpose, participation, potential, possibility. To doing and being and becoming. And to 'the contribution care and support can make to people's equality of opportunity to participate and contribute fully in society' (Equality and Human Rights Commission, 2009).

Us, not them and us

To deny people their human rights is to challenge their very humanity.
–Nelson Mandela

(UNITED NATIONS, N.D.)

The focus on needs divides people into them and us.

Those with care and support needs.

Them.

In contrast, rights are universal and apply to everyone.

Us.

However, there is currently a dangerous political narrative around human rights. As Amnesty International observes,

'the consequences of "us vs them" rhetoric setting the agenda in Europe, the United States and elsewhere is fuelling a global pushback against human rights' and 'instead of fighting for people's rights, too many leaders have adopted a dehumanizing agenda for political expediency. Many are violating rights of scapegoated groups to score political points, or to distract from their own failures to ensure economic and social rights' (Shetty, 2017).

This divisive rhetoric – echoed in sections of the media and influencing public attitudes – could easily be seen as a reason to steer clear of the language of rights in relation to care and support. *Or* as a very valid reason to firmly embed rights into our language, purpose, and practice.

We can choose to perpetuate an approach based around needs, screening, eligibility, gatekeeping, and them and us. Or we can choose instead to grow an approach based around rights, advocacy, participation, citizenship, and all of us.

From Industry to Ecosystem

Relationships need to be tended and nurtured – we don't even have the language for this type of activity in our public policy, which eschews the metaphors of the garden for the warlike vocabulary of targets and the front line or a mechanistic language of levers.

(COTTAM, 2018)

We talk about social care as an industry.

It's an apt description.

We operate social care sorting offices, processing 'cases' along the conveyor belts of our system. Our focus, like that of the industrial production line, is on efficiency and pace. Throughput. Flow.

Social workers are required to 'think and act fast' and 'progress cases efficiently' in a 'fast-paced environment'. We measure how long people wait, and how quickly cases are closed. We rarely stop to ask how people feel, and whether anything has really changed for them.

Efficiency is prized over effectiveness.

There's no room for personality, individuality, or creativity on assembly lines (and little in our current 'system'). Parts (people) are directed down conveyor belts (pathways). If they don't pass the checks (assessments) they're thrown out (turned away). If they do, they continue down the line (workflow) to be assembled (fixed). Labels (yup – loads of those) are applied. The product (outcome) is standardized. One size fits all.

Creating coordinated systems requires the suppression of the individual in favour of consistency and efficiency. Over time, organizational apparatuses grow so large that they squeeze out the personal. This trend, while understandable, is particularly unsettling when our purpose is people. (Tulloch & Schulman, 2020)

116

Rewilding social care

Nature has the power to heal itself and to heal us, if we let it. That's what rewilding is all about; restoring ecosystems to the point where nature can take care of itself, and restoring our relationship with the natural world. Reconnecting with what matters.

(REWILDING BRITAIN, N.D.)

Rewilding is about reconnecting with what matters, which is absolutely what we need to do in terms of the way we think about, and work within, social care. So, I'm interested to explore how our practice could change if we eschewed 'the warlike vocabulary of targets and the front line' and the 'mechanistic language of levers' and focused instead on 'the metaphors of the garden'.

If we viewed social care not as an 'industry', but as an ecosystem.

Ecosystems

The recent discovery that the roots of mature trees grow towards each other in a complex and inter-dependent ecosystem that, through its deep connectedness which allows each tree to stand tall and mature, serves as a metaphor for our new understanding of human development.

(COTTAM, 2020)

Our current practice treats people as isolated individuals.

Our current practice treats people.

The medical, mechanical model of care dominates. We work in institutional silos, discrete 'professionals' swooping in – usually at times of crisis – to patch and mend, 'to fix discrete bodies and body parts as if our lives are not inter-connected' (Cottam, 2020).

And yet everything *is* connected.

Our role should be to recognize, embrace, and enhance those connections, and in turn sustain and enhance people's lives.

'When organized well, social care helps nurture an ecosystem of relationships and support in our local communities that we can draw on to live our lives in the way that we want to, whatever our age or stage of life' (Crowther & Quinton, 2021).

Nurturing

When a flower doesn't bloom, you fix the environment in which it grows, not the flower.

(DEN HEIJER, N.D.)

We know that plants need light, air, water, nutrients, and space to grow. If a plant isn't thriving, we automatically assume the conditions aren't right – not that there's an issue with the plant itself – and we try changing the environment it's in. Maybe it needs more water or light. Maybe we need to improve the soil it's growing in or create more room around it.

Contrast that with our approach to supporting people, where we view them as problems and set about fixing them, paying little or no attention to the environment around them.

Yet it's obvious that people, like plants, will only thrive if we're in a nurturing environment where all – not just some – of our needs are met. A plant may survive for a while in rich soil with plenty of space around it, but if it lacks sunlight and water it will start to fade away. And equally, if we have our physiological needs met, but don't feel safe and secure, or lack loving relationships, recognition, and purpose, we won't flourish either.

Flourishing

Had the system, in its quest for standardization, fairness and clarity, squeezed out too much personality, zest and colour?

(TULLOCH & SCHULMAN, 2020)

The natural world is a joyous riot of colour, particularly in the spring, as an abundance of blossom clings to tree branches, vivid green shoots emerge from rich soil, and daffodils carpet the ground. And good lives are a joyous riot of colour too. Vibrant. Messy. Glorious.

But our current 'system' with its one-size-fits-all solutions is a monotonous monochrome. People are reduced to numbers on spreadsheets and dashboards. Curiosity, creativity, and compassion are crushed by commands to 'close cases'. Opportunities and possibilities are dismissed as we focus on reducing risks and 'managing expectations'.

Our goal should be for people to flourish.

To lead gloriously ordinary lives.

Roots

I wish I could have told him that loneliness is a human invention. Trees are never lonely. Humans think they know with certainty where their being ends and someone else's starts. With their roots tangled and caught up underground, linked to fungi and bacteria, trees harbour no such illusions. For us, everything is interconnected.

(SHAFAK, 2022)

I think the term 'belonging' encapsulates all that social care should be about. Living in a place that feels like home, being with the people and things you love, doing what matters to you. Included and affirmed. Anchored. Rooted.

Our current practice is fixated on individuals and self-sufficiency, on resilience and 'managing without support'. It's unrealistic and ableist, and perpetuates the loneliness and isolation that plagues so many of our lives.

Roots give trees and plants stability and security, and the soil they reach down into enables them not just to survive but to thrive.

We need to identify and strengthen people's roots by shifting our focus to building, maintaining, and restoring connections. We thrive through our relationships – we need to support them to flourish. And 'flourishing...depends on systems designed to reinforce relationships rather than individuals' (Cottam, 2020).

Sunlight

Social care exists in the shadows. Gloom and negativity pervade the national narrative, with an obsessive, doom-laden focus on what's broken and failing. Our practice focuses on the dark side too – abuse, risk, anticipating what could go wrong. And too many people are hidden away – separated, excluded, 'placed' elsewhere.

We need to shine a light on all that is good about social care and ensure that people drawing on support take centre stage and share the spotlight. Our practice needs to shift to a genuinely strengths-based approach and build on what is strong.

The sun gives plants energy, and they grow towards the light.

Illuminating what's good and what's possible gives us all energy too, and fosters hope and belief in a brighter future for all of us.

Seeds

Seeds are magical. All that potential and possibility captured in a tiny pod.

Our human equivalent is our ideas and aspirations, those personal dreams we hold on to.

Like seeds need the right amount of warmth, light, water, and air to sprout, we need the right environment to realize our dreams.

Our conversations with people seeking support should start by identifying the seeds, then aim to create the conditions for them to germinate and grow.

And our working environments must enable tiny ideas to grow too, with enough autonomy, trust, and permission to try.

'Exploring new ideas, talking about them, trying things a little differently – this is how we produce new possibilities, new rhythms and in time, new cultures' (Tulloch & Schulman, 2020).

Diversity

Because a person's needs are specific to them, there are many ways in which their needs can be met. The intention behind the legislation is to encourage this diversity, rather than point to a service or solution that may be neither what is best nor what the person wants.

(DEPARTMENT OF HEALTH AND SOCIAL CARE, 2023)

Diverse ecosystems provide stability, resilience, and the ideal conditions for growth, and in turn the diversity of individuals and communities should be recognized and viewed as a strength (Think Local Act Personal, 2018).

Support options should be as diverse as the people seeking and drawing on support. And the involvement of a diverse range of people with diverse lived experience and as such, diverse knowledge, skills, and ideas is essential to ensure that support options are co-produced.

Evolution

Nature is diverse, dynamic, unpredictable and complex so there's no one-size-fits-all route map to rewilding. It's about taking a holistic approach that lets nature lead the way as much as possible – to grow, evolve and change on its own terms.

(REWILDING BRITAIN, N.D.)

If we're really going to reimagine – or indeed rewild – social care, we need to shift from the dominant, industrial, Chronos time approach to practice and to practice change, and work instead in Kairos time – the time of nature, seasons, weather, tides.

There's no one-size-fits-all route map to rewilding, or good lives, or practice change.

The change we need can't be described in a plan or scheduled with a calendar or measured by a clock. This is change that spreads slowly but reaches deeply.

It is organic, experimental, fluid, human.

* * *

Rewilding is a 'story of hope' (Rewilding Britain, n.d.). And at its best, social care is also a story of hope.

So, let's leave behind the divisive language of the battlefield and the mechanistic language of industry, and be influenced instead by the bountiful, beautiful, and optimistic language of the natural world.

Reconnect with what matters.

Rewild social care.

PART THREE

CHANGING OUR PRACTICE

From Transactions to Relationships

What's needed to stimulate growth and actualization is profoundly different from what's needed to secure safety and stability. What's needed is nothing less than a reimagination of what we do.

(TULLOCH & SCHULMAN, 2020)

If you google the term 'practice', the following two definitions (Oxford Languages, n.d.) come up.

1. The actual application or use of an idea, belief, or method, as opposed to theories relating to it.
2. The customary, habitual, or expected procedure or way of doing something.

In this part, I'll demonstrate how our language exposes our mechanistic approach to practice, and how the second definition above reflects our dominant way of working, with a focus on procedures rather than principles. On doing things right, not doing the right thing. On doing to, not working with.

On transactions, not relationships.

If we agree that our purpose is supporting people to live flourishing lives, we must shift our language, and our practice, to focus on the actual application of this idea, this belief.

If our vision is good lives, we won't get there through standardization. We'll get there through liberation.

Clarity of vision alone won't change attitudes, power dynamics, or systems. Freedom to work towards this vision is essential. Values need to be demonstrated, not just described. Principles need to be observed across the board.

If we're guided by what matters most to people, we must have the flexibility to work together to achieve that.

Instead of processes and panels to make sure we do things right, we need to keep things simple, work together, trust each other to do the right thing. And trust people, families, and communities to know, and do, what matters most to them.

Cede control. Learn when to step in to nurture connections and make sure sufficient resources and support are in place, and when to step back and get out of the way.

So, of course, just changing our language is not enough. We also need a radical shift in our knowledge of and relationships with people and communities, the way we share power and responsibility, how we make decisions, what we record, measure, and understand, and how we design, commission, fund, and evaluate support.

We often change our language without making these much bigger changes. So, in this part I'll also expose how the language associated with the buzz words we so readily adopt to signal new approaches reveals the same old assumptions and power dynamics beneath the surface.

We must change our language to change our practice, and we must also change our practice to change our language.

Identity

The Covid-19 pandemic and the measures introduced to control the spread of the virus challenged all our identities.

We gained labels that changed the way we were seen, and the way we saw ourselves. Vulnerable. Shielding. Furloughed. Keyworker. Carer. Hero. Isolating. Isolated.

We lost loved ones. Livelihoods. Connections to the people and places that form – or formed – vital elements of who we are.

We lost opportunities, choice, hope. Vital elements of who we could become.

For many of us, this was a temporary state. A lockdown with an end in sight.

But for too many older people and disabled people, the lack – or loss – of identity, and in turn the lack or loss of connections, of choice, of hope, is permanent.

If we work in social care, we often meet people during periods of huge change. Chaotic, scary, bewildering times. These dramatic life events change how people see themselves and change how they are seen. They attach new labels, add a new layer of identity, or strip several layers away. But in our fleeting encounters we barely scratch the surface – focusing on a problem to be solved, a risk to be managed, a need to be met, rather than seeing and understanding the whole person, who they are, were, and want to become.

Too often our current practice ignores, and indeed erodes, people's identity.

If we really want to rewrite social care, we need to pay far more attention to identity.

Lenses and layers of identity

Often by the time we meet you, you've been screened, triaged, discharged to assess.

We've identified you as vulnerable, at risk, in need.

You've ticked the right boxes.

You've become a referral, an allocation, a concern, a case.

We've read details about your problems from forms. Our records reflect your life through the lens of (often multiple) 'professionals'. We're already forming an impression of you, possibly already determining your (our) outcome.

'The majority will be your four calls a day stuff.'

Our assessments allow us a snapshot of you, a glimpse in an intense, pressurized situation. You – or people close to you – answer predetermined questions about what's wrong and what you can't do. You're under pressure to say the right thing, without being totally sure what the right thing is.

To score enough points to proceed.

If we identify you as 'eligible', we plan and provide services to maintain your existence, to keep you alive, then close your case and move on.

If we decide you're 'not eligible', we signpost you elsewhere, then close your case and move on.

Labels as the enemy of identity

Our labels strip people of their unique identity. Hopes, desires, fears, and potential are obscured by the labels, assumptions, and judgements we attach.

We talk of being strengths-based, but our language shrieks deficits.

We talk of being person-centred, of putting the person first, but the person is nowhere to be seen.

Our labels strip away the unique identity of the people close by too. Family members and friends are identified as carers, representatives, appropriate individuals, not as human beings with desires, fears, needs, and potential of their own.

These labels make our social care world go round. Our sorting office approach relies on them. It depends on categorization, standardization, lists, forms, and one-size-fits-all solutions.

Blurred identities suit our system.

This distancing protects us too. It shields us from feeling too distressed or helpless ourselves, as we process people along our work-flows and down our pathways.

And in turn we become 'other' to the people we're here to support. Dehumanized. Robotic.

'Professional.'

Our own identities hidden behind our own labels, and all the stereotypes, assumptions, judgements, rules, and boundaries they bring.

Ubuntu: I am because we are

Of course, our identity isn't just about who we are as individuals. It's intrinsically linked to how we're connected to people and to places. We're daughters, sons, sisters, brothers, mums, dads, partners, friends, neighbours, colleagues. We live in homes, on streets, in communities, in cities, in countries, in virtual worlds.

Our relationships make us stronger. Help us feel we belong. Feel known. Feel we have a place in the world.

If we don't have these connections, or we lose them, we're missing part of ourselves too. Yet still too often the essential role of friendships, relationships, and love is overlooked in social care, as we commission, plan, and provide services to keep people alive but ignore the connections vital for people to thrive.

The scaffolding of the self

> It's not only other people who hold us in our identities. Familiar places and things, beloved objects, pets, cherished rituals, one's own bed or favourite shirt, can and do help us maintain our sense of self. And it is no accident that much of this kind of holding goes on in the place where our families are: at home. –Hilde Lindeman
>
> (CROWTHER, 2020A)

Living in a place we call home, and doing the things that matter to us, are also important elements of our identity. Belonging, meaning, and purpose are key, and too often these things are absent in people's lives if they draw on social care.

Our most vulnerable

Our othering extends to the collective identity of people who draw on support.

'The vulnerable.' 'The most vulnerable,' 'Those who are vulnerable,' 'Our most vulnerable,' 'Society's most vulnerable.'

This dehumanizing language often sits alongside equally dehumanizing stock images of disembodied body parts. Anonymous. Invisible.

Why does it matter?

This lack of identity matters because it impacts on pretty much every decision that's made at every level within and about social care.

It matters because it means people are left out of conversations, and decisions are made about them, not with or by them.

It matters because it means people are expected to be passive recipients of services, losing choice and control as assumptions are made, pathways are followed, and solutions are prescribed based on labels and classifications rather than personalities, preferences, and aspirations.

It matters because it means people are not valued. Not respected. Ignored. Neglected. Rights are not upheld, and barriers are not removed. Histories are denied, and futures are destroyed.

It matters because it means people who currently draw on support are rarely visible in strategic decision making about local policies and services that affect their lives, and are largely absent from discussions at national conferences, seminars, and webinars about the future of social care.

It mattered during the pandemic, at horrific cost, as the Care Act easements, blanket 'do not resuscitate' notices, hospital discharge policies, and distribution of personal protective equipment prioritized protecting the NHS over the lives of people who draw on and work in social care.

And it matters for the future of social care, because when the people who draw on and work in social care are barely visible, where's the public pressure and the political will to invest, to reform, to change?

Acknowledging and affirming identity

We have an opportunity – and a responsibility – to create a better, brighter, kinder, and more human social care future where we acknowledge and affirm identity.

Where we have the time and space to really listen. To learn. To understand who and what matters to people to maintain, or reclaim, or renew their identity.

A future where we are *all* seen, heard, valued, and loved for who we are, and who we can become.

From Robots to Humans

Social services spoke to me in checklists, mechanical, like talking to a robot. –Rhiannon

(PIERRE, 2024)

Social work is fundamentally about people working alongside other people as fellow human beings. About rights and relationships. Connection and creativity. Advocacy and activism. Humanity and hope. Or is it?

A not very scientific but reasonably extensive trawl through job adverts for social workers suggests that, despite the very explicit shift away from care management signalled by the introduction of the Care Act 2014, the industrialized approach to social work still dominates.

In this chapter, I'll show how the language of social work job adverts reveals that we're basically just recruiting robots to process referrals through the machine of social care. Baggage handlers to carry cases on and off the conveyor belts of our system. And I'll suggest how our language, and practice, must change if we want to regain our humanity, and be more human.

You will be responsible for...

Adverts for social workers tend to focus first on the tasks and duties you'll be required to undertake. Here's a sample of phrases from the adverts I looked at.

You'll be responsible for:

- 'reviewing waiting lists for prioritization and screening'
- 'screening and risk assessing cases'
- 'assessing service users'
- 'reviewing placements'

- 'carrying a caseload of service users'
- 'managing complex cases'
- 'helping to achieve the 28-day performance targets, while reducing the waiting time for new referrals'.

You will be required to...

- 'undertake screening and duty work'
- 'work with complex cases in accordance with statutory responsibilities'
- 'deal with complex and varied cases'
- 'be responsible for a non-complex caseload'
- 'hold a reduced caseload with a higher proportion of complex and contentious cases'
- 'hold long-term cases that are complex in nature and may include hoarding, non-engagers, deprivation of liberty safeguards challenges and court cases'
- 'carry a caseload of highly challenging complex cases with multifactorial needs'
- 'manage a caseload of service users'
- 'work autonomously with highly complex needs'.

Screening. Prioritizing. Assessing. Reviewing. Managing. Dealing with.
'It is a fast-paced team, and you don't hold cases for long.'
Busy, busy.
'You will ensure that all cases are progressed efficiently through the system within this fast-paced environment.'
The language of transactions.
Conveyor belts.
The social care sorting office.
While the 'p words' (pathways, processes, packages, placements) sum up the transactional nature of the role, it's the 'c words' that really grate: case, caseload, complex, challenging.
Dehumanizing, blaming terms appeared repeatedly across the adverts I looked at.

You will be working with...

Here's a selection of the phrases used in the adverts to describe who social workers will be working with (doing to):

- 'customers and potential customers'
- 'patients'
- 'vulnerable adults with mental health'
- 'some of society's most vulnerable individuals'
- 'vulnerable service users'
- 'service users with a range of complex needs'
- 'complex cases'
- 'challenging cases'
- 'safeguarding cases'
- 'the most complex and challenging adult cases'
- 'those who access services'
- those
- others.

Okay, so I added the last couple of bullet points. But effectively that's what these adverts are saying.

What's happened to 'strengths-based' practice? What's happened to our basic humanity?

You will need to have...

So now we've established that the social worker role is to screen, assess, and manage challenging, complex cases, who are we looking to recruit?

If, like us, you believe that social work is a vocation, a strong impulse or inclination to follow, a path rather than just a career, then you must also understand that the social worker is who you are, not what you are... Social work is about having an innate value base and a fire in your belly to live it and practice it. (James, Mitchell, & Morgan, 2019)

Actually, we're not really interested in who you are...just what you hold.

You'll need to have:

- 'a recognized social work qualification'
- 'a valid Social Work England registration'
- 'a valid UK driving licence and vehicle'

- 'access to your own laptop and mobile phone'
- 'the right to work in the UK'
- 'IT skills preferably experienced with Mosaic'
- 'experienced knowledge with Liquid Logic'
- 'clear and valid DBS disclosure'
- 'satisfactory references'.

Basically, our adverts suggest we're more interested in whether you can use our IT system and have a car, than in who you are and what you believe.

We care more about the paperwork in your hands than the passion and principles in your heart.

I'm not dismissing or devaluing qualifications, registrations, and references – just reflecting on the prevalence of these lists of commodities in the 'essential requirements' section of our adverts, and the lack of equivalent detail about required values and behaviours.

Scanning through numerous job adverts to write this was like playing words that make me go Hmmm bingo. Several terms were overwhelmingly present in the bland, generic adverts: case, caseload, vulnerable, complex, service user, challenging, screen, assess, process. Several terms were glaringly absent: people, relationships, rights, advocacy, trust, compassion, curiosity, hope.

For a profession that is (or should be) fundamentally about people and relationships, most adverts focused on processes and transactions. There was little evidence of the human qualities required in social workers, and even fewer references to the unique identity and humanity of the people they're being recruited to serve.

There were some glimmers. Some adverts gave me hope, but I couldn't find a standout job advert which really conveyed the purpose and possibility of the social work role, and the passion and principles required. So, I wrote my own. It's by no means perfect, but it doesn't contain any of the dreaded 'p words' or 'c words' – or the ubiquitous 'v word'!

Job vacancy: social worker
We want the people we serve to live gloriously ordinary lives in the place they call home, with the people and things that they love, in communities where they look out for one another, doing what matters to them.

We're looking for social workers to work alongside people seeking or drawing on support to live the lives they choose to lead, whatever their age or stage of life.

You'll be responsible for:

- building trusted relationships
- having conversations with people and families that are led by what matters most to them
- making sure people's wishes, feelings, and beliefs are central to decision making
- ensuring people have control over where they live and who they live with
- connecting people to wider networks of opportunity and support
- increasing people's hope and self-esteem
- responding quickly in a crisis and sticking with people until things are better for them
- being involved in people's lives in the least intrusive way – and always in their best interests
- keeping in touch with people to check how they are, how things are going, and if anything needs to change.

You will be required to:

- listen
- respect the dignity and diversity of the people you're working with
- understand and respond to people's unique needs and aspirations
- be curious, useful, and kind
- uphold human rights and social justice
- question the status quo
- do no harm.

Essential requirements include:

- recognizing that people are the experts in their lives
- communicating respectfully with and about people
- thinking and acting creatively

- challenging circumstances and environments that marginalize, exclude, or oppress
- critical reflection and a desire to keep learning.

This advert isn't saying anything new, or anything radical. The responsibilities and requirements within it are embedded in – and extracted from – legislation, professional standards, and established definitions of social work.

And despite what the job adverts say, as I said in Part One, those of us who work in social care don't join the workforce to process cases through a system. We do so because we believe in human rights, social justice, families, friendships, love.

We believe in people. We want to make a difference. We care.

Rewriting job adverts is the easy part.

The challenge lies in dismantling the sorting offices that still exist within our councils and liberating social workers from the process and bureaucracy of the current care management machine.

But we can only build a more human, humane approach if we each have the courage and support to be more human ourselves. And if we create spaces and places where people feel like human beings and feel they can be human too.

So, here's my starter for ten...my non-exhaustive list of the values and behaviours I believe are core characteristics of human organizations, with a very big nod in the direction of the 'Be human movement' principles, and their assertion that being human 'means treating the person as human not a widget or a cog in the system' (Be Human, 2020).

I couldn't agree more.

Trust

Trust flows from the experience of being treasured, not measured.

(RUSSELL, 2020)

First up is trust. Trust is fundamental to healthy relationships, and if we want to create a more human, relational way of working, we must acknowledge the vital importance of trusting each other. Because right now we don't. People don't trust institutions and/because institutions don't trust people, including the people working in them. So, we create and impose more and more rules processes restrictions boundaries checks hierarchies.

Measuring, not treasuring.

We misplace trust, believing in policies and procedures, not people and communities. We don't trust that people know what will work best for them, will make the right choices, are the experts in their lives. Yet we're happy to trust that our safeguarding processes keep people safe, that our signposts point to a solution, that our referrals get picked up, that the services we prescribe will meet the outcomes we define.

And we say no, repeatedly, until we finally say yes – prompted either by a crisis ('come back when things get worse') or after complaints, appeals, investigations, inquiries, and months and years of exhaustion, stress, and distress.

Without trust we can't build and maintain relationships. We can't be flexible. We can't promote autonomy, or innovation. We can't take risks. We can't share.

Without trust we can't break free from the dehumanizing shackles of our systems.

Without trust, we can't change.

Honesty

To build trust we need transparency. As Simon Sinek says, 'Trust is built on telling the truth, not telling people what they want to hear' (Sinek, 2020).

Honesty *is* the best policy.

Blagging, bluffing, distracting, and deceiving arouse suspicion and resentment. Build walls where we need to build bridges.

We can't work together as equal human beings, can't co-exist comfortably, or co-design better futures if ideas, knowledge, and learning aren't shared, and when agendas remain hidden.

And as well as telling the truth, we also need to be able to be true to ourselves.

Belong, not just fit in.

Challenge

In social care serviceland, to be 'challenging' is A Bad Thing. 'Challenging behaviour' is something that must be controlled, managed, and modified to become more acceptable, more 'positive'. People and families who question the status quo are labelled 'difficult' and 'non-compliant'. Workers who challenge current practice or decisions are 'disruptive' or 'troublemakers'.

But this behaviour is usually an indication that something is wrong, something is failing, something needs to change. The communication of frustration and distress. Of not being listened to or heard or understood.

We need to question everything we do. Challenge each other and be open to challenge. Encourage feedback. We need to Admit to ourselves and each other when things don't feel right, and that certain ways of working aren't working.

Instead of fearing change, we need to fear what will happen if we don't change.

Curiosity

I remember talking with a social worker several years ago about the concept of focusing conversations on what matters most to a person or family. The social worker wasn't keen on this approach.

'What if they ask for something I can't deliver?'

This exposes our expectation that 'the system' has the solutions, and that services *are* the solution. Our assessment for services approach means that questions are posed by our forms, and answers are predetermined by the drop-down options in our 'case management' systems. Our preoccupation with 'needs' and what's missing obscures gifts and potential, overlooks what is present, and writes off dreams as 'unrealistic expectations'.

There's no place for curiosity – or creativity – in the confines of this system, which traps us in the role of commissioner, provider, deliverer, not enabler or connector. There's no space for imagination. And there's no option for people to have any sense of choice or control over the support they require. No opportunities to have influence or ambitions. To have a life.

We need to make far more space for listening to what matters most to people. Talk less and listen more to what is said, what is not said, the way things are said, and what is communicated without words. We need to Listen without assumptions or judgement, without an agenda or an answer, but with a clear commitment to people living the life they choose to lead, as equal, valuable, valued human beings.

Learning

When we listen more, we learn more.

Our current learning tends to focus on how to do things right, and we have endless procedures, forms, checklists, how-to guides, and training to prevent us from getting things wrong. We spend less time focusing on how to do the right thing, on learning from and with people, families, and communities.

And human beings *do* get things wrong. It's one of the many things that distinguishes us from robots. From machines. Mistakes are part of being human, and part of how we learn.

What's not human is the way we defend our position, deny responsibility, shift blame, continue to believe and assert that we are right.

To be human is to say sorry. And mean it. Not the classic, non-apologetic, 'I'm sorry you feel...' or 'I'm sorry if...' Not the passive, vague 'mistakes were made'.

Just, I'm sorry. We're sorry. I made a mistake. We got things wrong. And then to ask what should be different? What have we learned? How can we make things better, together?

Vulnerability

Vulnerable is a word that pervades social care and the wider human services. A label we readily slap on to people, families, groups, and communities to justify restrictive practice, rationalize decisions made about people without them, and imply inevitability when things go wrong.

The term suggests weakness exposure danger other and as such it's a label no one wants to wear.

But being vulnerable also means being open about how we're feeling. It allows us to let people in to see who we really are, not what we're pretending to be. It means we can say, 'I don't know', 'I'm not sure', 'What do you think?', 'Can we look at this together'. 'Can you help?' And that's powerful, and essential, because that's how we open up possibilities and opportunities.

That's how we break down barriers.

That's how we connect as human beings.

Presence

Not too long after I published my first blog post, I received a direct message on Twitter from someone who I now know and greatly admire.

She'd messaged me to share her positive experience of support from a social worker. She concluded her message by saying, 'We have a life because she stood by my side and didn't judge, she simply had an invisible hand on my shoulder saying, "I've got you", and we are thriving because she believed in me.'

The importance of connection and consistency is overlooked in our industrial approach to practice, with its unrelenting focus on efficiency. Where fast equals good. Where we deal with, fix, solve, end our involvement, close the case, and move on.

Instead of managing and measuring time, we need to invest time and hold space.

Slow down. Be alongside. Be present. Be there.

Kindness

Interference, hostility, cruelty, disinterest, brutality, and inhumanity are terms that are frequently applied to institutional behaviours. And all terms that are antonyms to 'kindness'.

From individual acts of indifference – not acknowledging the person waiting at a reception desk, a dismissive 'that's not my job', 'my hands are tied', 'there's nothing more I can do' – to the blanket rules, bureaucratic processes, and divisive policies that lessen people's sense of identity, agency, and choice, our institutions are not kind.

So, kindness is crucial – but it comes with a big note of caution.

Kindness isn't a word that sits comfortably in our conversations. It's easily dismissed as 'soft and fluffy', 'non-essential'.

> Usually there is a strong sense that the person mentioning kindness has unhelpfully interrupted the adult flow of conversation about public policy. About planning targets, and about economic benefit, and value for money. Somebody is bringing a fairy tale to a meeting about Real Things. (Unwin, J., 2018)

Assertions to 'be kind' also have negative associations with the patriarchal mantra stitched on to 'girls' clothes' and into their minds, along with hearts, rainbows, flowers, and butterflies (while 'boys' clothes' carry phrases like 'unstoppable', 'awesome', 'ready for adventure').

And there's the 'bad kindness' Maff Potts talks about, which lessens people's own sense of identity, agency, and choice. Patronizing, sympathetic, pitying, charitable, interfering kindness 'drenched in "I'm the benefactor, you're the helpless beneficiary. You're grateful and I'm amazing"' (Potts, 2020).

The kindness we need to cultivate is the loving kindness highlighted by the Archbishops' Commission on Reimagining Care:

> It is about an attitude that is oriented towards the good and flourishing of the other. It is a primarily relational concept. It is not simply used as a one-off act of kindness. Loving kindness is therefore not simply a choice but an obligation to act with justice and kindness towards others over time... Loving kindness is a call to wider society to be organized for the long term flourishing of every person. (Archbishops' Commission on Reimagining Care, 2023)

Empathy

To empathize is to identify, understand, and feel the emotions of fellow human beings. But if we don't view the people we serve as fellow human beings, it's unlikely we can show empathy. If we frame people as less than human, we perpetuate an approach based on charity and sympathy instead.

Cormac Russell writes that sympathy:

> divides the helper and the helped, the haves and so called have-nots, the good guys and the bad, the rich and the poor, the needed and the 'needy'... Sympathy creates soup kitchens and traditional food banks; empathy creates community kitchens, where the harvests of local foods are prepared by neighbours, where everyone's gifts are needed to create the feast. (Russell, 2020)

Caring

Empathy fits hand in hand with parity, mutuality, and reciprocity. With caring about and supporting each other. With the relational approach we are seeking, not the transactional approach we have now.

'Care is an art, a craft, a relationship. It is about entanglement in the lives of others and in emotions that are not always comfortable' (Cottam, 2021).

Caring is acting with love. Understanding. Nurturing. Tending. Wanting the very best for people, to see people flourish and thrive.

And to really care, we need to feel we're cared about too.

❀ ❀ ❀

These ten values and behaviours are essential to strong, healthy, recip-rocal relationships. Colourful, liberating, open, real, raw, exhilarating *human* behaviours that offer sharp contrast to the uniform, sterile, closed, predictable, computer says no, dehumanizing, and inhumane systems we've created.

They are at the heart of co-production and the core of rights-based/strengths-based/personalized/person-centred/relational practice.

However, like all those terms they are in danger of becoming empty buzzwords if we just keep slapping them on posters or in charters and continue to maintain the status quo. If we don't reflect on them, invest in them, nurture them, experience them, and demonstrate them in everything that we do.

We must change our practice to change our language.

We must change our practice to ensure we can be human.

Frontline

The frontline.

It's 'a place where opposing armies face each other in war and where fighting happens' (Cambridge Dictionary, n.d.).

It's 'the military line or part of an army that is closest to the enemy' (Oxford Languages, n.d.).

It's 'an area of potential or actual conflict or struggle' (Merriam-Webster, n.d.).

It's the term we attach to the people who work at the core of health and social care.

A place where fighting happens

Ironic, isn't it, that we use the term frontline – so imbued with aggression and conflict – to describe people dedicated to sustaining and enhancing life?

Or maybe not, when so much of serviceland does resemble a battleground. Where often it feels we spend more time defending our budgets and processes than people's rights. More time fighting with people than for them. More time 'on duty' than meeting our statutory duties. More time creating barriers and boundaries than crossing them.

The term frontline suggests invasion, assault, attack. It's an all too accurate reflection of the power dynamics at play. The judgement involved in our assessment. The threat of the review. The fear of budgets being cut, and support being removed.

Authority and control sit with 'professionals' on the frontline, while 'service users' are the passive recipients of decisions made about them, and services delivered to them.

Often, of course, the power is even further from people seeking or drawing on support, as in reality it doesn't sit with 'frontline' workers, who are caught in the crossfire, defending their decisions to panels and the decisions of panels to people seeking support. Who are the passive recipients of 'innovation' and 'transformation', battered by an onslaught of 'change' imposed from above. Who are constrained by perpetual process and bureaucracy and defeated by impenetrable IT systems.

Opposing sides

As well as reflecting the battlegrounds and barriers in our current system, the use of the term 'frontline' perpetuates and reinforces the idea – and reality – of 'them and us', of opposing sides.

The people on the frontline are 'professionals'. 'Key workers'. On the other side: 'service users', 'the vulnerable', 'the cared for', 'those'.

Frontline heroes

I would urge anyone who is thinking of a career in care to come forward and join this heroic workforce. –Boris Johnson
(DEPARTMENT OF HEALTH AND SOCIAL CARE, 2021)

People working 'on the frontline' are frequently referred to as 'heroes' – a narrative reinforced with vigour during the Covid-19 pandemic. But as the 'vulnerable' label frames people as problems, deflecting attention from the politics, policies, prejudice, and power dynamics that cause and perpetuate vulnerability, the hero label shifts the focus from long-term failures to properly acknowledge and reward people who fulfil these roles.

These military metaphors also extend to unpaid carers, who are often referred to as an 'army'. As with the hero label, there's the implication of bravery and sacrifice – that battling is part of the role, not the result of decades of failures to adequately fund and reform social care.

Invisible heroes, a hidden army, and the forgotten frontline

'Invisible heroes.' A 'hidden army' of carers. Campaigns to gain recognition and reward for people working in paid and unpaid roles in social care frequently suggest they are invisible or hidden.

However, most attempts to raise the profile of the 'forgotten frontline' bring us back once again to the 'them and us' narrative. From Jo Brand's reference to the 'hugely demanding, arduous, sometimes repetitive, often boring, thankless nature of the work that care workers do' (Brand, 2021), to Unison's description of 'the day-to-day challenges of caring for vulnerable people' (Unison, 2020), TUC's reference to 'emotionally and physically draining' work (TUC, 2020) and multiple references to the 'burden' of caring, all too often this narrative involves blaming and dehumanizing people drawing on support, further eroding their identity.

> The truth of the matter is that the low status accorded to care workers derives from the low status accorded to people who draw on care and support and in turn to supporting people to live their lives. Reinforcing such thinking helps no one. (Crowther, 2021a)

* * *

'Frontline' is a term that doesn't sit comfortably in a relational approach. It doesn't belong in our more human future. It reflects division and conflict and perpetuates a power dynamic we need to move beyond.

We need to be on the same side. Our battles should be for better lives, for human rights and social justice – not with each other.

We need to let down our defences, stop fighting each other, and start looking out for one another.

Be curious, not furious.

Build bridges, not walls.

From Referrals to Connections

Today the welfare state concentrates on the efficient delivery of inputs and outcomes, trapping us in the cultures and mechanisms of transaction and limiting human connection. In contrast, new systems emphasise relationships, starting with the premise that everyday human connections matter...

(COTTAM, 2018)

Our current practice is dominated by hand-offs and referrals. The social care sorting office approach.

As Gord Tulloch and Sarah Schulman observe, 'routine and redirection [have] become ubiquitous features of services'. They cite 'insufficient public funds' and 'greater demand for social services' as reasons for this, but also note that 'too few are asking whether the current system ought to be sustained as it is. Is it working? Is it performing well enough that all it needs is more money to extend its impact? We don't think so. It's not that simple' (Tulloch & Schulman, 2020).

I agree, it's not that simple. Ploughing more money into our industrialized, transactional system with 'routine and redirection' at its heart is not the answer, because the focus of this system is efficiency. On 'stabilizing crises and maintaining minimum levels of service for the most people possible, no matter how vapid and generic those services may be' (Tulloch & Schulman, 2020).

We need to shift from referring to connecting. Here's why.

Referring

Right now, our 'system' actively discourages connection.

Our single, centralized 'front door' is separate – removed from neighbourhoods, reliant on people coming to us rather than us making the effort to get closer to them. In theory, this makes it easier for people to contact us: a single phone number, a sole email address, one doorway, one way in. In reality, channelling everyone through a single point of entry makes it easier for us to 'screen' and 'triage' – and to refer people on to someone else's door.

We exclude people through eligibility determinations and financial thresholds. Our 'transfer protocols' describe how we pass people on. Who we let in. Who we turn away.

We structure teams around specialisms, with 'pathways' between them, waiting lists to get near them, admissions criteria to get a foot through the 'front door', and 'duty functions' to screen and triage. To assess who gets to pass go, and who gets referred elsewhere. Our departments are not structured to help us work together, with 'whole people', families and communities, to build good lives. Instead, they're designed so we can each play our part in providing services to meet a fragmented set of needs.

We spend our time arguing with other teams and 'partner' organizations about referrals and responsibility – passing 'cases' backwards and forwards.

We work in silos – we know our part in the 'process' but the next stage is in another department, behind another door.

We employ 'navigators' to join the dots, make the referrals, fill in the endless forms.

We invest in new 'case management systems' with multiple pathways and workflows.

We impose restructure after restructure, endlessly searching for the perfect alignment of fragmented, 'specialist' teams and services.

And we map this complexity in flowcharts, with 'swim lanes' to indicate the worker or team responsible for processing each 'case' through each part of our system.

But what our neat process maps don't show is how readily we block people's entry because they haven't knocked on the right door, phoned the right number, filled in the right form, ticked the right boxes, met the right criteria. They don't show the speed with which we move people through our system, or the number of people waiting in line. They don't show how readily we pass people back because they're 'inappropriate referrals', or pass them on, once we've completed our tasks, because we have no idea what to do next.

We invest so much time, money, and effort in the management of

146

'cases' and 'referrals', in the maintenance of thresholds, services, and structures that trap us *all* in hopeless cycles of bureaucracy, draining hope from people seeking some support, joy from workers, and money from our budgets.

Our impenetrable forms mean that time is tangled up in the complexity of our 'computer says no' system. Time we could and should be spending alongside people, listening liberating loving connecting caring.

If I have any regrets, it's every single minute that I didn't spend holding his hand because I had to go and write an email, I had to go and make a phone call. Having to fight the system that should be there to catch you when you fall but feels when you're going through it like it's there to catch you out. –Kate Garraway (ITV, 2024)

Signposting

Signposting: A social care sat-nav to nowhere.

(NEARY, N.D.)

Our 'front door teams' aim to 'signpost enquiries to other organizations'. 'A multidisciplinary social care team at the first point of contact...is able to more effectively signpost and screen demand.' 'Without Adult Social Care specialists working within the front door, the team could not effectively triage and signpost people.'

We're basically encouraging people to come and tell us their story so we can pass them on somewhere else to tell their story again. And again.

We attempt to 'manage demand' by strengthening our front door. We 'navigate' people to 'other organizations (e.g. in the voluntary sector) that might be able to provide assistance', and redirect 'those considered to have a low need'.

We signpost people to 'the community' with a leaflet or a phone number.

With no idea what happens to them next.

We report 'performance' in terms of the number of 'clients' we have 'signposted to other services'. We measure 'success' by the percentage of people we redirect: '60% of contacts successfully triaged at front door', '25% increase in calls signposted to local communities by the front door'.

Success for who exactly?

As Mark Smith notes, 'The logic is plausible. By making it harder to access services, we can use what little resources we have supporting those that need it the most. "Come back when you're worse", we say' (Smith, 2022b).

But while we may record handing people a leaflet or dictating another number to ring as a satisfactory conclusion to our 'front-door process' ('no further action', 'involvement ended', 'case closed', job done), we're effectively saying, 'Off you go, you're on your own, start again.' And how many people don't, or can't, start again?

> When someone gives me a telephone number as a means of access and tells me to ring it myself, I don't ring it. They don't know about the anxiety. That you're already overwhelmed in that space and then to have to do that and explain it all again and do it all again. It's like, just leave it. I'll just sit in this problem. I can't be bothered. –Issachar John (Adult Social Care Making It Real Board, 2024)

This approach has an 'incalculable human cost', and a significant financial cost too, because 'systems that exclude by design or default are extremely expensive' (Cottam, 2020). When people do come back when things are worse, things *are* worse! And options are reduced. Support is more reactive. More intensive. More restrictive. More expensive.

But perhaps the main issue is that we're ignoring the main issue. We're blithely overlooking the fact that our current ways of working aren't working. We're not admitting that we're defending a system that is 'mostly focussed on time and task, life and limb care [that] isn't something any of us want for ourselves or our loved ones' (Social Care Future, 2024) – summed up succinctly by 'someone very sage' who once told Angela Catley that 'social services spend a huge amount of time and effort trying to stop me having what I didn't want anyway!' (Catley, 2023b).

We're not listening to the people who are living this 'experience', who are too often absent from conversations and decisions. Impacted most. Mostly ignored.

And in our obsessive focus on what's missing and what's wrong, we're overlooking what we have, and what is strong.

Connecting

As the Covid-19 pandemic demonstrated all too starkly, we really do need each other, and our lives are better when we're connected.

Our focus in our better, brighter future must be to bring people together, and to connect with people too. To weave webs of relationships and support in our local communities. To help connect the threads, tie the knots, untangle the messy bits, and mend those parts that are torn.

Instead of investing in redirection, we need to invest in connection. Invest in our own relationships with people and families and with colleagues and communities. Invest in connecting people to other people to find friendships, relationships, love, and peer support. Invest in co-creating the conditions for people and communities to thrive.

Social work and social care should be right at the beating heart of communities, the core of a pulsing, shifting, growing network of connections and relationships that benefit us all.

The need is immense, the potential is huge, and the rewards are clear. So, what are we waiting for?

We can all play our part in building our better, brighter, more human future.

All of us, together. One connection at a time.

From Segregation to Belonging

ood social workers will carefully check themselves to make sure that...they aren't becoming street-level bureaucrats... whose actions to protect people involve taking them away from the very thing that we all strive for: a place where they feel settled, accepted, wanted and loved – a place where they belong.

(JAMES, MITCHELL, & MORGAN, 2019)

If there's one word that encapsulates all that social care should be about, it's 'belonging'. Love. Home. Safety. Meaning. Purpose. Connection. Identity. Inclusion. Rights. Family. Friendship. Hope. All right there, in one word.

And yet belonging – like love – is not a word that appears much in our legislation or guidance.

'Love and belonging are words that you very rarely see in assessments and support plans' (James, Mitchell, & Morgan, 2019).

In fact, our practice often reflects and reinforces the opposite.

Segregating

Perceived difference has historically been met with fear and loathing, evidenced in this chilling extract from Virginia Woolf's diary, written back in 1915:

> On the towpath we met and had to pass a long line of imbeciles. The first was a very tall man, just queer enough to look at twice, but no more; the second shuffled, and looked aside; and then one realized that everyone in that long line was a miserable ineffective shuffling idiotic creature with no forehead, or no chin, and an imbecile grin, or

a wild suspicious stare. It was perfectly horrible. They should certainly be killed. (Unwin, S., 2022)

Around the same time, the eugenics movement was gaining momentum. Eugenicists believed that anyone disabled or 'deficient' was a threat to the 'health of the nation'. The aim of eugenics was to remove human 'defects' altogether, segregating and preferably eliminating disabled people in the name of building a stronger society and 'perfecting' the human race.

In the same period, the Mental Deficiency Act 1913, which aimed 'to make further and better provision for the care of Feeble-minded and other Mentally Defective Persons', became law. The Act – which replaced the Idiots Act 1886 – stated that 'a person who is a defective may be dealt with under this Act by being sent to or placed in an institution for defectives or placed under guardianship...' (Mental Deficiency Act 1913).

Dealt with. Sent to. Placed.

Separated.

Removed from public life.

'They' don't belong here, with 'us'.

Then, in 1948, 'in the same year as the NHS began to great fanfare, its sister legislation, the National Assistance Act quietly slid onto the statute book' (Humphries, 2022). The Act gave local authorities the power to make 'welfare arrangements for blind, deaf, dumb and crippled persons' (National Assistance Act, 1948). It introduced a: 'duty of every local authority...to provide residential accommodation for persons who by reason of age, infirmity or any other circumstances are in need of care and attention which is not otherwise available to them' and 'also placed a legal duty on councils to recover payments from a person provided with residential accommodation and to assess their ability to pay if they were unable to pay the full cost' (Humphries, 2022).

So, the classification and segregation of 'others' was written into law, and the language and regime of assessment and means-testing was also established – firmly embedding judgements about 'eligibility' into practice and locating power and control over people's lives in the hands of 'professionals' and institutions.

Who's in, who's out? Who qualifies, who doesn't? Who stays, who goes?

Who do we not save?

The practice of separating and excluding older and disabled people remains to this day. Asylums and workhouses have been replaced with assessment and treatment units, residential care homes, supported living schemes, retirement villages.

People separated from the place they call home and the people and things that they love. Losing privacy, dignity, autonomy, identity, control. And yes, it may be a choice for some people, but even then, is that 'choice' due to the financial cost of alternatives? The lack of alternatives? The emotional and physical cost to family members – or pressure from them? Loneliness? Isolation?

Is it an inevitable consequence of an insufficient ecosystem of community-based support? An inevitable consequence of pervasive and enduring attitudes about who matters, and who doesn't?

Othering

'Othering' is 'a process whereby individuals and groups are treated and marked as different and inferior from the dominant social group' (Oxford Reference, n.d.). 'Othering can be as simple as speaking of a group of people as "them" in relation to another's "us", or even putting the definite article *the* in front of a label' (Merriam-Webster, n.d.).

'Othering' is rife. We don't talk about people. We say – and see – others. 'Service users.' 'Customers.' 'Clients.' 'Cases.' 'The elderly.' 'The disabled.' 'The vulnerable.' 'Those.'

In an article entitled 'Us v them: the sinister techniques of "Othering" – and how to avoid them', john a. powell observes how language 'not only activates people's anxiety and fear around a perceived Other, it creates new processes of exclusion and dehumanization' (powell, 2017).

Of course, we don't always choose our words with conscious intent to divide and exclude, and we may be totally unaware of the messages we're receiving and transmitting. But there are also too many examples throughout history of the very deliberate and dangerous use of language to incite division and dissent.

It's easier to frame people as something different to us, to despise and dismiss someone as being something other, than it is to consider them as equals in the common human cause, a person with the same desires as you, me and other human beings. If we consider people who require social care as people like us, it forces us to consider the totality of that. This leads to a risk that people might possibly be loved. Love and belonging in social care anyone? (James, Mitchell, & Morgan, 2019)

But surely social work and social care are all about human rights and social justice? Inclusion? Ordinary, equal lives? Our language reveals otherwise, exposing and perpetuating the 'them and us' attitudes that pervade serviceland – not just a denial of belonging, but an active barrier too.

Our jargon and labels are fuelled, perpetuated, and amplified by politicians and in the media, and heartbreakingly adopted and repeated by people they're attached to – leading to further division and exclusion. The recent Scottish Care Review highlighted that care-experienced children are singled out and bullied by other young people for 'speaking in social work jargon', using words like 'unit', 'placement', 'sibling', and 'contact'. The review 'heard repeatedly from children that using these words, and system language like them, often compounds a sense of being different' (Naysmith, 2018; Independent Care Review, 2020).

How can we promote and support belonging if we don't believe ourselves that everybody should belong?

The opposite of othering is not 'saming', it is belonging. And belonging does not insist that we are all the same. It means we recognize and celebrate our differences, in a society where 'we the people' includes all the people. (powell, 2017)

Siloing

The labelling and classification of people provides structure to our organizations, segregating the adult social care 'workforce' in local councils into 'reactionary silos' (Russell, 2020). 'Older Adults Team.' 'Frail Elderly Team.' 'Dementia Team.' 'Physical Disabilities Team.' 'Learning Disabilities Team.' 'Vulnerable Adults Team.' 'Entrenched Rough Sleeper Social Work Team.' 'Complex Adults Team.' 'Complex Needs Team.' 'Complex Cases Team.' 'Complex Lives Team.' 'Complex Under 65 Team.' I promise I'm not making these up! Of course, there are also first contact teams, front door teams, reablement teams, hospital discharge teams, long-term care and support teams, safeguarding teams, occupational therapy teams...

A fragmented jigsaw of 'specialisms' fragmenting human lives.

This siloed approach adds layers of bureaucracy, removes accountability and continuity, and means people are trapped in an endless cycle of referrals and repetition. And as Cormac Russell highlights, 'this approach has led to ghettoization and inadvertently to the further erosion of communities of place' (Russell, 2020).

Gatekeeping

The system is built to say no and turn you away.

(ROBINS, 2020B)

Being welcomed and feeling welcome are key elements of belonging. But we're not very good at welcoming people. Sometimes it feels as if we focus more on exclusion than inclusion, with our 'front doors', screening, signposting, waiting lists, eligibility criteria, and 'come back when things get worse' approach.

We're quick to close our doors to 'those' who don't meet our thresholds, and we inadvertently close more doors with our stigmatizing entry conditions.

> We had a Public Living Room in a big NHS hospital and the chalkboard sign outside said, 'Come in, relax, look out for each other'. Our invisible infra-red counter on the door showed approximately 1000 people per week were visiting it. One week the management in the hospital changed our sign to say 'It's time to talk — #MentalHealthAwarenessWeek'. When we checked the counter the numbers visiting fell to 40 for that week. (Potts, 2021a)

If people do manage to defy our barricades, we still don't really welcome them. We merely fit them in.

Fitting in

The opposite of belonging is fitting in... Fitting in is assessing and acclimating. 'Here is what I should say/be, here is what I shouldn't say, here is what I should avoid talking about, here's what I should dress like/look like,' that's fitting in. Belonging is belonging to yourself first. Speaking your truth, telling your story and never betraying yourself for other people. True belonging doesn't require you to change who you are, it requires you to be who you are.

(BROWN, 2022)

'Fitting in' pervades every element of our practice. Our 'contact centres' resemble sorting offices where we swiftly slot people into a category, attach a label, and assign a 'next action', a 'referral route', or a 'pathway' – preferably to the nearest exit. If we can't 'signpost' people away, we add them to our waiting lists, fit them in when we can.

People know they need to adapt their language – and adopt our language – to proceed. Use the magic words. Say the right thing.

We don't just fit people into our categories and processes; we fit them into services too. Despite the clear directive in the Care Act guidance that 'local authorities must consider how to meet each person's specific needs rather than simply considering what service they will fit into' (Department of Health and Social Care, 2023), fitting people into service solutions and schedules still dominates our practice.

This fitting in extends, of course, to the 'workforce' too. How many people working in social care can genuinely, hand on heart, say they can be who they really are at work?

Can you?

Welcoming

Being welcomed and feeling welcome are key elements of belonging.

This isn't rocket science. It's about creating open and appealing places for being, and spaces for listening, not fixing. Removing our labels, lanyards, jargon, forms, and agendas, and replacing them with curiosity and compassion. With tea, and with time.

'No more glass screens, waiting rooms with plastic chairs and forms to fill in. More fairy lights and sofas please' (Potts, 2021a).

Connecting

Our role is to stretch beyond giving help and instead connect people with a life outside of programs and services – with meaningful jobs, friends, activities, and places where they experience belonging.

(TULLOCH & SCHULMAN, 2020)

Our role as connectors is crucial. In our traditional, transactional approach, we don't connect. We signpost, triage, and refer.

But in our better, brighter future, we develop and maintain trusted connections with people and families and help to weave webs of relationships and support in local communities. And their communities are our communities – because 'you can't be of value to people and families who are disconnected from community if you are also disconnected from community' (Bartnik & Broad, 2021).

Whether we call it 'place-based', 'patch-based', or 'locality-based' working, organizing our approach around human geographies and communities rather than by a 'service label, eligibility, and service first' system enables us to focus on 'the whole person (their aspirations, strengths, connections, contribution) within the context of their family, relationships, contribution and mutual support within the community in which they live. Whole person, whole family, whole community, whole system' (Bartnik & Broad, 2021).

An approach based on relationships not transactions.

People not labels.

Inclusion not segregation.

Including

As Dr Chris Moore observes, 'inclusion should accept and celebrate differences. It should minimise "us and them" and maximise "us". It's not just about being in the room but feeling that you belong there' (Moore, 2022).

Article 19 of the United Nations Convention on the Rights of Persons with Disabilities recognizes the equal right of all disabled people to full inclusion and participation in communities. Everything we do should be about upholding this right. About dismantling barriers, not reinforcing them. Building bridges, not walls.

The 'nothing about us without us' principle should underpin our practice, making sure people are part of – and preferably leading – conversations and decisions about their own life and their support, and influencing and shaping wider support and services too.

We must value difference and diversity rather than fear it, and ensure that every human being is recognized and included as an equal citizen.

Anchoring

The people, places, and things that we love 'anchor us in the world and in our own selves. They reaffirm our identity and are what provide us with meaning, purpose and a sense of belonging' (Crowther, 2021d).

Without these anchors, we're drifting. In limbo. Lost.

We don't pay enough attention to identity in social care, to the 'scaffolding of the self' (Crowther, 2021c).

Too often we do more to erode people's identity and personhood than to honour it.

The goal of social care should be to help people to develop, maintain or repair the 'scaffolding' and to remain firmly anchored. And that is what 'personalized care' must mean too: not the narrow idea of delivering a transactional service in a more 'customized' or slightly kinder and more responsive way, but about attending to the things that anchor us in the world and in our own selves. It is about starting with the question 'what matters to you'. (Crowther, 2021c)

Belonging

Ubuntu is very difficult to render into a Western language. It speaks of the very essence of being human... It is to say, 'My humanity is caught up, is inextricably bound up, in yours.' We belong in a bundle of life. We say, 'A person is a person through other persons.' It is not, 'I think therefore I am.' It says rather: 'I am human because I belong. I participate, I share.'

(TUTU, 1999)

Ubuntu: I am because we are.

The relationships we have with the people, places, and things that matter to us help us to feel welcome. Connected. Included. Anchored. Help us to feel we matter. We belong. And in turn they help us to contribute, to be part of communities where we look out for one another, to build a 'larger us'.

Our role should be to honour and nurture these relationships, to honour and nurture belonging, and to remove the obstacles that get in the way – including those barriers our current practice imposes and perpetuates.

Stop segregating.

Stop othering.

Stop gatekeeping.

Stop fitting people in.

And stop fitting yourself in.

Question. Challenge. Be creative. Think differently.

Find a better way – because there's always a better way. A way of working, and a way of being, where we all have a seat at the table.

Where everyone belongs.

From Fear to Love

It was love's absence that let me know how much love mattered.
(HOOKS, 2016)

While we talk endlessly of safeguarding and keeping people safe, we don't talk anything like enough about fear or acknowledge how it dominates. And we don't talk much about love or acknowledge its absence. But love must be a fundamental part of our social care future. If we're serious about shifting our focus from transactions to relationships and supporting people to have a life not a service, we must recognize the influence of fear and create far more time and space for love.

The presence, and influence, of fear

Fear is 'to be worried or frightened that something bad might happen or might have happened' (Cambridge Dictionary, n.d.).

Fear casts a shadow over the public perception of social care and social work, and the dominant narrative helps fuel anxieties.

The overwhelmingly deficit-based, dehumanizing, and othering rhetoric around ageing and disability leads to fear of both. Language that implies older and disabled people are 'dependent' associates requiring assistance with being a 'burden', and social care with decline.

The media portrayal of social workers as adversaries, not allies, translates into a very real fear of 'social services', and endless stories of horrific abuse and neglect in institutions connect care with cruelty.

Successive governments have emphasized the need to 'fix social care' so people don't have 'the fear of having to sell their home to pay for the costs of care' – associating the need to draw on support not just with loss of savings, but also loss of freedom and the places people call home.

And crisis communications in the media emphasizing the

'demographic time bomb' and the 'silver tsunami' threaten that worse is yet to come.

For people who draw on support, there is the constant fear of that support being removed or becoming more restrictive. Despite the clarity in the statutory guidance that 'the review must not be used as a mechanism to arbitrarily reduce the level of a person's personal budget' (Department of Health and Social Care, 2023), reviewing 'high-cost packages' frequently features in plans to improve 'cost-effectiveness'. As such, the fear of assessments and reviews is very real.

> A lot of us who use social care fear our hours being cut. It makes me feel sick to think that my review is coming up because it is so out of my control, and those hours could be cut. I know many people who have had their hours cut, often by up to a third, just like that. That is a third less life that that person can effectively be getting on with and living. –Anna Severwright (House of Commons, 2020)

And inevitably this fear impacts not just on people's perception of social care, but on people's relationship with services too.

> Another barrier that I would like to highlight, which is not necessarily as obvious, and is more like a hidden influence and pressure, is a concern or fear that I have, which many other people in my position have, that when I contact social care because I need a review, or advice or support, my budget will be cut. Just by contacting them and them getting more involved in my life, suddenly things might start getting pulled away. That means I would not contact social care unless there was a serious problem that I needed to deal with. –Andy McCabe (House of Lords Adult Social Care Committee, 2022)

Fear is heightened by the tangle of bureaucracy that people find themselves caught up in. And by language that confuses, threatens, and excludes.

The fragility of budgets and support means that despite our talk of 'strengths-based practice', we're trapped in a place where fear of further cuts means we can't celebrate what's working well, and what is strong. People are forced to emphasize what's wrong to ensure 'eligibility' for support. Social workers emphasize 'complexity' and 'vulnerability' to persuade panels to approve 'packages'. Senior/'sector' leaders emphasize what (and who) is broken to retain the budget they have, or put in a plea for more.

This fear also stifles challenge and honest conversations, as people and families are afraid to speak out or to say 'the wrong thing', for fear of support being removed and more labels ('difficult', 'aggressive'...) being applied in its place.

And family members fear what will happen when they are no longer able to support and advocate for the people they love.

As well as impacting on perceptions of social care, too often fear drives practice.

There's the fear that asking, 'What matters to you?' exposes ambitions and desires that can't be 'delivered', expectations that can't be 'managed', so the belief that social workers have all the answers, and that the answers lie in services, keeps conversations within the confines of the boxes on our forms.

There's the fear of getting too close, too involved; of crossing boundaries and being 'unprofessional', caring too much, showing you care. And so 'boundaries' become impenetrable walls, built ever higher to 'maintain an acceptable distance'. Natural, human emotions are stifled to remain 'professional'.

There's the fear of 'demand' – adding physical barriers to emotional ones as doors are closed and gates are locked, and we screen, triage, signpost, refer, redirect, look away.

There's the fear that people will misuse scarce resources – particularly in relation to direct payments, which leads to restrictions on their use and excessive, intrusive monitoring and control.

There's the fear of 'hostile' 'aggressive' 'angry' 'challenging' 'non-engaging' 'clients' – people labelled by a system that ignores our own influence, that blames people rather than acknowledging what's happened to them and is happening around them. A system that does more to create than challenge the circumstances and environments that marginalize, oppress, and exclude.

There's the fear of questioning the status quo, despite the desperate need for change. And the desperate fear of change for people comfortable with the status quo.

And above everything, there's the fear of mistakes, of missing something vital, of getting something wrong. So, we escalate decisions, wait for permission, risk assess everything, restrict opportunities, tighten procedures, impose more rules. We create more audits, more governance, more scrutiny, more regulation, more suspicion, and more bureaucracy.

And we have less and less time for the things most likely to ensure safety, wellbeing, and flourishing lives.

For creating safe spaces to meet in the middle 'where we have a real chance to connect, differences aside, as humans first' (Chapple, 2023).

For building and sustaining trusting relationships.

For considering what could go right and what's possible, not what might go wrong.

For acting with love.

The absence of love

Love is a central feature of family life and yet remains invisible in health and social care services, practice and research. Where is the love? And why is this word erased in the professional arena?

(RYAN, S., 2021)

It's a brave professional who talks about love and social care in the same sentence.

(FOX, 2010)

While Rob Mitchell describes love as 'the essence of humanity', he acknowledges it's 'something that health and social care isn't comfortable with' (Mitchell, R., 2018). And Alex Fox refers to the 'abhorrence of love' in our invisible asylum of public services (Fox, 2018).

So why is this? If our aim is to support people to achieve the things that matter most to them, how can it be that we must be brave to talk about love?

When I refer to love, I mean love in all its guises.

The intimate physical passionate aching shaking constantly on your mind dizzying desiring adoring anticipating sleepless soaring non-stop smiling type of love.

The affectionate, gentle, easy, settled, content, held, familiar, familial, belonging type of love.

The 'I've got you', on your side, looking out for you, dropping everything for you, challenging, enthusing, encouraging, admiring, accepting, laughing, crying, and just being there when you need them friends type of love.

The hopeful, hopeless, maybe, maybe not, one-sided, lonely, rejected, foolish, unrequited type of love.

The lost gone broken sobbing desperate empty distraught raw grieving type of love.

And the escaping, returning, just being, compassionate, listening to, connecting with, believing in, respecting, and accepting yourself and who you are and who you want to be type of (self) love.

I also mean love in the sense of '*what* matters to us' as well as 'who matters'. The pleasures, joys, and sensations of the things we love seeing, doing, anticipating, reflecting on, being part of, and fighting for. Our passions, desires, hobbies, and interests. The causes we campaign for. The places we feel we belong. And the pleasure in the everyday. For me, that's waking up to blue sky and sunshine. Swimming in the sea. Seeing magnolia trees blossoming in spring. Hearing my children laughing. Cooking colourful food. Creating. Writing. Connecting. Hugs and being held.

People take pleasure from different things. We all have our own public, and private, passions. We all love differently. That's one of the fabulous things that makes us all unique. But one of the core things we all share is our desire – and our human right – to love and to be loved.

'The main thing is love. Food, shelter and warmth are important but it's lack of someone caring that leads to despair' (Fox, 2018).

For all our talk of needs in social care, love rarely features on the list. We're stuck at the bottom of Maslow's hierarchy – focusing on people's basic requirements for food and drink, clothing, shelter, and safety but paying little or no attention to people's needs for love and belonging, or to their hopes and dreams. If we do consider relationships at all, it's often in the context of the people who are 'willing and able' to provide care – so we don't have to.

Despite the Care Act 2014 shift to promoting wellbeing, our focus is still very much on providing services to help people to survive. But what use is surviving without the passion, desire, and joy that gives us all a reason for living and a feeling of being truly alive? Okay, so maybe love isn't all we need, but just maybe it *is* the main thing we need.

Instead of focusing on love in social care, we focus on the shadows. Safeguarding. Abuse. Neglect. Risk. Threat. Danger.

But our pathways, manuals, regulations, and procedures don't keep people safe. Our institutions don't keep people safe. People keep people safe. Kindness, compassion, connections, friendship, and love keep people safe.

We talk about appropriate professional boundaries and the dangers of getting too close. But what about the consequences of our distance? What about the dangers of not having honest conversations about relationships, sex, sexual identity, and sexual health?

What about the risks of a life without love?

'Why is it more important that someone gets training to teach them how to use a bus than having someone to hold hands with on their bus journey?' (Marriott, 2019).

Conversations about love and relationships take a whole lot of time, and a whole lot of trust.

'Intimate and private lives cannot be explored in a single visit, especially not one where the agenda is predetermined by a script to be followed as laid out in a large assessment document' (James, Mitchell, & Morgan, 2019).

Support for people to find love takes time too. Relationships don't come in 'care packages'. There's no referral form for romance. There's no brokerage team for love. But when the clock is ticking and our waiting lists are lengthening, we don't have time for love. We don't have time to explore all the options, so we focus instead on the services we know, the support we can buy. But often these services don't make space for friendships to develop, love to flourish, or ambitions to be realized. They have rules and ratios. Single beds and curfews. Constant supervision.

Yet while we claim to be too busy for love, we spend plenty of time fighting. Indeed, the statutory social care sector is more akin to war than love, as we work on the 'frontline', maintaining our defences against people fighting for support.

And our language is often cold, passive, and devoid of love. The language of an enemy.

We refer to people as numbers, cases, referrals, and describe family and friends as 'carers', 'next of kin', 'representatives', 'appropriate individuals'. There's no category for 'lover'. There's no box to tick for 'soulmate'.

We have comprehensive safeguarding procedures and extensive risk assessments, but no guidance on romance. No policies on love.

Any reference to love in the legislation or literature is often implicit. The Care Act 2014 refers to 'emotional wellbeing' and 'domestic, family and personal relationships'. The Human Rights Act 1998 includes the right to respect for private and family life, and the right to marry and start a family. The Mental Capacity Act 2005, under the heading 'Family relationships etc', refers to marriage, civil partnership, and sexual relations, but in terms of consent, not love. The Care Quality Commission has guidance on relationships and sexuality in adult social care services – but the document doesn't mention love.

In response to an observation that 'there's no romance or sex in Making It Real,' Kate Sibthorp acknowledges 'it's not immediately obvious...however, it's all there if you look more closely' (Sibthorp, 2019).[1] And it is. But maybe instead of all these implied, veiled, indirect references, we need to start embedding love much more blatantly at the heart of our policies and practice.

Embracing love

It is people's human right to have a relationship. It shouldn't be a 'nice to have', but something that adds value to people's lives. We are social animals; if you don't see someone in that way, then you don't see them as human. –Claire Bates

(SALMAN, 2019A)

It seems to me that if you believe in love, value love, and trust in love, you make time for love, and you fight for love. So, is the stark reality that we've distanced and othered 'our service users' to such an extent that we don't see them as human beings with human desires? Have we stepped so far into the 'system' that we've forgotten our own passion for social justice, equality, and human rights? Blocked out our own humanity? Forgotten about love?

We offer people seeking support a service, when often what they want more than anything is a relationship.

To fully embrace love, we need to recognize that the people we're working alongside are first and foremost *people*. Human beings with human desires, human passions, human needs, and human rights. And we need to remember we are human too. We must stop acting like robots processing widgets in a factory. Quit being the baggage handlers carrying cases on and off our conveyor belts.

Love is complicated. Relationships are messy. Connections take time. A relational approach does not fit easily within our current linear,

---

1   Making It Real is a set of co-produced 'I' and 'We' statements, published by Think Local Act Personal (TLAP), that describe what good care and support looks like.

process-driven system. But you know what, we *are* the system. And we can be the change.

However...

Apologies for throwing in an element of caution – but it matters.

There is a danger that a focus on love and relationships without associated funding, and devolution of power, shifts ever more unsustainable responsibility towards families and communities.

> Intentions to put 'love for children and families at the heart of our care system' are well meant. But the sector doesn't need more empty promises of 'love' (which, when used in isolation, seems to be a euphemism for 'cheap'). It needs urgent investment, in all areas, from children with special educational needs and disabilities to mental health services. (Pierre, 2023)

It's no use if love features in our language but doesn't translate into action.

No one needs more empty promises.

'We need to reclaim the concept of love, not as an abstract, all embracing, fantasy but as a set of ethics, principles, values and behaviours. A love that is justice in action...' –bell hooks (Parker, 2019).

It's never *just* about words.

To love is to act.

From Assessment to Understanding

*W*e refer to social workers as 'social care assessors' or 'assessment officers'. We have assessment teams and assessment forms. We measure 'performance' in terms of 'waiting times for assessments' and 'number of assessments completed'.

Assessments define our purpose and our identity, while the purpose and identity of 'the assessed' is overlooked in this 'process'.

It's time to flip this language, and this practice.

Stop assessing.

Start understanding.

Assessment: The gateway to care and support

Assessments are a way into packages, pathways and protocols. They result in either a screen out ('Come back when you're worse'), a referral ('Go and have an assessment over there...') or some action, which will be a package or pathway about the bits of your story that fit the service boundary. If you need more, you'll need to have a different assessment and more referrals.

(SMITH, 2022B)

The Care Act guidance is clear that the assessment 'should not just be seen as a gateway to care and support'. Language matters – and the 'just' in that sentence is key, because ultimately its presence confirms that the assessment is a gateway – the gateway – to care and support.

The guidance states that 'the outcome of the assessment is to provide a full picture of the individual's needs so that a local authority can provide an appropriate response at the right time to meet the level of the person's needs' (Department of Health and Social Care, 2023).

As 'assessors' we identify, and provide, the 'appropriate response'. We decide the 'right time'. We fix the 'level'. We determine the 'needs'. And as such we hold the keys to the social care door.

The power is well and truly in our hands.

The assessor and the assessed

The Money Advice Service website claims that 'many people are put off by the idea of an assessment, but it's not something you should worry about. A social care assessment is not a test you can pass or fail' (Money Advice Service, n.d.).

If only that was true.

Any kind of assessment is a test, and tests are generally nerve-wracking experiences, particularly when we know that the outcome will have a significant impact on our lives. Tests have right and wrong answers. You can pass or fail.

Our social care assessment *is* a test, and the result either opens or closes the door to support. And as such, the power imbalance between the assessor and the assessed is stark. In the world of social care, we control people's futures. Sounds scary, doesn't it? And it is.

> Steven has been very anxious and destructive all week. It might be the stopping of the medication. It might be anxiety about the house move. It might be that he knows that assessments can turn his life upside down. It was probably all three. I find the pre assessment anxiety unbearable. (Neary, 2016b)

To assess is to judge

The dictionary definition of assessment is 'a consideration of someone or something and a judgment about them' (Collins, n.d.).

To assess is to judge. As assessors, we judge needs, risks, eligibility, capacity, best interests, finances. And regardless of our Care Act duties, we're quick to walk away if we judge that people's needs aren't 'eligible', or if their eligible needs are met by family or friends, or if they can fund their own support.

Our decisions are influenced by thresholds, checklists, calculators – not by our principles, our values, or our hearts. And as such we've detached ourselves sufficiently to think we have the right to assess and judge people against predetermined criteria and rules, while we get on with pursuing our own ambitions, building (and breaking) our own relationships, taking our own risks, making our own unwise decisions, living our own lives.

The assessment form: Set questions and tick boxes

It just seems to me though, if services weren't spending so much time and energy on my paper-self, they could perhaps see me. They could perhaps hear me. They could perhaps help me.

(WREN, 2021)

When our assessment is based on set questions from a generic form, we're setting the agenda for, and limiting the scope of, our conversations. If we ask (often intrusive and unnecessary) questions about 'personal care' needs, we get answers about personal care needs.

Despite the Care Act guidance suggesting the assessment should be a 'critical intervention in its own right', in reality our assessments are often rushed and usually take place in response to a crisis. As a result, we glean a 'snap-shot' of a person's life, and all too readily reach for our standard service solutions to fix the problems we've defined.

Assessing needs

I am struck by the fact that there is no discussion, no talk of what could be changed. There is just the recording of facts, the processing of problems. It's a tetchy interview, not a conversation.

(COTTAM, 2018)

Our social care assessment is an assessment of need. We focus on what people struggle with and can't achieve. We see problems, not people. 'We lose the person in the very process designed to find them' (Fox, 2018).

We're so caught up in screening, assessing, labelling, and processing that we believe if we've met basic safety and survival needs, we've done our job, and we can move on to the next 'case' on our waiting list. But in focusing just on basic, functional, personal care needs, we fail to see, hear, or understand the person.

We fail to talk about what really matters.

These conversations require time. Time to establish the trust required for the person to tell their story. Time to listen. Time to understand what's happened to make them who they are now, and what needs to happen to enable them to be who they want to be. Time to explore how we can be most useful. Time to stick around and see the difference. And the reality is that in our current system, time is scarce.

But it's not just time that's the issue. These conversations also require us to be curious, and increasingly it seems as if we've just lost interest.

'I didn't ever really feel like the case workers who came to visit me cared about me; they cared about paperwork' –Rhiannon (Pierre, 2024).

The assessment process

At the end of the day the assessment is just that – a process.

It's a 'document and a stage in the IT system that is needed to unlock other stages' (Pitts, 2018).

It's a cog in the social care machine.

The assessment process is our process. The assessment form is our form. Its completion and approval allow us to progress to the next stage but hold little value to the people who are desperate for us to put down our pens, look up from our checklists, listen to what really matters, and act on what we hear.

Conversations

To escape the dehumanizing bureaucracy of rigid assessments, some local authorities are adopting a more conversational style of assessment, captured on 'conversation records', not on lengthy tick-box forms.

While an assessment is prescriptive and narrow in its reach, these conversations can be more open-ended, and led by the person, not the questions on a form. They 'can help people to explore their own aspirations, the things they're good at, the experiences they've had, the people they care about and what matters to them, as well as their support needs' (Skills for Care, 2018).

And yet, however open and honest these conversations are, they take place within a system full of assessments and tests. We still judge whether people's needs are significant enough to meet our criteria. Our forms may be replaced by records, but we still write for panels, to justify our decisions and their associated costs. And if we decide people have sufficient needs, we apply a means-test to their finances to determine how much they'll pay.

'Conversations' are nothing more than assessments with a shiny new name if they aren't accompanied by an associated shift in thinking at all levels, including nationally. As long as we have a system based on eligibility, the power dynamic remains. We are still assessors. We are still judging people. Our function is still to process people through our system – if we permit them to enter at all.

We still hold the keys to the social care door.

Understanding

Assessments are about accessing resources rather than working out what matters to someone. Understanding starts with a blank sheet rather than a checklist that you might find in an assessment. It starts with 'what matters to you?', 'what does a good life for you look like?'
(CHANGING FUTURES NORTHUMBRIA, N.D.)

Assessments are designed to classify, categorize, and channel, so by default they reduce people's lives to lists. We assess to fit people into boxes, pathways, and services, with the associated boundaries defining and limiting the scope of our conversations. Of our interest.

Assessments don't exist in our better, brighter future. There's no place for tests. Instead, we build relationships of trust where we recognize and respect people as experts in their own lives. We listen to what they, and the people who know them best, say about the support they know they need to live the life they want to lead. We shift the power, so instead of us judging people, we let people judge how we can be most useful. The barriers we can help to remove, the rights we can uphold, the connections we can make, the doors we can open, the opportunities we can bring their way.

We understand and respond to stories and aspirations, rather than expecting people to understand and respond to the questions on our forms about what's wrong.

Without an assessment, we focus instead on what needs to happen next – for the subsequent hours, days, weeks, or months. Not a plan for services, but a plan for a good life, well lived. A plan owned by the person and developed in collaboration with people who genuinely care about them.

We're in that team. We're on their side. We're by their side. And what matters most to us is what matters most to them.

So, let's revisit the Care Act 2014 and shift our attention away from the sections on assessing needs and determining eligibility, and back to the start – to the core principle of promoting wellbeing.

Let's liberate people from the dehumanizing constraints of the assessment process and liberate ourselves too.

Rather than setting the tests and asking all the questions, let's focus on the answers, and let's be part of the solution.

Strengths-based

Some words we use in social work and social care literally make me cringe when I hear or read them. 'Strengths-based' is different though. It's a term that genuinely does make me go 'Hmmm'.

I'm all for the shift away from a paternalistic, deficit-based, transactional, care management approach, with its focus on problems, labels, and tick boxes. On assessments for services and one-size-fits all solutions. On doing to and fixing.

I wholeheartedly believe in the key elements of strengths-based practice. In the vital importance of recognizing and responding to people as unique human beings, as the experts in their lives, and in the context of their whole lives. Of listening hard – with no assumptions or judgement – to understand what matters most to people. Of flexibility, proportionality, collaboration, and trust. Of identifying, and responding to, the capabilities, aspirations and potential of people, families, and communities. Of creativity and possibility. And – above all –relationships.

But.

I'm uneasy about some of the stated ambitions of a strengths-based approach – or at least our interpretation of them. And I also think we throw the term strengths-based around, drop it into our narrative too easily to put a new shine on our practice, without realizing very many of those key elements. Without changing very much behind the scenes.

A 'new softer-sounding language adding a coating of irony to unyielding bureaucracies' (Fox, 2018).

Glossy wallpaper covering up the cracks in a wall built on crumbling foundations.

Let me explain what I mean.

Independence

The strengths-based approach is about reducing dependency and challenging 'prescription culture'. Crucially, it is about protecting and promoting the person's independence, resilience, choice and wellbeing.
(SOCIAL CARE INSTITUTE FOR EXCELLENCE, 2015)

Strengths-based approaches are frequently defined as aiming to 'promote independence' and 'reduce dependency'. In this narrative, reliance on other people is seen as a negative, undesirable state, and independence equates to 'managing with minimal or no support'.

These ambitions, however, are far from the Article 19 definition of independent living and its focus on equal rights, equal choices, inclusion, and participation.

Drawing on support doesn't prevent independence; it allows it. We all depend on other people. None of us functions in complete isolation. We know we need each other to thrive.

We must flip the widely misinterpreted narrative of independence, and talk instead of the importance of relationships, connection, and inclusion. Of continuity, stability, safety, and belonging…a place to call home, people we love, communities where we look out for one another. And we must recognize and uphold people's rights to choice and control, and to the support we all need to live ordinary, *interde*pendent lives.

Resilience

Strength-based practice is a social work practice theory that emphasizes people's self-determination and strengths. It is a philosophy and a way of viewing clients as resourceful and resilient in the face of adversity.
(DEPARTMENT OF HEALTH AND SOCIAL CARE, 2019)

Resilience means 'the ability to become strong, healthy, or successful again after something bad happens' (Britannica Dictionary, n.d.). 'People and things that are resilient are able to recover easily and quickly from unpleasant or damaging events' (Collins, n.d.).

Resilience is the process of adapting in the face of trauma, being able to 'bounce back' when times are hard.

A strengths-based approach 'helps create, develop and support "resilient individuals" – people who can manage independently even when their needs may be increasing' (Think Local Act Personal, 2016). Changing people, rather than addressing the causes of stress and trauma. Absolving our collective responsibility, rather than challenging the behaviours, environments, and structural inequalities that cause harm.

Instead of 'creating' 'resilient individuals', who 'manage', 'cope', and survive, let's turn our attention to creating compassionate, welcoming, and accepting ecosystems of support, where everyone can thrive.

Empowerment

Strengths and asset-based approaches are ways of working to empower and support people to lead good quality and fulfilled lives.

(SKILLS FOR CARE, N.D.)

'We empower our customers to take care of themselves.'

'We empower our service users to make positive decisions.'

Argh.

Our 'customers'. *Our* 'service users'. Remind me again where the power lies?

Our use of the term 'empowerment' suggests people don't already have power, and it's our actions that give them power. So, who has the choice and control here?

We've turned empowerment into a transaction. A service. We give people power. It is our gift to (choose to) give (and take) away. How benevolent of us. How kind.

For all of us to have genuine power, we must address the politics, policies, and prejudices that remove choice and control. We need to devolve decision making, shift resources and responsibility out from the institutional core, and work alongside people as equals.

Signposting

Strengths-based approach/practice is NOT about signposting and providing less support.

(DEPARTMENT OF HEALTH AND SOCIAL CARE, 2019)

Strengths-based practice is NOT about signposting. Except it is, for the councils investing in their 'front door' under the guise of a strengths-based approach, to 'manage demand' and redirect people elsewhere, either a website or, usually, The Community – that abundant, welcoming, accepting alternative to services, brimming with opportunity.

The pot of gold at the end of the signpost.

We view increases in the number of calls 'signposted to other services' as an indicator of success.

We wave people off from our front door with a cheery, 'Come back if things get worse.'

We need to stop signposting and start connecting. Introduce, not refer.

To do this, we need to be based within communities, know (and be known in) communities, and above all – *invest* in communities.

Assessment

> *There is increasing interest in 'strengths-based' approaches to assessment – where the focus is not on what the person can't do, but on where their strengths lie and the supports they have around them in their family and the community.*
>
> (HARDY, 2017)

Ahh...the paradox of the strengths-based assessment.

We 'start with what's strong', but our assessment only begins because something is wrong.

We focus on capabilities, aspirations, and potential, then determine eligibility for support on levels of need and 'outcomes' that people are unable to achieve.

> Like so many others in my position, now that I have secured the level of support that I need, I don't want to do anything that will threaten this. And so I have learnt to only talk about what I can't do; I have learnt not to mention my skills, my experience and my abilities. I have learnt not to mention my dreams, my ambitions and my intentions. More than that, I try to make sure that those who assess me have no idea that these dreams aspiration and intentions even exist.
> (Sutton, 2014)

We consider how family and friends can help, then – despite strengths-based practice NOT being about 'shifting responsibilities to carers and family/friends' (Department of Health and Social Care, 2019). Where carers are able and willing to continue, we reduce or remove support.

'The quickest way to be denied or lose support is to offer to do the caring yourself' (Fox, 2018).

We refer to people as 'the experts in their life', but decisions about their future are made in conversations about them, without them.

We 'empower' people to have choice and control about their support, then prescribe from a limited menu of services, or offer a direct payment we don't trust people to spend.

We talk of people as equals, but a strengths-based assessment is still an assessment, and any kind of assessment is a test. Tests have right and wrong answers. You can pass or fail. One party is the judge, the other, the judged.

And when we get round to reviews, if things are a bit better and support is working well, the threat of cuts to budgets is never far away.

Outcomes

A strengths-based approach is goal orientated and outcomes focused.
(DEPARTMENT OF HEALTH AND SOCIAL CARE, 2017)

Outcomes is a lovely bit of social care jargon, isn't it? I have plans, hopes, daydreams, and endless to-do lists – and maybe the odd New Year's resolution I make and promptly forget about, but I don't think or talk about my 'outcomes'.

But strengths-based working is all about outcomes – and when we say outcomes, we don't mean vague ambitions, or pipe dreams, or wild fantasies. Outcomes must be personal, and measurable, and – even better – 'SMART'.[1]

Just whose outcomes are we talking about here?

Why do learning disabled people always have to be working towards an outcome? Why do learning disabled people's lives have to be in a permanent state of being measured? Why do learning disabled people

---

1   Specific, Measurable, Achievable, Realistic, and Time limited.

have to succumb to professionals deciding whether they've achieved something? (Neary, 2016a)

Training

A strengths-based approach to care is a collaborative process that draws upon an individual's strengths and assets and those within their community. Learn how to put this approach into practice and maximise an individual's independence.

(SOCIAL CARE INSTITUTE FOR EXCELLENCE, 2022)

Ahh, training. A half day here, a full day there. Let's 'roll out' mandatory strengths-based training and change the world...or at least change our practice. Just. Like. That.

Easy.

Except, of course, it's not.

This isn't about training. It's about liberating workers from the processes, forms, and bureaucracy that have smothered values, crushed hope, and stifled curiosity. It's about freeing workers up to explore communities, make connections, build relationships, uphold rights. It's about permission to try, to be creative, make mistakes, and try again. It's about unlearning one way of working and learning another way – not in a classroom or in front of a computer but by being alongside people, families, communities, and colleagues, to agree what good looks like and how we can work together to achieve it.

Focusing on strengths-based training also absolves organizations of any responsibility for systemic change – which is why it won't work.

We tried in vain to explain that more money was not needed, nor were new professionals required. What was needed was permission to free those at the front line to work in new ways – ways in which they want to work. (Cottam, 2018)

Our communities don't need to be trained to help each other, because that's a human thing – that's a very human thing. –Karen, People Focused Group (Social Care Institute for Excellence, 2021b)

❋ ❋ ❋

As I said, the term 'strengths-based' makes me go 'Hmmm'.

It's too widely misinterpreted. Too easily misused.

We talk about 'what matters to you' but we're still doing what matters to us. We're still concentrating on doing things right, not on doing the right things. We've added layer upon layer of complexity and jargon to describe good practice. We have handbooks, models, theories, and policies to help shape and improve what we do and how we do it, but somewhere along the way we've forgotten *why* we're here.

We don't need more glossy wallpaper. We need to acknowledge the cracks, dismantle the walls, and rebuild the foundations.

As Hilary Cottam writes, 'to create change we need a guiding vision, and the vision we must aim for is good lives well lived' (Cottam, 2018).

If 'good lives well lived' is our 'why', then good practice really comes down to one simple question. A question that the Care Act guidance suggests is 'a good starting point for a discussion' (Department of Health and Social Care, 2023).

A question that encapsulates listening, curiosity, meaning, purpose, hope, ambition, relationships, inclusion, choice, control, connection, and collaboration.

What does a good life look like for you and your family, and how can we work together to achieve it?

Does it really need to be any more complicated than that?

From Doing to, to Working With

*W*hat does a good life look like for you and your family and how can we work together to achieve it?

(DEPARTMENT OF HEALTH AND SOCIAL CARE, 2023)

The principle of working together – of co-production – is explicit in the statutory guidance. The guidance states that 'local authorities should ensure that individuals are not seen as passive recipients of support services, but are able to design care and support based around achievement of their goals', that 'local authorities should actively promote participation in providing interventions that are co-produced with individuals, families, friends, carers and the community', and that 'strengths-based approaches might include co-production of services with people who are receiving care and support to foster mutual support networks' (Department of Health and Social Care, 2023).

The principle of working together – of co-production – should underpin everything we do.

Alex Fox suggests 'strengths-based working and co-production are inextricably linked' (Fox, 2023). Both terms refer to working alongside people, with a focus on what matters and a shared role in producing something valuable and valued. Shared power. Shared decisions. Mutual trust. Respect. A shift from providers and passive consumers – saviours and 'the saved' – to reciprocity and interdependence. To seeing all people as equal human beings with ideas, talents, knowledge, passion, and dreams. To creativity and possibility. Connections and relationships.

Working with, not doing to.

Nothing about us without us.

But over 20 years ago, Edgar Cahn identified that 'words like "strength-based" and "asset-based" had been turned into a mantra by social welfare professionals – an obligatory incantation recited to prove that "one was in the know".'

'Use of buzzwords certified one as morally pure and appropriately avant-garde. Behind the curtain, though, business was proceeding as usual: preserving one's turf, creating dependencies, and protecting a livelihood earned by catering to people's needs, deficiencies and problems' (Cahn, 2000).

I've already suggested we throw the term strengths-based around, drop it into our narrative too easily to put a new shine on our practice, without changing very much behind the scenes. That the words associated with 'strengths-based' expose our (mis)interpretation of the approach and reveal the same old power dynamics and divisions that exist 'behind the curtain'.

And if we unpick the language relating to 'co-production', we find much the same. It quickly becomes clear that while the meaning of the term couldn't be more explicit, we've largely managed to miss the point in our interpretation. We're still in charge. We're still 'doing to'.

Professionals and service users

There are *a lot* of definitions of co-production out there, and many of them refer to 'professionals' and 'users'.

The term 'professionals' suggests status, authority, and expertise, while the term 'users' implies an absence of power and agency. Passive receipt.

'Professional' offers people working in organizations an identity, while 'users' remain an anonymous, dehumanized, 'other' group.

The powerful and the powerless.

So, we've already failed. Instead of working together as *equals*, our basic definitions imply and perpetuate difference and inequality. Us and them.

These definitions also reinforce stereotypes and stigma by implying that people who draw on support aren't professionals, and that professionals aren't people who draw on support.

And what if you can't 'use' a service? If you're not allowed in? If you're not eligible? Who is 'engaging' with you then?

Improving services

The purpose of co-production is invariably described in terms of better services, not better lives. This interpretation confines ideas of co-production – and indeed of social care – to the realm of serviceland and 'the market', where 'care' is a task delivered in a package, or a destination with no return.

Of course, there's plenty of room for improvement in services, but this narrow lens ignores the vital, everyday role of families and communities in caring for and about each other.

Most care and support is already 'co-produced' in our homes, streets, and neighbourhoods.

People looking out for one another.

Nurturing. Tending. Loaning. Mending.

Webs of support and relationships in local communities.

So, if we're serious about building better lives and stronger communities, our thinking about co-production must start with people and relationships, not services and institutions. We must recognize and value the love, compassion, energy, and potential in communities, and work out together how we can be most useful – as public *servants*, not masters – in support of local people and local places.

Engagement

'Engagement' is often described as a 'stepping stone' to co-production, a rung on the ladder. But if we're thinking in terms of 'engaging' people, we're stepping off on the wrong foot.

The dictionary definition of 'engagement' is 'an arrangement to meet or be present at a specified time and place' (Merriam-Webster, n.d.).

In other words, when can you – over there in your 'marginalized group' or your 'vulnerable population' – show up (at a time and place convenient for us) to help us?

Not, how can we step in to be most effective? How can we step up to ensure that sufficient resources and support are in place for you to live the life you choose to lead? How can we step back and get out of the way?

'Engagement' is something we do to people, at a fixed time, for a fixed purpose. There's no sense of an evolving, organic, long-term relationship, where trust is built and where genuine, human connections are made.

There's also the association of the term 'engagement' with battles – 'a hostile encounter between military forces' (Merriam-Webster, n.d.), which may be apt given the language of war that threads through our practice (frontline, duty, officers...) and the exhausting reality of fighting for support, but is obviously not the intention.

Empowerment

'We empower people with lived experience to use their own voice.'

'We want to empower our service users to work as equal partners with us.'

Argh.

We – the 'professionals' – give you – the 'users' – power. If we feel like it. Maybe. Sometimes. Or maybe not.

We see power as ours to give away.

And, by default, to take away.

And you are 'ours'. We own you. We control you. We're in charge.

'Empowerment: An illusory gift from professional to a not quite human' (Neary, n.d.).

We absolutely need to talk about power. We need to be aware of – and honest about – the power we hold in different roles and remove the obstacles to power being shared (including by paying attention to the way our policies, practice, and language divide and exclude). But by talking about 'empowering people' and 'giving power to people' we are further embedding the very power dynamic we're (in theory) aiming to remove.

Voice

The way we talk about 'voice' really makes me go 'Hmmm'.

There are the dehumanizing references to 'voice' detached from any sense of a person. 'We will actively recruit or involve diverse voices in a meaningful way.' 'Advocating for a lived experience voice to be involved...'

There's the noble act of 'giving people a voice'. 'We will be running events to give disabled people a voice.' 'Giving voice to those who often aren't heard or often don't engage.'

And there's the generous act of people speaking on behalf of a collective group of 'others'. 'The voice of lived experience', and – squirm – 'the voice of the voiceless'.

Like engaging and empowering, the way we talk about 'voice' reveals and perpetuates deep divisions, a sense of superiority, and a paternalistic approach.

The focus on voice also implies that meaningful contributions can only be made by people who communicate verbally – and retains the focus on 'talking' rather than producing something together.

You said we did

'We will empower our residents, listen to their voices, and act on what they say.'

You told us some things and we went away and did stuff without you.

Erm – so much for *co-production*.

Managing expectations

'Managing expectations is crucial.'

'We need to be realistic about what we can offer.'

'We can't promise the world because we can't do everything.'

Ooof. This is not co-production. Where is the trust? Where is the transparency? Where is the shared vision? 'Managing expectations' is a term I'd happily bin – and it certainly has no place anywhere near co-production.

Also – 'what we can offer'…'we can't do everything'?

Point entirely missed.

Co-production leads, strategies, frameworks, policies, etc...

We're approaching co-production in the way we approach strengths-based working. Recruiting a lead, writing a strategy, sending workers off on a half-day training course, and expecting the world to change – without making any effort to change our world. We're viewing co-production as an add on. A nice to have, over there, located in a meeting room, led by someone else, while we keep doing 'the day job'.

But co-production isn't *extra* work; it is *the* work. It's not something to be confined to the remit of a lead or board, or constrained by a strategy, framework, or policy. It's an ethos and a value-base that should run through everything we do.

As Edgar Cahn suggests, it is 'a different imagining of the world we know' (Cahn, 2000).

* * *

The core elements of co-production are the same elements of a better, brighter social care future. Seeing people with gifts and potential, not problems and needs. As resourceful human beings – not 'non-human' resources.

Nurturing relationships and connections, not delivering services. Promoting reciprocity so people have a chance to 'give' as well as 'get' support. So people feel needed and valued, not needy and devalued.

And building and sustaining communities and better lives, not institutions and better services.

Like 'strengths-based', the term 'co-production' is too widely mis-interpreted and too easily misused.

I think we're spending too much time talking about the future of co-production, and not enough time co-producing the future.

So, I'm tempted to suggest we drop both these 'buzz words' from our vocabulary and focus instead on making sure our one simple ques-tion underpins everything we do.

'What does a good life look like to you and your family, and *how can we work together* to achieve it?'

From Blame to Curiosity

The language of social care is filled with words that blame people seeking and drawing on support. Our so called 'strengths-based' practice drips with deficit-based terms that stigmatize people as problems. Our 'person-centred' approaches are infused with phrases that marginalize.

Let me explain what I mean by discussing ten familiar words and phrases, unpicking what they suggest about our practice, and considering how we can shift from blame to curiosity.

Hard to reach

Labelling people as 'hard to reach' implies they are deliberately avoiding contact, keeping their distance, staying away. It places the blame entirely with them. But how hard are we really trying before we slap on that label as a convenient excuse?

Hard to reach? Or easy to ignore?

And couldn't the 'hard to reach' label be just as easily applied to us? Our lack of accessible information and reasonable adjustments. Our jargon and acronyms. Our eligibility criteria. Our thresholds. Our waiting lists. Our 9 to 5, Monday to Friday opening hours. Our city centre offices with security guards on the doors.

We blame people for being hard to reach, from behind our impenetrable walls.

Refuses to engage

We use the term 'refuse' a lot. Refused an assessment. Refuses services. Refusing treatment.

Refuse suggests defiance, stubbornness. Blaming, again.

What about 'chose not to'? 'Decided against'?

What about some acknowledgement of informed decision making by the person? Of agency? Of control? What about some evidence of a conversation? Of capacity to decide? Weighing up options?

Advocacy?

Choice?

Was there any?

And what of the classic 'refuses to engage'? We condemn people for not responding or participating. Not getting involved. But hang on, who exactly should be engaging here? We're public servants – here to serve, not to get people to serve us. We should be focusing on what matters to people, instead of blaming people for not doing the things that matter to us.

> Again look at the question: 'how do we get ppl to engage?' With respect you don't get ppl to engage. You listen to what they care about enough to act on, and then support them to work with others to do what they care deeply about. It's not about getting ppl to do what we want. (Russell, 2022)

Frequent flyers

We blame people for not responding, not doing what we ask, not being where we want them to be. And we blame people for being too present. For ringing up too often. For coming back too regularly. For asking too much. 'Frequent flyers.' 'Revolving door customers.' 'High intensity users.'

Behind these derogatory labels are human beings with hopes, fears, worries, aspirations, and fluctuating needs for care and support. Are we really listening? Are we really meeting people's needs and supporting them to get on with living their lives? The fact they're coming back again and again suggests not. So, who exactly is to blame here?

Carer breakdown

Our statutory guidance requires that we offer an assessment 'where it appears that a carer may have needs for support (whether currently or in the future)'; that we establish 'not only the carer's needs for support, but also the sustainability of the caring role itself'; that we determine 'whether the carer is, and will continue to be, able and willing to care for the adult needing care' (Department of Health and Social Care,

2023). Yet when someone is no longer able or willing to continue in their caring role, we're quick to apply the 'breakdown' label.

We refer to carers 'struggling to cope', 'breaking down', and 'burning out'. Carers 'struggling to cope', or people exhausted, worried isolated ignored lonely confused angry grieving frustrated abandoned desperate scared just trying to do their best for the people they love – or don't love – and facing so many too many hoops to jump through, forms to fill in, boxes to tick, phone calls to make, battles to fight.

'Carer breakdown' or people we've failed to identify, listen to and support?

'Carer burnout' or people we've failed?

Bed blockers

Bed blockers. Such a hideous, dehumanizing term applied to people who are 'medically optimized' and no longer meet the 'criteria to reside' but can't be discharged from hospital for any number of reasons – usually nothing to do with their needs and wishes, and everything to do with failures in communication and coordination in the wider 'system'.

This is the language of widgets, processes, targets, and flow, not of compassion and humanity.

Challenging behaviour

The 'challenging behaviour' label is, well, challenging.

The phrase labels people's behaviour as problematic, as something that must be controlled or managed, so they behave more 'appropriately'. But who defines what is 'appropriate'?

> Somebody has decided that my behaviour, or the person's behaviour, needs to be modified. Needs to be improved, mainstreamed, made less extreme. So, there's a power differential right there, isn't there? And the person's agency to behave in the ways that are most comfortable for them is taken away. (Quinn, 2022)

'Problems' require solutions, and too often having identified 'challenging behaviour', our response is to increase medication, restriction, or restraint. Separation. Seclusion. The classic medical model of treating and fixing rather than understanding what's happened to, and is happening around, the person.

All behaviour is a form of communication. If I suggest your behaviour is 'challenging', I'm either failing to understand – or deliberately ignoring – what you're communicating, and why.

Maybe you're scared? Excited? Frustrated? In pain? Angry? Bored? Lonely? Hungry? Sad?

Maybe something has happened or there's something going on around you that's causing you to lash out or to retreat?

Maybe it's my behaviour that's challenging you?

Even when we do acknowledge the communication element of a person's behaviour, we still manage to twist this to blame the person, whose 'challenging behaviour' is attributed to their 'difficulty' in communicating – not our failure to meet their communication needs, our legal duties, or their human rights.

And no, 'behaviour that challenges' or 'behaviours of concern' aren't any better, because they're still loading blame onto the person. And while referring to 'distressed behaviour' (hopefully) shifts the focus to understanding the reason for the distress and (hopefully) prompts some wider changes to relieve it, it's still a label. And anyway, maybe the person isn't communicating distress at all.

I can remember meeting an Afro-Caribbean man having treatment on a mental health ward. He told me that one day he was starting to feel better, so he started singing loudly in the corridor. For him this was an expression of joy. But in reserved Britain, staff interpreted this as unusual behaviour and upped his medication. (Hammond, 2020)

Non-compliant

Compliant means obedient, submissive, biddable. It means you do what you're told. You do what is expected of you, what we think you should be doing. So, if we label you as 'non-compliant', we're effectively saying you're not doing what we want you to do. Because we know best. Obviously.

Complex

Complex cases. Complex individuals. Complex health conditions. Complex lives.

Real lives *are* complex. Messy. Rainbow coloured crayon scribbles on crinkled and torn pages. Stuff happens – or doesn't. Too much. Not enough. It Stops. Starts. Loops back. Dead ends. Creeping, miniscule shifts. Rapid, devastating changes. Balancing. Juggling. Waving. Falling. Drowning.

Real lives don't fit the straight lines of our 'system', or the black and white boxes on our forms.

Our processes and pathways require a single label at the start. One 'primary support reason'. One 'service user group'. Go.

Too many labels = too many boxes ticked = too many pathways = too many professionals = too many conversations = too many options = too much time = not enough time = not enough options = 'complex'. And then often, 'too complex'.

Of course, 'complex needs' is the classic. As I noted in Part Two, we've even built complexity into the term 'complex needs', as the multiple references in the Care Act statutory guidance illustrate. 'Multiple complex needs.' 'Highly specialized and complex needs.' 'Less complex needs.' 'More complex needs.' 'Particularly complex needs.' 'The most complex needs' (Department of Health and Social Care, 2023).

The guidance refers to 'Isabelle [who] is 15 years old with complex needs' and 'Maureen [who] is 72 years old...with complex care needs'. We don't find out what their needs are, just that they are 'complex'.

Like 'challenging' and 'vulnerable', 'complex' is a meaningless term, used repeatedly to convey – well, what exactly? Yes, people's lives may be complicated, but people's basic needs are simple. Somewhere to call home and to belong. Someone to love, and to be loved in return. Something to do. Something to look forward to.

Stop using labels as excuses.

Difficult

What starts as a note stating I cried in an appointment, becomes a letter that details a 'difficult appointment', which takes flight as a descriptor of me as a 'difficult person', which ultimately leads to a doctor I only just met describing me as 'difficult – as expected'.

(WREN, 2021)

Tricky discussions. Feedback we find hard to hear. People experiencing tough times. Difficult conversations and difficult situations quickly morph into just plain 'difficult'...and yes, it's pretty much a catch-all term for all the other blaming words and phrases listed here too.

Difficult case. Difficult service user. Difficult customer. Difficult patient. Difficult family.

Labels stick.

Vulnerable

And finally, the v word. Although I've already written at length about the term 'vulnerable', it's worthy of a mention here – partly because it's so ubiquitous, but mainly because it points the finger squarely at the person as the problem and stops any consideration of the external factors that make people vulnerable. And in turn this prevents any focus on – or attempts to change – the situations or circumstances that create vulnerability.

Such a divisive and dangerous narrative.

* * *

These terms don't just feature in our conversations and our records. We recruit social workers to work with 'non-engagers', 'the most complex and challenging adult cases', and 'some of society's most vulnerable individuals'. We have policies for 'dealing with difficult families' and guidance on 'engaging hard to reach groups'. We have 'complex needs teams' and 'challenging behaviour units'.

The irony, of course, is that so many of these blaming terms can just as easily be applied to 'serviceland'. Hard to reach? Yep. Challenging behaviour? Oh yes. Difficult? Sure. Complex? Absolutely.

The language we use reflects our attitudes and influences our behaviours. So, what does this blaming language tell us about our current practice?

Labels close minds. Once applied, they stick, and lead to assumptions and prejudgements. These terms become not just part of the person's record, but part of their identity. Become their identity.

After a while, it feels as if you actually cease to exist, swamped by this paper version of yourself which somehow takes on its own life. After a while, it is your 'paper-self' who is risk assessed, diagnosed, and treated. After a while, you realise there's nothing you can do to stop the rise of your paper-self, because every word, every action, every movement you make only adds to its ever-growing and everlasting presence. (Wren, 2021)

If we hear or read labels like 'frequent flyer', 'difficult', 'complex', or 'challenging' before we've even met someone, our response is preloaded with assumptions, meaning we fail to properly listen, observe, or understand what's happening, and why.

And this leads to solutions that don't address the underlying causes, which can have devastating consequences.

> Imagine feeling severe pain and not understanding what is happening, nor even being able to ask for help and information. That is frequently the case for people with profound learning disabilities who cannot communicate verbally. Yet when distress and anxiety alter their demeanour, it is often dismissed as 'challenging behaviour' until the illness causing the pain reveals itself in some other way. (Morris, 2018)

Labels like 'vulnerable' prevent us from acknowledging and addressing external causes of vulnerability – and may prevent people from seeking support too. And terms like 'difficult' undoubtedly prevent people from raising concerns – not just for fear of being stigmatized, but also for fear of support being removed.

Describing people as 'non-compliant' exposes our fixed expectations about what 'should' be happening and the 'we know best' power dynamic. 'Carer breakdown' and 'bed blockers' shifts attention from the failures of our services and support. And terms like 'hard to reach' or 'refuses to engage' make it easy for us to walk away.

These blaming terms demonstrate and perpetuate the 'them and us' divide that pervades our practice. They highlight the power imbalance that dominates, the sense of superiority and expertise.

We know that relationships must be at the beating heart of our better, brighter future. That we must share power, trust each other more, and acknowledge people as the experts in their lives. And we also know that blame destroys trust, stifles curiosity, and sabotages relationships.

So how do we shift this narrative?

How do we move beyond blame?

Accountability

When something doesn't turn out in the way we hope or expect, instead of asking why, we ask who? Whose fault is it? Who can we blame?

There's some element of failure behind every one of these blaming words and phrases. While we're busy blaming people for failing to show up, cope, or behave, we're missing the basic point that much of the failure lies with us. Failure to ask, understand, and do what matters most to the people we serve. Failure to identify, listen, empathize, and respond compassionately. Failure to relinquish power and control. Failure to comply with our statutory duties and uphold people's human rights.

Failure to acknowledge where, how, and why we're failing.

Accountability is essential, but that doesn't mean we start pointing fingers at colleagues. The blame culture is already far too prevalent and damaging within our organizations. It doesn't mean we blame 'the system', because, well, we are the system. And it doesn't mean we add more tick boxes to our forms to justify our every move.

It means we know and follow the law, we're transparent about our responsibilities, and we're honest about our mistakes and where we need to do better. We acknowledge that we're still learning, and we welcome – and act on – suggestions about how we improve.

Curiosity

Blame prevents curiosity, learning, change.

We need to question these blaming words and phrases when we hear them, read them, or use them ourselves. Ask what's really going on here? And why? What's happened – or is happening – to this person? What are they communicating? What's important to them? What would they like to happen next?

Ask what these labels say about our attitudes and assumptions. And in turn, what does that tell us about the wider system? About where the power and control really lie?

We blame people when things don't turn out as we expect and when things don't go to plan. But whose expectations are these? Whose plan are we following? Whose needs are we really meeting?

We must shift our focus from correction to connection. We must move from expecting people to 'fit in', 'engage', 'behave', and 'comply', to meeting people where they're at, and on their terms. We must understand, accept, be curious, and care about people for who they are, and want to be, not who we think they are or should be, or how we think they should behave.

No assumptions.
No judgement.
No blame.
Just a question.
Why?

From Placements to Home

*W*e all want to live in the place we call home, with the people and
things that we love, in communities where we look out for one
another, doing the things that matter to us.

(SOCIAL CARE FUTURE, N.D.)

We all want to live in the place we call home.

It's a core element of a shared vision of our social care future –
something we can all relate and aspire to. But home, like love and
belonging, is a word that is too often missing from our vocabulary –
and the language we do use in relation to the places people live exposes
our 'them and us' divisions, and our transactional approach.

Putting something somewhere

Placement means 'the act of putting something or someone somewhere' (Cambridge University Press, n.d.).

In social care, people don't move house. We move people. We
'place', 'transfer', 'discharge', 'admit', and 'refer' people.

Putting someone somewhere.

Even when we talk about people living 'at home', our language still
suggests we make the decisions. We pull the strings.

We aim to 'keep' people at home. We 'enable' people to 'stay at
home' for 'as long as possible'. We 'allow' people to live in their own
home 'for longer'.

Do we ever actually ask people where they want to live, or what
'home' means to them?

The Social Care Future vision starts, 'We all...' But our language is
about others. Them. Putting *someone* somewhere. ('Someone' is used

to refer to a single person when you do not know who they are or when it is not important who they are' (Cambridge University Press, n.d.), which says it all.

Maybe it's easier to 'place' people when we don't recognize them as humans? When we don't know them as people? When it's not important who they are?

And we're putting someone *somewhere*. Accommodation. Arrangements. Units. Schemes. Properties. Developments. Beds. Care settings. Housing with support. Residential care. Bedded care facilities. A vacancy. A void.

Somewhere nobody calls home.

We use the phrase 'own home or a care home' repeatedly in our practice guidance, professional literature, and public information. We don't identify these 'settings' as people's 'own homes'. They are places (placements) for care if you are 'finding it difficult to live in your own home' or you can 'no longer manage in your own home'. When your 'needs are such that you can no longer be supported in your own home', or 'when living in your own home is no longer the best and safest option for you'.

Wherever people live should *feel* like their own home.

'She has lived in lots of services. She wants somewhere to settle' (Fox, 2018).

Living 'in care'

People live 'in care'.

Our language reinforces the view of care as a destination – the end point of a 'journey'.

Care and support plans say '24-hour residential care'. Full stop.

Not a plan for a life, for living. Just a plan for 'care'.

Written up. Signed off. Written off.

Social care should be the vehicle, not the destination.

Living 'in the community'

In our social care world, you either live in an institution or in 'the community'.

Our standard alternative to 'putting people into care' is home care – care at home.

'Four calls a day', 'time and task', 'life and limb' care.

Too often, our social care 'interventions' involve either removing people from the place they call home or turning people's homes into places that no longer feel like home. Places with strangers, uniforms, rules, routines, and restraints imposed and enforced.

'How could this place be the home she used to have control over? My mum's home had become a service – she knew it, she felt it, and we just didn't see it' (Maguire, 2020).

And living 'in the community' just means you don't live in 'residential care'. It doesn't mean you're part of a community, that you feel connected, that you belong.

A home is a place to live. Social care should support people to *live* in the place they call home.

A place that *feels* like home

Many rough sleepers decline or underuse accommodation offered to them. A big reason for this is that once established in a rough sleeping community, social bonds are forged and become difficult to break. Housing is about more than shelter. We must feel connected to feel secure.

(MCGARVEY, 2018)

Home is where the heart is. So the saying goes. And our hearts – our emotions – are fundamental here. The place we call home is so much more than just the physical environment in which we live – the place we own or rent, the space we're physically in. Home is just as much about a feeling as a place.

And while home looks and feels different to all of us, fundamentally feeling 'at home' is feeling safe. Feeling secure. Feeling settled. Feeling connected and involved. Feeling loved. Feeling you belong.

It is that true belief you're exactly where you're supposed to be, and that you don't need to be somewhere – or someone – else.

If we're genuinely going to shift from 'placing' people 'in care' to caring about people living in the place they call home, we need to take time, and have time, to find out what home really means to people, then support them to find, remain in, or return to a place that *feels* like home.

From Chronos Time to Kairos Time

Care is not an activity that can happen by the clock... Care belongs in the world of Kairos time (measured by flow and connection) as opposed to Chronos time (the industrial time measured by minutes and deadlines). Care is not the same as cure – yet it so often seems we have confused these categories. This is why our care systems 'think' in terms of an activity that is costed, rationed, and meted out in response to a specific need or life moment, as opposed to an ongoing human activity.

(COTTAM, 2021)

Care *belongs* in the world of Kairos time, but our language reveals how Chronos time dominates the world of social care.

Fast-paced environments

When I studied the language of social work job adverts, one thing that really struck me was the emphasis on speed.

- 'You will ensure that all cases are progressed efficiently through the system within this fast-paced environment.'
- 'We want you to think and act fast to support the most vulnerable people in our population.'
- 'The team works in a fast-paced, highly pressurized environment.'

Fast. Quick. Efficient.

The language of transactions, production lines, sorting offices.
Standardized, managed, linear, controlled, quantified.

The social care 'industry'.
Industrial time.

Busy teams

Our teams are busy.

- 'You will be working within a busy team and be expected to work at pace while maintaining a high standard of practice.'
- 'This is a busy team with a fast throughput of work.'

Research by the British Association of Social Workers suggests that social workers spend close to 80% of their time on admin, while only 20% of their time is spent working directly with children and families (British Association of Social Workers, 2018).

So busy screening, triaging, assessing, processing, purchasing, placing, recording, reviewing, and reporting. Too busy for people.

> I spend so much time recording and writing reports that I feel like I'm in an admin role rather than a social worker. It's horrible and not what I signed up for. I get reprimanded if I choose to prioritise time with clients over recording. (British Association of Social Workers, 2018)

Waiting

Despite this pace, this industry, the queues are growing.

The Association of Directors of Adult Social Services reported that in August 2023, 470,576 people were 'waiting for an assessment, care or direct payments to begin or a review of their care plan' (Association of Directors of Adult Social Services, 2023).

Almost half a million people waiting.

And even though the statutory guidance states that 'it is critical to the vision in the Care Act that the care and support system works to actively promote wellbeing and independence, and does not just wait to respond when people reach a crisis point' (Department of Health and Social Care, 2023), we do wait.

Too busy reacting to be proactive.

Too busy responding to crises to prevent them.

We won't wait for long, though. If you 'refuse to engage' or you don't 'comply', we'll remove you from our waiting lists, close your case, and move on.

Immediate needs and quick fixes

Care decisions are often made quickly and at a time of crisis.

(DEPARTMENT OF HEALTH AND SOCIAL CARE, 2023)

We work in the moment, in the present time, responding to crises, new requests for support, 'unplanned reviews'. We focus on 'immediate needs', prescribe sticking-plaster service solutions, and move on as quickly as possible to the next 'case'.

There's no sense of any connection or continuity. No ongoing conversation, collaboration, or curiosity. Just a series of transactional starts and stops.

Episodes

Care is described – and measured – in 'episodes'. Short-term. Time-limited. Discrete. Disconnected. 'Episodes of social care support.' 'Brief episodes of care.' 'Planned and unplanned hospital episodes.' 'Episodes of respite care' (NHS Digital, 2022).

We dip in and out of people's lives as if we're watching just a couple of shows from a multi-season television series or reading only one or two chapters of a novel. No chance to get to know the characters, understand the setting, interpret the narrative, or follow the plot twists (though we're pretty good at deciding what should happen next without knowing the full story).

Time and task

'Care' is prescribed, commissioned, 'packaged', and 'delivered' in hours and minutes. Rotas and schedules dominate, and time is money.

It's a 'time and task model of care where both clients and staff are reduced to numbers, activities and timing on schedules' (Hannan, 2019).

People working in social care juggle and justify time.

Care worker Latif Choudhray describes how he often only has 15 minutes in someone's home. They expect more from us but we don't have the time. If we put in extra time we don't get paid for it. They want to talk, they miss their family. They cry, they beg us to stay. It's challenging and very emotional... You want to help but there are so many restrictions on time. (Cox, 2022)

And people drawing on support are made to juggle and justify time:

My life got split up into chunks. How long will it take me to have a shower? How long do I need to get dressed? How long for food preparation? That is not what I want my life to be about. I find myself in the position quite regularly where I have to think, 'Well, I only have two hours left this week, so do I want to do food shopping, have another shower or go and meet up with a friend?' It is quite a hard place to have to live your life when you have to quantify the things you want to do into a small number of hours a week. –Anna Severwright (House of Commons, 2020)

Zero hours and part-time work

Skills for Care reports that around a fifth of people who work in adult social care, and a third of all care workers, are employed on zero-hours contracts. Half the workforce is part time, rising to 88% of personal assistants. Hourly rates of pay for care workers are among the lowest of the economy in general (Skills for Care, 2023).

In theory, it's a flexible career choice and a fluid workforce, ebbing and flowing to suit the lives and needs of people working in, and drawing on, care and support.

In reality, it's an insecure and inflexible option for social care workers and for the people they support.

Visiting times, mealtimes, and bedtimes

Set times structure the lives of so many people who draw on support. Home care is timetabled. Visiting hours are set. Mealtimes are fixed, and often the menu is too. Bedtimes are generally early. Too early.

One person told us... 'I don't like going to bed at 7 o'clock at night. Carers come at 8.30am – 9am in the morning so I asked if they could come later, they said 'No' because everyone has a set time and it can't be changed.' (Care Quality Commission, 2022a)

Living (barely) by the clock.

Days and weeks scheduled to suit providers, not people.

No choice.

No control.

No life.

Free time

The provider had asked people what activities they wanted to take part in. People fed back they would like to go to the cinema, theatre, the seaside, shopping and going out for a meal. There was no evidence from the daily notes that these activities had taken place.

(CARE QUALITY COMMISSION, 2022B)

The Care Act is clear that wellbeing includes participation in recreation, personal relationships, and people's contribution to society. Friendships are started and sustained in 'free time'. Love sparks and blooms. It's time for adventures, dreaming, becoming, returning.

Time for doing the things that matter to us.

Leisure time, and the opportunity to fill it, is not just a nice to have, an optional extra. It's essential to citizenship, human rights, and ordinary, equal lives.

And yet care plans and care 'packages' still focus on survival, and rarely on reasons to stay alive. On 'activities of daily living' but not the things that make life worth living.

Measuring time

We measure what we do in days and hours, minutes and deadlines.

- Percentage of assessments completed within 28 days.
- Percentage of annual reviews completed on time.
- Proportion of older people (65 and over) who are still at home 91 days after discharge from hospital into reablement/rehabilitation services.
- Number of homecare hours delivered.

Quantitative measures that add numerous tick boxes to our forms (keeping social workers busy). That populate charts and graphs to evidence 'performance' (keeping team managers busy). That are scrutinized, disputed, and manipulated (keeping performance teams and senior leaders busy).

Quantitative measures that give no indication of people's experience and wellbeing.

Measuring outputs, not outcomes. Quantity, not quality.

* * *

It's clear that Chronos time dominates our industrialized approach. Processes, transactions, and measurements rule. Care is 'packaged' and 'delivered' in hours and minutes. Workers are reduced to robots, and people seeking or drawing on support to widgets.

All time is accounted for.

All eyes are on the clock.

It's a race against time, that nobody wins.

It doesn't have to be like this.

Care *belongs* in the world of Kairos time. Kairos time is fluid. It's the time of nature, seasons, weather, tides. Of creativity. Possibility. Opportunity. Serendipity.

The time of flow and connection.

If we're ever going to achieve more relational, human ways of working, we must move away from the industrialized 'care system' dominated by the clock, to a world where we have a different relationship with time.

From Chronos time to Kairos time.

Early 'intervention'

Rather than focusing on approaches to delivering care that intervene at a time of crisis, care and support services should intervene early to support individuals, helping people retain or regain their skills and confidence, and prevent needs from developing.

(DEPARTMENT OF HEALTH AND SOCIAL CARE, 2022)

'Early intervention' is another jargon term we throw around. However, behind the jargon lies a fundamental shift from our 'come back if things get worse' response, to a more open, visible, proactive, and timely approach.

Earlier conversations create space for aspirations to be considered, options to be explored, and choices to be made.

I'm not a huge fan of the term 'intervention' – to me it suggests interfering. This is not, and cannot be, about a 'professional' wearing a lanyard and an air of superiority wading in to take charge and prescribe. Instead, it's about partnership, trust, choice, and control. It's about listening to people and families to understand what a good life looks like, and working alongside them to ensure they can live their chosen life.

We need to open the gates, go outside and seek people as early as we can find them. If we have time to understand what they really want and need in life, our services will be a vital – but small – part of it. (Fox, 2018)

Time for stories

We need to spend more time finding out who [people] are and who they want to be in the world.

(TULLOCH & SCHULMAN, 2020)

Our current approach involves people 'telling their story' time and time again to multiple different professionals. 'I should only have to tell my story once' is a familiar and justified aspiration of people exhausted by repetition, and of national and local ambitions for reform. Too often though, this 'story' isn't a story at all, but a fragmented list of labels, problems, and risks repeated in response to a narrow, deficit-based, and potentially traumatic line of questioning. Obviously only having to answer the same questions once rather than multiple times is an improvement. Having a coordinated plan in response is better too. But it's not enough.

When we can tell stories about our lives to someone who is genuinely curious, who listens with no agenda, judgement, or interruption, and who recognizes what we don't say as much as what we do, it's powerful.

People are stories, and knowing these stories gave more agency and currency to help than any assessment I'd ever seen in my whole career. People were helped out of decades-long slumps because they were understood, and time was invested in them. (Smith, 2022b)

We need time to listen to stories, and time to build the trusted relationships required for people to share them, and to know they will be heard.

Lifetimes

Despite being homeless, it started with sorting his teeth. Then a better sleeping bag. Then a bicycle (we scourged[sic] a free one) and then a place to stay. This was his order of things. We don't know best. He's stopped offending and [is] getting help with his addiction, but crucially he's thinking longer term. We're working with him at his pace. There's a relationship and support, where there used to be (non) eligibility criteria and transactions.

(SMITH, 2022A)

We need to shift from our focus on the present moment, on quick fixes for immediate needs, and see people in the context of their whole lives. Look back, be aware of and informed by what may have happened before. Appreciate and harness the experiences, skills, and knowledge people collect and carry with them. Look around, consider – and challenge – the barriers. Be alert to, and embrace, the opportunities. Look ahead – be curious about, and prepared for, what could happen next. Understand the hopes, desires, wishes, and dreams people cling to. Create the space and time for the past to be acknowledged, the present to be explored, and the future to be imagined.

(Safe) waiting

David Oliffe describes 'safe waiting' as 'a stance, like a professional position, that we can take when supporting someone. It's kind of a commitment you make with that person to stick with them while life unfolds, whatever pace it wants to go at' (Oliffe, 2021).

Safe waiting is about being present – for as long as that presence is needed. It's not about rescuing or fixing. It's about walking alongside people at a pace determined by them, not by a process or a performance indicator.

It's about waiting for the right moment and recognizing that takes time.

Pausing

The power of a pause. It takes a moment, but it can change everything. Pause, reflect and go again.

(CHAPPLE, 2021)

Our 'fast-paced environments' and 'busy teams' offer little, if any, opportunity to pause.

But pausing creates space for curiosity, connection, and compassion. It allows perspective and prevents snap judgements. Breathing space. Time to think, imagine, create, reflect, learn.

Indeed, pausing is built into our statutory guidance, which suggests 'the local authority may "pause" the assessment process to allow time for the benefits of [preventive] activities to be realized' and highlights opportune times during safeguarding enquiries for 'appropriate pauses for reflection, consideration and professional judgment' (Department of Health and Social Care, 2023).

Reflection time

A third of the social workers who responded to a British Association of Social Work survey said they spent *no time* on reflective practice per week, and 42% said they spent less than an hour. One social worker said 'it is interesting that you ask about reflective practice, once past the stage of ASYE [sic, Assessed and Supported Year in Employment] this is not seen as important as it doesn't relate to a PI [performance indicator]' (British Association of Social Workers, 2018).

Reflection time has been squeezed out as 'case management' dominates. But critical reflection is – well – critical. Time to reflect is essential for social workers to analyse and challenge their assumptions, beliefs, and values. To consider context. To speculate, and to learn.

Reflection time isn't just important for social workers; it's important for people and families too. It provides space to consider what matters, what a good life looks like and how it might be possible to achieve and sustain that good life.

The poignant part of all this is that the people we support, for whatever reason, may never have been given the opportunity to think about what would make a good life for them... It often takes time for an individual to think about what the real answer to the question is for them. (Broad, 2012)

Time to be human

The industrialization of care has suppressed individuals in favour of consistency and efficiency (Tulloch & Schulman, 2020). Identities are hidden behind lanyards and labels, and all the stereotypes, assumptions, judgements, rules, and boundaries they bring.

We can't work in a relational way without allowing time for relationships to form and grow. These relationships are built and maintained through trust, and trust can only be established and sustained through human connection. We can't work in a relational way unless we have time for empathy, honesty, kindness, vulnerability, love.

Unless we have time to be human.

Time to care

A discussion on Mumsnet about working in a care home includes the following comments: 'I have worked in a care home and hated it. Not enough time per resident it felt like a conveyor belt' and, 'There is no quality time spent with the residents, it's all about getting everything done and everybody done in record time.'

This is efficiency, not efficacy. Caring for, not caring about.

Care as a task or a service.

'Delivering care.'

We need to recognize care as a relationship and a vehicle, not a transaction or a destination.

And we must have time to care about each other, and time to care about ourselves too.

The right time

For everyone who draws on care and support – no matter their age or circumstances – achieving the choice, control and independence set out in our 10 year vision starts with making sure they are listened to, understood, and get the right care, in the right place and at the right time.

(DEPARTMENT OF HEALTH AND SOCIAL CARE, 2022)

The right time for conversations and support is personal and unpredictable. If we're ever going to achieve this relational way of working, our organizations need radical change. We need to open our doors, flatten our hierarchies, and step out of our silos. Listen rather than assess. Invest time instead of managing time. And recognize that not everything that can be counted counts, and not everything that counts can be counted.

* * *

This is not some fantasy world, an impossible dream.

The foundations of this world of Kairos time are built in existing laws and guidance. Our legislative and best practice frameworks advocate a more human, relational approach, and there are numerous examples of this approach in local areas, community groups, micro-providers, and social enterprises.

However, Chronos time undoubtedly still dominates.

If we're ever going to achieve more relational, human ways of working, we must develop a different relationship with time.

Shift from Chronos time to Kairos time.

And unless we begin to step into the world of Kairos time, we won't have time to pause and to reflect on what really matters. To listen to stories and to share experiences. To visualize this different world and to work together to achieve it.

We'll always have our eyes on the clock.

We'll always be too busy, and we won't have time for change.

PART FOUR

CHANGING OUR STORY

From What's Wrong, to What's Strong

*B*ut what if we wanted to change the way people thought about *Social Care? How would we do that?*

(MITCHELL, W., 2020)

Wendy Mitchell wrote those words in a blog post reflecting on one of several Social Care Future meetings that I was also in, convened by Neil Crowther as part of ongoing work:

> to develop and share a compelling new narrative to reframe the way social care is talked about, understood and valued by the public and policy makers...part of a wider strategy that is designed to create lasting change to the way care and support is organized, supported and valued. (Social Care Future, 2019)

Crowther sums up the current, dominant story:

> Social care, which fails to look after vulnerable people adequately, leaving them to be neglected and abused, is broken and in or on the brink of a crisis. The cost of social care is spiralling because there are growing numbers of older and disabled people and funding hasn't kept pace with demand. Councils, the NHS and providers are under severe strain. The system can't cope. Other valuable services are threatened. (Social Care Future, 2019)

Social care has got stuck in this deficit-based narrative. And there's no question that many aspects of the current social care 'system' aren't working. However, we know that if we only look at what's wrong, we ignore what's strong. If we focus on 'what's the matter?', we miss what really matters.

This is a book about change. Changing our minds, our purpose, and our practice. To achieve these changes – and ultimately to ensure better experiences and better lives for all of us, we also need to change the story we tell about social care, and about social care reform, and indeed about change.

And we need to start with – and build from – what's strong, not what's wrong.

Changing the Story of Social Care: From Care for Others to Caring About Each Other

Stories can change the world. And social care needs a better story.
(SOCIAL CARE FUTURE, 2023)

A quick Google News search for 'social care' gives a good overview of the prevailing narrative. Top results include references to 'society's most vulnerable', 'looking after some of the most vulnerable people in society', 'care in old age', 'personal care for the elderly and disabled', 'those in care', 'delivering care services', 'lack of social care blocks beds in hospitals', and 'frail elderly people...forced to sell homes in order to fund care'.

It's time to flip this narrative and tell a different story about social care.

From 'society's most vulnerable' to all of us

Back in 2018, when FrameWorks Institute researchers 'took a snapshot of what the British public thinks when they hear the words "social care"', they summarized the collective response as 'we don't know what social care is, exactly...but we know it's for the vulnerable' (Hyatt, 2018).

This perception is fuelled by the narrative of local government and echoed by the media.

Scan through council websites and you'll see numerous pages with headings like, 'Are you concerned about a vulnerable adult?' 'Tell us about a vulnerable person.' 'Help for vulnerable just a click away.'

Pay attention to references to social care in the news and you'll get used to stock photos of wrinkly hands. Bodies without heads. The backs of figures retreating down empty corridors. Single human forms silhouetted against windows.

This tells a story of 'others' – them – diminishing not just the identity of people drawing on support, but also the prospect of any significant reform.

The alternative story of social care is a story of us. Human beings with hopes, fears, wishes, dreams, gifts, and potential. Human beings with human rights.

I'm not comfortable with arguments for social care investment or reform because 'you or your family' might need it one day. This just perpetuates them and us thinking. 'I'm only interested if it directly affects me or the people I love.' That's not okay. Investment and reform are needed not because any of us might need support one day, but because many of us require support to live good lives right now.

This is a story of all of us, not them and us.

From 'looking after some of the most vulnerable people in society' to looking out for each other

The framing of people who require support as 'vulnerable people who can't look after themselves' locks in the perception that people need to be cared for and protected. Looked after. Indeed, the purpose of social care is invariably described as 'protecting vulnerable people' and 'keeping vulnerable adults safe'.

Instead of looking after 'others', the alternative story is of people looking out for each other. It's a story of reciprocity, community, and love. Of freedom, inclusion, equality, and rights.

One of the core messages from the Covid-19 pandemic was just how much we need each other. And, during the pandemic, alongside the horrifying narrative of institutional care, there was another narrative of genuinely *social* care. Of an amazing collective, collaborative response which demonstrated the power of communities and just how much we do care about one another.

This is our social care future.

This is the future we need to invest in.

From 'care in old age' to support at every age and stage

'Care in old age.' 'The elderly.' 'Looking after ageing parents.' The story of social care focuses on older people, illustrated with gloomy images implying loneliness and despair. There are rarely any references to, or images of, younger people – ignoring the 'working age' adults who draw on, and benefit from, care and support to lead the lives they choose to lead. This associates social care with decline and the end of life, not with possibilities, opportunities, and flourishing lives – at every age or stage.

And older people are generally blamed for much of what's wrong – with predictable references to 'increasing demand from an ageing population'. As well as overlooking the benefits of longer lives, as with other blaming language, this frames people as the problem, suggesting an inevitability to the situation and deflecting attention from decades of limited investment and imagination.

From surviving ('support with things like washing and dressing') to thriving

'Adult social care can include assistance with activities of daily living such as getting up, washing, getting dressed, eating, going to the toilet...'

There's so much more to life than meeting our basic needs. But the story of social care so often stops here. Descriptions of adult social care generally concentrate on 'personal care for the elderly and disabled'.

We focus on the mundane stuff that keeps people alive, not the glorious stuff that makes life worth living. And we frame social care as a safety net to catch people when they fall, rather than as a springboard to a better future.

From a destination ('those in care') to a vehicle

In our current story, social care is a destination. An outcome. We assess people for care, plan for care, and 'place' people in care.

Care is something you get or somewhere you go.

But if we recognize social care as the connections, relationships, resources, and support that enable us all to live our lives the way we want to, we shift this narrative to care and support as a vehicle.

Instead of focusing on the support people need, we focus on the lives people want to lead, and the role of care and support in enabling people to live equal, flourishing lives.

From 'delivering care services' to nurturing relationships and connections

The framing of social care invariably focuses on services, and on care as something that's 'delivered' by 'providers'.

The 'social care industry'.

'Packages' of care.

This reflects and reinforces the perception of care as a one-way transaction. Care 'provided' to passive recipients. And the focus is often on the 'ability of social care providers to continue delivering services' and 'the financial sustainability of providers', making 'the sector' the story.

But if we shift away from this transactional view of social care, if we widen the focus of our lens, we reveal a different, more hopeful story that highlights the abundance of support available in communities. Instead of dividing people up into providers and consumers of services, we recognize what people can and could contribute, and the mutual benefits of mutual support.

In the same way that health is much broader than the NHS, social care is not, and cannot be, confined to a 'sector' or an 'industry'.

'Social care happens throughout society and communities, in living rooms, on street corners, at work, in colleges and even in the pubs and night clubs across the land' (Harvey, 2020).

From hospital discharge ('lack of social care blocks beds in hospitals') to the place we call home

Hospital discharge increasingly dominates the discourse.

Social care is blamed for 'delaying discharges', and 'vulnerable patients' are blamed for 'blocking beds'.

People getting in the way of process. Disrupting the 'flow'.

The language of production lines. The health and social care sorting office.

One out, one in.

There are calls for reform to 'relieve pressure on the NHS'. There is talk of expanding 'services to keep vulnerable out of hospital' and prioritizing 'those approaches that are most effective in freeing up the maximum number of hospital beds and reducing bed days lost'.

In this discourse, social care is tied to the NHS – and always in its shadow, and the focus is on investment in health and care services, not on people's health and wellbeing. Not on people finding, remaining in, or returning to the place they call home.

From cost and spending ('frail elderly people...forced to sell homes in order to fund care') to value and investment

When Boris Johnson announced his plan to 'fix social care' back in 2019, it came with a commitment 'to protect you or your parents or grandparents from the fear of having to sell your home to pay for the costs of care' (Prime Minister's Office, 10 Downing Street and The Rt Hon Boris Johnson, 2019).

Sally Warren noted then:

> The new Prime Minister is now joining a long line of politicians, going back to Tony Blair in 1997, who define the problem as 'removing the fear of selling your house to pay for care' in older age. This is an extremely narrow frame of reference. (Warren, 2019)

The cost of care for people and families remains a strong element of the public narrative, as does the current and future cost to local authorities.

Headlines like 'The cost of social care is bankrupting local councils and threatening the NHS' and 'Billions needed to fund rising cost of social care' are common in the media.

Yet again there is often a strong element of blame in this narrative, which is generally accompanied by references to – for example – the 'ageing population', 'disabled people living longer and with increasingly complex needs', and 'the burden of disability in the UK population'.

The fact that adult social care employs over 1.5 million people in England (more than the NHS) and contributes £55.7 billion to the economy (Skills for Care, 2023) is missing from this story. As is the value of social care to the people who draw on support.

No one would deny we need to talk about money, and about the way social care is funded. But we need to focus the conversation on investment, not spending, and on the value of care and support rather than the cost.

* * *

Stories matter. They can trap us, but they can also inspire us. The stories we tell shape how we see ourselves, and how we see the world. When we see the world differently, we begin to behave differently, living into the new story... The new story becomes an invisible force which pulls us forward. Imagining the future makes it more possible. (Alexander, 2022)

The Care Act 2014 begins with the general duty of local councils to promote wellbeing. The very first point of the associated guidance states that 'the core purpose of adult care and support is to help people to achieve the outcomes that matter to them in their life' (Department of Health and Social Care, 2023).

Yet despite this clear focus on wellbeing and on what matters most to people, we've got trapped in a narrow, deficit-based story of looking after our most vulnerable washing and dressing delivering care services getting care going into care the sector blocking beds freeing up beds selling homes spiralling costs fix social care now.

Oof.

Maybe it's the *narrative* of social care that is broken?

If we really want to achieve the ambitions of the Care Act, and indeed our own ambitions for better lives and brighter futures, we must tell a different story. Reframe social care as something for – and about – all of us. As the web of connections, relationships, resources, and support in our communities that ensures we can *all* live the lives we choose to lead, in places that feel like home, with the people and things that we love, doing the things that matter most to us.

Social Care Future's research with Equally Ours and Survation found that not only does this alternative narrative 'help shift mindsets about what social care is and its value, people also attach more importance to investment and reform after being presented with such messaging when compared with their default understanding' (Social Care Future, 2023).

So, let's all do what we can to flip the narrative and tell a different story of social care – for all our futures.

Changing the Story of Working in Social Care: From Delivering Care to Promoting Wellbeing

'Workforce' is another term that dominates the narrative of social care. So, let's unpick this a little to understand the story we're currently telling about working in social care, and how that needs to change.

First, though, a note on the story of social work.

Recent research into 'the language surrounding the profession of social work in the media' identified 'four times as many negative stories as positive ones' (Leedham, 2023). To counteract this largely negative narrative, The British Association of Social Workers (BASW) launched the BASW Social Work Journalism Awards, the Social Workers Union issued 'media reporting guidelines for cases involving social workers', and Social Work England is campaigning to 'change the script on social work'.

Ironically, the stories shortlisted for the first journalism awards in 2023 almost all appear to tell a largely negative story of social work! They include features on 'social workers in England quitting in record numbers', 'impossible workloads', 'hundreds of jobs vacant', 'high stress, high demand, high burnout', and 'the social care system in crisis' (British Association of Social Workers, 2023).

The media guidelines emphasize that 'it is important that social workers are portrayed fairly and accurately in the media...to prevent damage to the recruitment and retention of social workers', then refer to 'unmanageable caseloads', social workers 'crying/feeling unwell at least once a week', and 'half of social workers considering leaving their posts' (Social Workers Union, 2022).

And the Social Work England campaign was launched alongside the findings of research into how social workers feel about their profession. The research includes a case study about 'former social worker' Andy, who says, 'the culture is toxic', 'people are constantly stressed', and that he 'wouldn't touch that profession again with a bargepole' (Social Work England, 2024).

All these attempts to shift the narrative focus on social workers at the expense of the people they serve. The winning article in the 'print – news' category of the journalism awards describes social work as 'a demanding but rewarding job protecting and helping some of Wales' most vulnerable'. The media guidelines begin with 'Social workers are on the frontline of helping the most vulnerable in society.' And the Social Work England campaign refers to 'dealing with cases' and 'very difficult cases'.

In a further layer of irony, the media guidelines emphasize that 'journalists should consider whether language used generalises social workers unfairly', in a document that uses language that unfairly stereotypes and dehumanizes the people who draw on their support.

It seems there are lots of people suggesting we need to tell a different story, then repeating the same old deficit-based narrative.

What's wrong, not what's strong.

The wider story of working in social care is equally deficit-based. There are endless references to low pay and low skills, 'the day-to-day challenges of caring for vulnerable people', the 'challenges faced by the sector in delivering care as a service', vacancies and recruitment difficulties, and care workers either being exploited and abused, or exploiting and abusing.

We need to tell a different story, and we need to begin in a very different place.

From care to self-directed support

The wider workforce portrayed in the dominant narrative is not very wide at all. The depiction of the 'workforce' in both discourse and imagery is largely limited to residential and home care workers, invariably shown in uniforms, often wearing masks, and with their arms around anonymous shoulders, or clasping wrinkly hands.

Not only does this fail to convey the diversity of roles, and of the people who benefit from support, it also severely limits the conversation around reform. As Neil Crowther observes:

The workforce being imagined is one for the local authority commissioned institutional and time and task sausage machine. It's for 'an industry', it's not part of building the wellbeing ecosystem that will permit us all to reap the dividend of our longer lives. (Crowther, 2023a)

This focus on care and carers inevitably places people who require support in the background, and in the passive role of 'the cared for'.

We need to shift this narrative and start instead (as per the Care Act 2014) with wellbeing. With the rights of disabled people to independent living, and to the 'personal assistance necessary to support living and inclusion in the community' (United Nations, 2006). With the principles of self-directed support. And with what great support looks like, from the perspective of people who draw on it.

From tasks to values

Descriptions of working in social care usually start (and end) with details of the tasks involved in 'delivering exceptional care to service users' and 'helping vulnerable people live as comfortably as possible'.

Job adverts for care workers include lists of 'duties' like 'assisting patients with grooming and personal hygiene', 'assisting with bodily functions such as bathing, washing, feeding', 'aiding with toileting during the day', 'administering medication to service users', and the 'dressing and undressing of clients'.

It's a narrative of functional, scheduled, life and limb care. There's little or no reference to supporting people to do the things that matter to them, with the people who matter to them. To enjoy life. To thrive.

And adverts say things like 'any relevant work experience with looking after vulnerable people would be an advantage', 'experience of looking after the elderly preferred', 'experience of caring for others would be useful'.

In contrast, talking about her experience of recruiting personal assistants to support her family, Tricia Nicoll says:

I look for and I try to attract people who have never worked in social care before… Our interview process is focused on human values, and then the three of us and great outside trainers can teach people anything else they need to know. (Nicoll, 2021)

At an Adult Social Care 'Festival of Practice' in Doncaster in 2022,

Wendy Sharps said a very similar thing, speaking of her experience of recruiting a new personal assistant (PA):

I just advertised my own job on Facebook and I shoved it in the middle of everybody's business. 'Wendy wants a PA.' I had loads of people saying, 'I've worked in hospital' and this and that and I'm thinking, oh no, I don't want a sergeant major working for me. I want somebody flexible because you see I've worked with people like that, they don't want to bend. They want to come in [and say] 'you're having your dinner at this time, you're going to be doing this at that time'. [But] you can't put me in a time slot. It don't work. So, when Kyla came and she'd never done care before, I thought, this is great. I can mould her. She can learn her job and we can learn together, you know? Her qualifications weren't as good as what the other people had got, but she asked me questions and she were interested in me. I thought, bless her, she really wants it and she's hungry for it. I thought, we're going to be a good team.

While the 'sector' continues to talk about tasks and 'the right skills', people seeking support are often far more interested in finding people with the right values.

From vacancies to opportunities

- 'Vacancies in social care are now the highest on record.'
- 'Social care: The £600m jobs emergency that isn't going away.'

There's much talk of 'vacancies' and problems with recruitment and retention. But there are multiple issues with this persistent narrative. Vacancies are often presented as a challenge for 'the sector', rather than for people seeking and drawing on support. 'Without a long-term plan to solve care's staffing crisis, the sector will remain many thousands of employees short.' 'We will see care homes closing and care companies going bust.' 'Bed blocking up by a third as social care jobs go unfilled.'

There's little mention of the impact on people's lives beyond the 'vulnerable adults left without care'.

The repeated references to challenges with recruitment sit alongside equally ubiquitous messaging around low pay, high pressure, stress, and the 'hugely demanding, arduous, sometimes repetitive, often boring, thankless nature of the work that care workers do' (Brand, 2021).

And, as with the whole narrative of 'workforce', we're limiting the conversation to a very narrow range of job roles. As Community Catalysts note, 'narrow definitions of "social care" restricting to "time and task" & "personal care" create perceptions of limited support' (Community Catalysts, 2023a).

By persistently talking about vacancies, we're focusing on what is missing, not what is present. We're 'squeezing the abundance out of view' (Catley, 2023b).

So how about we focus instead on telling positive stories of people who are living good lives and benefitting from brilliant support from the millions of people who *are* working in roles across social care. Positive stories about the wide variety of roles, and the rewards of working in them. And tell a very different story to, and about, the people who *could* work in social care in the future.

> I really really have to make it easy for people who've never seen themselves as wanting to work in social care to become part of the team that I employ. So that means I've got to actively recruit differently and describe the job differently, and to make the job a very different job. (Nicoll, 2021)

From pay to reward

- 'Half of care workers in England earn less than entry level supermarket roles.'
- 'It pays more to be a warehouse packer than a care worker.'

Of course, people working in care and support should be paid more. But focusing on pay suggests that's the only reason people don't apply for, or stay in, social care jobs, and that if the pay was better, all problems would be solved. This squashes conversations about wider terms and conditions that also need to change and ignores the rewards of working in social care at its best.

It may well be possible to earn more per hour in your local supermarket or pub, but the endless comparisons suggest the jobs are comparable.

Where is the narrative of the flexibility and autonomy that different support roles can provide? The sense of purpose, achievement, and fulfilment they offer? The variety? The relationships? The laughter? The joy?

> I've never done anything like this before. I've always worked in pubs and stuff like that. And coming from an environment like that to here, it's just amazing. Even if we just go to the shop or go out for the day or we go for some food or we watch a film together, things like that, it makes such a massive difference to Wendy's life, but it does to mine as well... For me, it's not about the money. I enjoy this job. I like seeing Wendy be a mum, seeing her be a granny, seeing her be a wife. I've seen all of it and it's just amazing that she's had the opportunity to still be able to do these things because she hasn't changed. She's still Wendy and all she needs is support, and that's what I'll do for her. (Kyla, Wendy's PA, speaking at Doncaster's Festival of Practice in November 2022)

✳ ✳ ✳

The story of the social care workforce has become curiously detached from the story of the lives people want to lead, and the resources and support we need to draw on to lead them.

The dominant narrative of workforce reform focuses on narrowly defined, paternalistic care roles, and on preventing things getting worse, rather than on the wealth of great examples of brilliant support, and on promoting wellbeing.

The stories of good lives and good support are not mutually exclusive. They are the same story. A story of autonomy and flexibility. Choice and control. Dignity and respect. Meaning and purpose. Recognition and reward. Connections and relationships. Capabilities and possibilities. Love and belonging. Hope.

This is the story we need to tell, and the future we need to build.

Changing the Story of Social Care Reform: From Crisis to Opportunity

*T*o *be truly radical is to make hope possible, rather than despair convincing.*

(WILLIAMS, N.D.)

In his final speech as Prime Minister, Boris Johnson listed 'reforming social care' among his achievements (Prime Minister's Office, 10 Downing Street and The Rt Hon Boris Johnson MP, 2022), a claim quickly and widely disputed and derided.

Social care 'reform' means different things to different people, and 'the right "fix" depends on your interpretation of the system's problems' (Alderwick, Tallack, & Watt, 2019). However, I think most people would agree that whatever reform looks like, it is much needed, and it hasn't happened yet.

The language of social care reform adopted by much of the media, 'sector leaders', and campaigning organizations is a catastrophizing, deficit-based narrative of ticking time bombs and the rising cost of care. It screams with urgency and demands for immediate action, and yet the same story has been told on repeat for years, if not decades.

We need to tell a different story about social care reform.

'Britain facing social care "time bomb"'

Medical leaders are warning that we are facing a 'ticking time bomb' in social care as chronic underfunding, severe staffing shortages and a growing elderly population means that many in the future will not get the care and support they need.

(BRITISH MEDICAL ASSOCIATION, 2022)

We see frequent references to 'ticking time bombs' in reports and articles about the need for social care reform, and headlines like 'Britain facing social care time bomb' and 'Social care time bomb set to explode' are common.

The 'rapidly ageing population' is often cited as a key pressure, and this 'demographic time bomb' narrative drips with othering and blame.

- 'An ageing population as well as a growing number of disabled people of working age, means problems are escalating.'
- 'London is facing a social care time bomb due to its ageing population.'
- 'The issue of coping with our rapidly ageing population is not going to go away.'

Instead of celebrating longer lifetimes, this blames people for living longer, growing older. The burden of an ageing population. Longevity as a threat. More 'demand' to manage.

How will we cope?

Where shall we put them?

'Where are these people going to go?'

The 'workforce time bomb' is another pressure, with articles calling for reform getting tangled in a contradictory 'Care work is low paid, low skilled, high pressure, stressful' versus 'We need to attract more people to work in social care' spiral.

And the 'financial time bomb' narrative threatens that 'people's homes will be sold and their lifetime's savings raided to cover their care costs' while also managing to blame people once again as 'millions ignore future costs entirely' and 'almost no one has made other plans' to cover the cost of care. There are warnings too that 'a bankrupt care system will undermine the NHS' and that 'widespread care home closures' due to the government 'seriously underestimating' the cost of reform 'could leave councils struggling to find beds for those who require care'.

The emphasis is firmly on the cost of ageing and the cost of care, rather than the benefits of longer lives, and the value of great care and support.

'A sector in perpetual crisis'

'A threadbare safety net.' 'A system on its knees.' 'Deeply flawed.' 'Ravaged.' 'Broken.'

The media, charities, and social care commentators delight in using dramatic language to describe the state of social care. Headlines scream of 'crisis', 'scandal', 'car crash', and 'disaster'.

While 'strengths-based' working is promoted throughout practice, the narrative around social care reform is overwhelmingly deficit-based. There's no mention of opportunities and possibilities. Just the dreary 'social care is broken' rhetoric on repeat.

This narrative presents a pleading 'fund a damaged system to prevent things getting worse for the vulnerable/the elderly/those who need care/the workforce/care providers/local authorities/the NHS' instead of painting an appealing picture of a brighter future for all of us, that's worth investing in.

'Reform social care for the elderly'

'Change is needed, and it is needed now, to protect some of the most vulnerable members of society.'

This narrative focuses on change for 'others': the 'ageing population', 'bed blockers', 'vulnerable patients', 'elderly residents', 'service users', 'those'. This othering elicits a variety of reactions – sympathy, pity, charity – but most often no engagement or response at all.

It's a narrative about them, not us.

We need to spend more time focusing our messages on the fact that we *all* have a right to a good, equal life, and to the resources and support to achieve that, and therefore social care reform matters to us all.

The great news is that [sustainable approaches that support people to have a life, not just stay alive] can already be seen in glimpses of the future around the country. To command public and hence political support, they need to be presented as for 'us' not 'them', about good communities and lives for all of us. (Routledge, 2022)

'Next PM must overhaul social care'

In the dominant narrative of reform, *only* the government can 'fix' social care. Talking about a fix is inevitable when the rhetoric focuses on how broken social care is, but there are numerous problems with this framing.

In this narrative, the fix is more money, and the reason it's needed is to:

- 'reduce the burden on the NHS'
- 'prevent further deterioration of services'
- 'alleviate the burden from local authorities'
- 'prevent people from having to sell their home to pay for the cost of care'
- 'drive down future demands on the health service'
- 'prevent widespread market collapse'
- 'reduce waiting times'
- 'close the gulf between demand and capacity'
- 'reduce workforce shortages'
- 'protect some of the most vulnerable members of society'
- 'prevent a widespread catastrophe within adult social care'.

It's a narrative with a confused/confusing message, focusing on what more money will prevent, not create. There's rarely any mention of equality or inclusion. Choice and control. Good lives. Human rights. In fact, there's little mention of people who draw on support at all, beyond references to 'the elderly' and 'the most vulnerable'. 'Those who need care.'

This narrative presents social care as a single entity – a 'sector', a 'system', a 'body', an 'industry'. Care as a noun, not a verb. Care delivered in a package, rather than care as the connections and relationships that we can all demonstrate, feel, and benefit from.

The suggestion that social care can be fixed 'once and for all' also gives the impression that a one-off wave of a magic wand (or a single shake of the magic money tree) is all that is needed, and all will be well.

In no way am I disputing the need for significant investment, but without much broader and deeper change, any increase in funding will quickly be swallowed up in maintaining the bureaucracy of the current system and lining the pockets of a few beneficiaries, with little impact on the experiences and lives of people seeking and drawing on support.

And claims that 'only the Prime Minister can fix this' place all the agency with the government. Like the superhero 'professional' swooping in as the expert to protect 'the vulnerable', we're waiting (still) for a prime minister to take charge and rescue the helpless, broken sector from the brink. Not only does this overlook the value of collaboration and co-production and the way we can all influence change, but it also absolves us all from any responsibility to play our part.

It ignores the agency we all have and the part we can all play.

'I don't feel the emphasis on fixing it is right. We need to think of cherishing, supporting, caring and enabling social care with the attitudes and behaviours of what's needed. It's a constant steer not a one-off fix!' (Patel, 2022).

'Social care "time bomb" means reform is urgent'

Collapse is imminent.

Devastation looms.

Reform is urgent.

Immediate action is needed.

FIX SOCIAL CARE NOW.

'There is a demographic time bomb set to go off in Herefordshire in just five years' time – and action is urgently needed to ensure it does not blow up in the faces of the most vulnerable.'

'There is a real feeling in the industry that we are at the cusp of a devastating wave that is about to crush the lives of thousands of vulnerable people.'

Such catastrophizing metaphors are common, and the threat of impending doom is clearly and repeatedly articulated by adult social care directors, medical leaders, care providers, and campaigning organizations, in increasingly desperate attempts to convey the need for investment.

However, the sense of necessity dissipates somewhat when reform has been described as 'urgent' for so many years. In a House of Lords debate in 2021, Lord Bichard observed 'as we all know, social care has been in need of urgent reform for a decade or more...' (Hansard, 2021).

There's a real danger that 'where messages rely on crisis and urgency...the impact on public thinking over time can be fatalism. In summary, public sentiment can shift from the sense that "something must be done" to a resigned view that "nothing can be done"' (Social Care Future, 2019).

A future to fight for, not just a present to fight against

We have to have a vision of a future to fight for, not just a present to fight against. And for that we need imagination, hopes and dreams in our kit bag as well as strategy, tactics and relationships. –Clare Wightman

(CLOUGH, 2022)

We need to tell a different story about social care reform. The dominant narrative isn't working. It's exhausting, and exhausted. It lacks vision and coherence – a confused and contradictory rhetoric where older people are simultaneously blamed as the cause of the crisis and presented as the victims, and where younger adults have no presence at all. Where campaigns to encourage more people to work in social care vie with commentary about how arduous and challenging 'care work' is. Where we emphasize how bad things are, rather than how good things could be. Where we claim that only the government can fix this, with no conviction that they will, and with no agency of our own. Where the goal of reform is more money, with little mention of better, more equal lives.

It's a narrative devoid of hope, focused on fixing a broken system rather than imagining a better, brighter future. On the growing cost of care, not the value of great support. On emphasizing how bad things are, rather than how good things could be. On what investment will avoid, not enable.

There's no sense of opportunity, or possibility. The core messages are all around reducing and preventing, not creating or building.

So is it time to stop talking about 'reform'? Because this language suggests fixing. Restructuring. Reinforcing what we have. Improving services, structures, systems, and a 'sector', not improving people's experiences and building better lives.

Should we be talking instead about 'reimagining' social care?

And indeed, is it time to stop talking about 'social care'? Is the term too deeply aligned in public and political consciousness with the NHS, care homes, providers, services, 'the vulnerable', wrinkly hands, 'ticking time bombs', crisis, abuse, cost, decline, despair?

Should we be talking instead about wellbeing and belonging? About good lives, well lived? About what matters to all of us?

To create change we need a guiding vision, and the vision we must aim for is good lives well lived. This bold vision – which creates a sense of purpose, sparks our energy and sets a shared direction of travel – returns us to the original intentions of the welfare state and reinvents them for our time. (Cottam, 2018)

We need to make hope possible.

And we need to recognize that yes, it's time for change, but that lasting change takes time. The substantial and sustainable reform we need doesn't have a set timeline or a fixed implementation date. It can't be planned with a calendar or measured with a clock. It can't be scheduled or, indeed, delayed.

In contrast to the Chronos time urgency of the dominant narrative of reform, this is fluid, organic, Kairos time change.

This is the change we need to see, and – as I'll illustrate in the following chapter – this is the way we need to see change.

Changing the Story of Change: From Transformation to Lasting Change

The vision of flourishing lives has been our joint North Star.

(TULLOCH & SCHULMAN, 2020)

I'm all for radical change in social care, and I also firmly believe in the potential for fundamental, lasting change at a local level. But I don't believe we'll achieve this lasting change through 'transformation programmes' led by 'transformation teams'.

I've looked at a significant number of councils' social care 'transformation' plans and strategies, and in this final chapter I want to unpick the language of change in relation to local authority social care, to illustrate where I think we've got stuck, and why I think we're trying to transform the wrong things, for the wrong reasons, in the wrong ways, with the wrong people, in the wrong places!

Then I'll go on to consider how I think we need to shift our language, and in turn our approach, to achieve lasting change.

To rewrite social care.

Transformation

While much of the national narrative around social care is about 'fixing', at a local government level there's a strong emphasis on 'transformation'.

The dictionary definition of transformation is 'a complete change in the appearance or character of something or someone, especially so that thing or person is improved', 'An extreme, radical change' (Cambridge Dictionary, n.d.; Vocabulary.com, n.d.).

Sounds good doesn't it, given the scale of reform needed? Ambitious. Hopeful. Revolutionary even.

Or not.

As ever, when we pay attention to the language, we illuminate the story we're telling, and in this case it's clear to see where we're going wrong.

Why?

Most transformation plans begin with the stick, not the carrot.

Documents which inevitably reference 'strengths-based approaches' invariably start with what's wrong, not what's strong.

The motivation for change is usually articulated in quantitative terms, and – like the national narrative – has a distinct undercurrent of blame.

Reasons include:

- 'An increase in older adults suffering with dementia.'
- 'An ageing population.'
- 'Increased complexity of cases.'
- 'An increase in people suffering from a moderate or severe learning disability.'

The anticipated result of the 'transformation' is usually articulated in quantitative terms too:

- 'To reduce demand.'
- 'To save money.'
- 'To avoid hospital admissions.'
- 'To ensure ASC is as efficient and as cost effective as possible.'

Reduce. Save. Avoid.

So, while the local narrative of change may have a glossier and more ambitious headline than the national message, the nuance is still the same. Things are bad. We need to stop them getting worse.

Overall, there's an absence of vision in these plans. There's no sense of possibility, or hope. There's little to grab our attention, pique our curiosity, or motivate us to get involved.

There's no North Star.

How?

So how will this 'transformation' happen? Well, through programmes and plans of course, and largely, it seems, through 'reviews'. The plans I looked at mentioned reviewing:

- 'our information and advice strategy'
- 'our workforce strategy'
- 'the front door'
- 'our crisis response arrangements'
- 'Direct Payment audit arrangements'
- 'respite'
- 'our day care offer'
- 'reablement services'
- 'high cost expenditure'
- 'lower cost expenditure'
- 'high cost packages'
- 'low cost packages'.

As well as reviewing literally everything there is to review, there's lots of emphasis on the transformational potential of 'strengths-based practice'.

Plans mention 'implementing a strengths-based approach to working with all service users', and 'embedding a strengths-based approach at every stage of the customer journey'. And if references to 'service users', 'customers', and 'journeys' aren't enough red flags, it's explicit in these plans that this emphasis on strengths-based practice is all about 'reducing care expenditure' and 'effectively managing demand'.

Training also features regularly in plans, with workers subjected to, for example, 'detailed behaviour change training', 'strengths-based practice training', and even 'training and supervision to divert people from statutory services appropriately'.

Sigh.

I agree wholeheartedly with Ewan Hilton's astute observation:

When we say we want 'change', all too often what we do is just train or re-train our frontline staff. We expect more from the people already doing the work. We don't even question if leadership, our organizational culture and our power structures are standing in the way of change. And we don't ask how these things can instead act as enablers. (Hilton, 2023)

There's no sense of any form of appreciative inquiry, of learning from and building on what's working well (although maybe – hopefully – this forms part of all those 'reviews'?). There's little mention of co-design or co-production.

There's no space or permission in the programmes and plans to experiment, be curious, share stories, challenge, make mistakes, try again.

There's no sense of any kind of organic, evolutionary approach to 'transformation'.

And as such we 'deliver' change like we deliver care, with plans and schedules. Structured. Linear. Measurable. Reportable.

Done to and for, not with or by.

Changing people – 'frontline staff' – rather than focusing on creating the right 'material conditions for people to start doing things differently or start doing different things. Material conditions not hot air. The new system has got to take the worker out of the factory as well as taking the factory out of the worker' (Holmes, 2023b).

What?

Innovation tends to proceed without an explicit ethical foundation, too often focused on coordination, efficiencies, and the exploitation of new technologies... An app on its own doesn't change the quality of the information collected, or who holds what kind of power, or the types of decisions that are made. If anything, it becomes one more system artifice that reinforces the way things are done.

(TULLOCH & SCHULMAN, 2020)

So, what is this 'transformation' going to achieve?

There's a distinct focus on 'more and better use of technology', to 'enable staff to work efficiently', 'to support people more effectively and efficiently', and 'to maintain people independently in their home':

- 'an e-marketplace'
- 'a front-end chat bot'
- 'an online self-assessment and screening tool'
- 'a library of useful apps'
- 'a new customer relationship management system'
- 'a new resident-focused performance dashboard'.

233

Technology isn't the only focus though. Social work practice, performance monitoring, financial management, and reporting are all in the mix too.

But there's no reference to any change in leadership style, power dynamics, or decision making. No mention of building trust, compassion, or connections. No sign of liberating people from the stifling processes, forms, and bureaucracy. Of freeing workers up to listen and to learn. To share ideas, explore communities, remove barriers, build relationships, and uphold rights.

If you ask, well, pretty much anyone seeking or drawing on support what they'd like to be 'transformed' about adult social care, you can pretty much guarantee that IT systems and performance monitoring won't be on their list.

And therein lies the problem.

We don't ask.

Who?

I've been involved in many change initiatives over the years, and mostly, that change was decided in one room, and then explained and trained in another set of rooms.

(STILLMAN, 2022)

The focus of 'transformation' is on what, not who. Process, not people. Efficient systems, not flourishing lives.

People who require support, and the people who directly support them in both paid and unpaid roles, are largely excluded from discussions and decision making. Instead, we have transformation teams. Heads of transformation. Transformation leads. Directors of transformation. Transformation managers.

The proliferation of these posts implies that 'transformation' is the remit of select individuals and teams, who will lead, manage, deliver, and evaluate 'change'.

This removes any sense of agency or influence from the people who are most likely to know best what needs to change, and how best to make those changes. It ignores – and in turn saps – their ideas, creative potential, energy, and vision. And, because we're 'engrossed in only grand things, we underappreciate (and under-resource) the small things, which can be mighty. We leave changemaking in the hands of a few giants rather than vesting it in everyone' (Tulloch & Schulman, 2020).

Where?

The majority of 'transformation plans' I read could apply anywhere and everywhere.

There was little sense of place influencing or impacting on plans, and little sense that 'transformation' would change anything very tangible beyond the office walls.

When?

'Our transformation projects have key milestone dates for each outcome that are monitored through our project management system.'

This is Chronos time change, with implementation dates and delivery dates.

Scheduled. Controlled. Predictable. Measurable.

Impossible.

'The only kind of change you can make happen suddenly, on a large scale, is destruction, whereas creation of anything real and valuable starts small, but ambitious' (Fox, 2018).

So?

So, how will we know when we've 'delivered' transformation?

Well, 'we have built several performance dashboards that provide a picture of how we are performing on a range of indicators.' 'We will have succeeded when...performance in key areas is sustained in line with the targets we have set ourselves.'

'The targets we have set ourselves.' Pretty much sums it up really, doesn't it?

How about we ask people drawing on support what 'success' looks and feels like?

How about we ask people drawing on support if things have 'transformed' for them?

Ah no – sorry, we don't have time. We're too busy ticking the boxes to complete the forms to populate the dashboards to provide the evidence that things have changed.

Lasting change

Despite the urgency, lasting change takes much longer than we appreciate.

Darn.

One way to counteract our impatience is to shift from Chronos to Kairos time. Chronos time is sequential time, measured by the clock, which seems to be speeding up. Kairos time bends and stretches, sometimes it even seems to stand still. Chronos is measured by the clock which many of us try to beat. Kairos unfolds like the seasons, following a natural rhythm and waiting for the right moment.

(ETMANSKI, 2015)

Our approach to delivering change mirrors our approach to delivering care. (The concept that either can be 'delivered' doesn't help!) We don't start with what matters most to people and families. We don't involve the right people in conversations. We have discussions in the wrong places. We make decisions about people without them. We make plans that lack imagination and insight and impose inflexible and inhumane schedules. We focus on changing people rather than creating the conditions for change to happen. And we concentrate on and measure outputs, not outcomes.

Our deficit-based reasons for reform, and our ambitions to reduce, avoid, and save, lead to transactional rather than transformational change. A focus on efficiency and processes, not wellbeing and better lives.

We need to reimagine social care.

We also need to reimagine change.

And we need to begin with these four little words.

What. Matters. To. You?

What *really* matters to you?

Because if we make time for those conversations, make space to listen, question, and learn, we'll identify the needs and desires we share and that connect us all. We'll understand what good really looks like. And then we can start to work *together* to achieve it.

Singing from the same songbook

The words we use matter. When we share our vision and truth, we can build powerful movements and win public policy and transformative changes we've been calling for. To do this, and create the space for massive gains, we need to sing from the same songbook – communities, allies and organizations alike. It's all about repetition – we tell our stories and show others how to repeat them. When we repeat effective messages we can shift public support and win transformative change.

(PASSING THE MESSAGE STICK, 2021)

If we want to win hearts and minds, and build support for change, we need to sing from the same songbook.

We need a shared North Star.

Don't we *all* want to live in the place we call home with the people and things that we love, in communities where we look out for one another, doing the things that matter to us?

We all need to tell our story

Stories make, prop up, and bring down systems. Stories shape how we understand the world, our place in it, and our ability to change it.

(SALTMARSHE, 2018)

Where stories feature in calls for reform, they are stories of institutions and stories of abuse. Ely Hospital. Winterbourne View. Muckamore Abbey. Whorlton Hall. Shocking, distressing stories that need and deserve to be told. But they've been told again and again and will no doubt – and heartbreakingly – continue to be told unless we make space for different stories.

These different stories are stories of difference. They offer glimpses of what's possible. Make that reimagined future a little bit more tangible. Help turn those dreams into reality. Help illustrate the path and illuminate the destination.

Human stories about gloriously ordinary lives and about the role that brilliant support can play in creating and sustaining them.

Colourful, beautiful stories of love. Belonging. Desire. Joy. Meaning. Purpose. Compassion. Inclusion. Laughter. Tears. Living. Dying.

As Glyn Butcher told a room full of social workers at the Adult

Social Care Festival of Practice in Doncaster in 2022, 'The point is...
we all need to tell our story.'

Listening to stories takes time

*Listening to stories takes time, but stories are abundant and in this rich,
unruly mix we find the seeds of ideas that can be grown.*

(COTTAM, 2018)

We need to ensure there are opportunities and platforms for people to
share their own stories, and we need to create the spaces for listening.

We need a diverse range of people to be heard, and a diverse range
of people need to listen.

And when stories have been shared and heard, and barriers start
to come down, and trusted relationships begin to form, and energy
starts to build, and momentum begins to grow, and the seeds of ideas
start to emerge, we need to make sure the conditions are in place for
those seeds to flourish.

We are the change

*Change will not come if we wait for some other person or some other
time. We are the ones we've been waiting for. We are the change that
we seek. –Barack Obama*

(NEW YORK TIMES, 2008)

In the dominant narrative of social care reform nationally, the prime
minister has all the agency, and 'only the government can fix this'. In
our local narrative we have transformation leads, imposing a structured, linear, and hierarchical approach to change. And in both the
national and local rhetoric, change is about others, those, them. This
framing removes any sense of agency and responsibility, and indeed
benefit, from too many of us.

But in our Kairos time approach to change, we're all agents of
change. We can – and must – be the change that we seek.

'Co-production' and the 'nothing about us without us' principles
are key here. We'll only ever achieve meaningful and sustainable change

if we share stories, ideas, knowledge, skills, passions, respect, and space with each other and work together as equals.

Good conversations about better futures should mirror good conversations at an individual level, focusing on what matters, what good looks like, and how we can work together to achieve it.

And conversations about change must be about we, our, all of us.

'Never doubt that a small group of thoughtful, committed, citizens can change the world. Indeed, it is the only thing that ever has' (Margaret Mead).[1]

Liberation

While our standard approach to 'transformation' focuses on programmes, plans, reviews, and training, and on new processes, products, systems, and structures, often the most impactful change comes from what we stop doing, rather than what we introduce.

When we strip back the layers of bureaucracy, the lengthy forms, the eligibility criteria, the labels, and the assumptions, we make space for human beings, and space to be human.

Small, but ambitious

It's worth remembering that it is often the small steps, not the giant leaps, that bring about the most lasting change. –Queen Elizabeth II
(ITV NEWS, 2019)

In the dominant 'transformation' narrative, 'big' change is required. Large-scale, whole-system fix social care now. But so often it's the littlest things in the smallest places closest to home that make the biggest difference.

It's the tiny seeds of ideas and little acts of kindness, curiosity, and challenge that create gentle ripples and then bigger waves, meandering through our consciousness and conversations and cultures, flowing and connecting and creating change along the way.

---

1   Original source unknown, but widely quoted online. You can listen to Anna Severwright quoting these words against the images of the brilliant #SocialCareFuture gathering 2023 (Social Care Future, 2023).

Because the change we need most begins in hearts and minds.

Lasting change takes much longer than we appreciate, but the sooner we start to tell a different story, the closer we'll get to reaching out and touching our North Star.

So, What Now?

I hope you've enjoyed reading this book. Perhaps it's affirmed much of what you've thought and experienced. Maybe it's made you think a bit – or a lot – differently. Possibly you're left thinking, 'What now?' I'm pretty sure you'll have some thoughts about changes you might want to make or to influence. Here are three things that work for me.

Be curious

I started my blog because I was curious. I knew I felt uncomfortable about a lot of the language of social care, and I wanted to delve deeper, to research and think and write about particular words and phrases to understand more about them, and what they represent and reinforce.

Often when we want to 'do something' about language, we create glossaries to explain, or lists of words to avoid and words to use instead. But straight switches can lead us into the realm of policing language and banning words – and while there are some words and phrases I'd love to see erased from our vocabulary, this approach is too blunt. Alternative words can easily become jargon themselves. 'People we support' is a classic example. The phrase is, in theory, a description of a relationship (rather than 'service users' or 'clients') but has become a label for a group of 'them'. I've seen the term capitalized ('People We Support'), hyphenated ('People-We-Support'), and condensed to one of those three letter acronyms we love so much. PWS. Argh. See also 'people with lived experience'. That's all of us, isn't it? But we're turning it into a label that means 'them'.

So be curious about what the words you hear, read, and use with and about people tell you about power and about relationships. Do they imply 'us' or infer 'them'? Do they acknowledge and truly reflect what's happening, or do they perpetuate assumptions and stereotypes that conveniently deflect and deny reality?

Reflect on the language used in relation to the purpose and potential of social care. Are we talking about people getting services, or living their best lives? Surviving or thriving? Safety net or springboard? Think about the words we repeat in relation to practice. Do they suggest doing to, or working with? Processing or connecting? Assessing or understanding? Be alert to those deceptive words, like 'prevention' (what are we trying to prevent?) and 'independence' (do we mean doing things by ourselves and managing without support, or having choice and control over our lives?).

And remember, we can't change our language without changing our practice. If we stop screening, triaging, signposting, referring, assessing, and placing, we won't need these words any more.

Challenge

If you're curious about language, dictionaries are your friend. As you've probably noticed, I've included dictionary definitions throughout this book, because so often the explanation of a word speaks volumes about the reality of our perceptions and our practice. 'Vulnerable' means 'in need of special care, support, or protection because of age, disability, or risk of abuse or neglect' (Oxford Languages). 'Respite' means 'a short period of rest or relief from something difficult or unpleasant' (Oxford Languages). 'Complex' means 'difficult to understand or find an answer to' (Cambridge Dictionary).

I just checked various definitions of my next suggestion, which is to challenge. While I'm not suggesting you 'call out to duel or combat', challenge also means 'to dispute especially as being unjust, invalid, or outmoded' (Merriam-Webster). If you're getting curious about the language you're hearing, reading, or using yourself, you'll want to start to call it out. I hope that what you've read in this book will help. Your own values will help you too, as will the law – both in terms of the principles of equality, dignity, respect, autonomy, and wellbeing enshrined in our legislation, and the actual language used too.

There's no reference to 'vulnerable' or 'respite' or 'complex' in the Care Act 2014.

Connect

Challenging also means 'something that is difficult and that tests someone's ability or determination' (Cambridge Dictionary, n.d.).

Challenging *is* difficult. I know, from years of trying!

When I left my post of Strategic Lead for Practice Development in Adult Social Care at Doncaster Council in September 2024, I posted the following on LinkedIn:

Last week, Phil Holmes compared me to that person in the 'first follower' video who starts dancing on their own in a field, and gradually people join in. It can be tough being the person who is always questioning, challenging, asking 'why?' But I was never really alone in that field. My 'team' in Doncaster have been the people with lived experience of care and support – Glyn, Val, Martin, Helen, Issachar, Wendy, Kyla, Zac, Emily, Karen, Claire, Debbie, Giovanni, Amy...who have shared not just their experiences but also their wisdom, passion, ideas, creativity, frustrations, trust, and love. I've learnt so, so much from them, and with them, and we've had a lot of laughs along the way.

Several years earlier, well before my time in Doncaster and when I was feeling a bit frustrated and fed up, Phil suggested that I 'find good people'. And you know what – I have! It's much easier to be curious and to challenge when you connect with people who are curious and keen to challenge too. So, find those people, if you haven't already found them. Seek them out, in person or online. Join conversations and find opportunities to start them.

And once you've found each other, I suggest you don't get too stuck in what's wrong, but instead ask one of Tricia Nicoll's most helpful questions: 'What would it take?'

Recommended Resources

There are some books, videos, and blogs that I return to and recommend, again and again. The authors have had a huge influence on me, and their words mingle with mine in my blog posts and on the pages of this book. They are just some of the 'good people' I've found through my writing.

If you haven't already discovered them, I suggest these pieces are an excellent place to start. Some of them expose the damaging futility of our dominant, dehumanizing, and bureaucratic approach. Others offer encouraging and inspiring glimmers of a far more human, humane alternative. Many do both.

Books

Maff Potts' beautifully human *Friends and Purpose* has only just been published, so as yet I haven't included any quotes from it in my writing. Let's change that. His chapter on 'Talking bollocks' explores 'the idea that how we speak to people is awful. Even the positive stuff'. He writes that 'deficit language is quicker and simpler and so the system loves it', but also suggests that 'the positive, "aspirational" language can be almost worse than the deficit words, because they are somehow more dishonest and manipulative'. I couldn't agree more. I also love his observation that 'when we organise we systemise and so we dehumanise' (Potts, 2025). Buy or borrow a copy of this book. Everyone should read it.

Edgar Cahn's *No More Throw-Away People* (Cahn, 2000) was published 25 years ago but remains just as relevant today. His writing helps us to understand what co-production really means, illustrating the importance of recognizing and valuing people as 'assets', not 'demand', and the shift from the transactional to the relational. From 'you need me' to 'we need each other'.

Gord Tulloch and Sarah Schulman's *The Trampoline Effect: Redesigning Our Social Safety Nets* (Tulloch & Schulman, 2020) is all about 'learning how to make our social systems more human'. The authors ask us to 'consider a basic question about the social services: are we only safety nets, holding and protecting the people we support, or are we also trampolines, launching people into flourishing lives?' Through a combination of quotes, stories, and suggestions, they demonstrate how, 'if we want to be trampolines, then we need to stretch what we do, how we do it, and who we are'.

Hilary Cottam's *Radical Help* (Cottam, 2018) exposes how 'our current welfare systems have a logic that runs like this: assess me, refer me, manage me'. She proposes a different logic through a set of five experiments, illustrating a shift from fixing problems to growing good lives, where instead of managing need, we focus on developing capabilities 'so that each and every one of us can thrive'. Instead of containing risk, we create possibility, and instead of transactions, we focus above all on relationships.

Videos

In her powerful TED talk, *Diversity is the key to our survival: The Shoeness of a Shoe* (Chapple, 2019), Elly Chapple describes what she has learned from her daughter Ella about the importance of listening, observing, connection, and trust. She highlights how and why we need to flip the narrative, dropping the 'ridiculous assumptions' we hold about people, and acknowledging that while we are all different, we're also all the same, because we are all human.

If you haven't come across Open Future Learning yet, now is the time to check them out. I frequently include their graphics in slides when I'm talking about terms like 'challenging behaviour' or 'special needs'. In their *Man w/ developmental disability will not bathe* video (Open Future Learning, 2024), Lynne Seagle illustrates the futility of the 'hassle, nag, document' approach to support, and describes what happens when the focus shifts from 'important for' to 'important to'.

Community Catalysts' short film *Exploring the idea of social care abundance and deficit with Mavis and Meena*, and Angela Catley's accompanying text (Catley, 2023b), illustrate how the dominant, deficit-based narrative of social care stems from a definition of social care which is limited to services and institutions, and how this narrow framing

– and associated practice – means we overlook the capacity of local communities, and 'squeeze the abundance out of view'.

Blog posts and articles

Whenever I talk to groups of social workers about the way they write about people in their records, I share Wren Aves' *Mental Health Clinical Notes: The Curse of the Paper-Self* (Aves, 2021). This post highlights the lasting, damaging impact of language and labels, offering a powerful account of how, in Wren's mental health notes, her own identity was erased by her 'paper-self'. She writes 'this is the curse of the paper-self. Despite literally being a pile of paper, she holds more authority than me on my own life, because she is sculpted with the thoughts and words of "professionals"...and in the end, they are the only thoughts and words which matter.'

I also frequently reference Mark Neary's writing, including the definitions in his brilliant and insightful *An A to Z of CareSpeak* (Neary, n.d.) Here are a couple to reflect on:

Choice: An opportunity to pick between one thing or nothing.
Measurable outcomes: Having everything you do logged and judged.

All of Neil Crowther's writing has had a huge influence on my thinking, and I love his blog posts. I think *Somewhere north of Preston* is my favourite – a powerful, personal musing on the importance of identity and personhood, which touches on the way 'language that displaces personhood and identity softens things up for violating human rights' (Crowther, 2020a).

Rob Mitchell and the rest of the Social Work, Cats and Rocket Science crew have written many raw, honest, and illuminating pieces about social work practice. Of them all, *Someone to Safeguard* (Mitchell, R., 2016) is the one I've returned to, and referenced, multiple times in relation to ideas about safety and safeguarding. It's a tough and essential read.

Mark Smith's *Eligibility criteria – what if we just turned them off?* (Smith, 2022b) sums up brilliantly just how futile and destructive our 'come back when things get worse', sorting office approach to public services is, and how this 'intended brake has become an accelerator', meaning 'there's more to do because we weren't engaging earlier'. Mark offers a 'bespoke by design' alternative – person-shaped not system-shaped – with understanding rather than assessment at its heart.

And finally, Social Care Future's *Building public support for a brighter social care future in 5 easy reframes – quick read* (Social Care Future, 2023) suggests five easy ways to reframe our messaging about social care to help shift the narrative and achieve that brighter future, where we can *all* live in the place we call home, with the people and things we love, in communities where we look out for each other, doing the things that matter to us.

References

Adult Social Care Making It Real Board. (2024, January). *Your Care and Support: Doncaster – Adult Social Care Local Account 2024.* Retrieved March 10, 2024, from City of Doncaster Council: www.doncaster.gov.uk/services/adult-social-care/your-care-and-support-doncaster-2024-adult-social-care-local-account

Alderwick, H., Tallack, C., & Watt, T. (2019, 30 August). *What should be done to fix the crisis in social care?* Retrieved 24 September 2022, from Health Foundation: www.health.org.uk/publications/long-reads/what-should-be-done-to-fix-the-crisis-in-social-care

Alexander, J. (2022). *Citizens.* Canbury Press.

Archbishops' Commission on Reimagining Care. (2023, January). *Care and Support Reimagined: A National Care Covenant For England.* Retrieved 11 June 2023, from Church of England: www.churchofengland.org/about/archbishops-commissions/reimagining-care-commission

Association of Directors of Adult Social Services. (2023, 16 November). *ADASS Autumn Survey – Part 2.* Retrieved 18 November 2023, from ADASS: www.adass.org.uk/documents/adass-autumn-survey-2023-part-2

Aves, W. (2021, 22 August). *Mental Health Clinical Notes: The Curse of the Paper-Self.* Retrieved 23 April 2022, from Psychiatry Is Driving Me Mad: www.psychiatryisdrivingmemad.co.uk/post/mental-health-clinical-notes-the-curse-of-the-paper-self

Bartnik, E. & Broad, R. (2021). *Power and Connection.* Centre for Welfare Reform.

BBC Newsnight. (2024, 27 March). *'When you're not perceived by other people...'.* Retrieved 29 March 2024, from Twitter: https://x.com/BBCNewsnight/status/1773126968025792595?s=20

Be Human. (2020). *The 7 principles of Be Human.* Retrieved 20 January 2024, from Be Human: https://be-human.org.uk

Belton, J. (2018). *It's words that I remember – language matters.* Retrieved 20 December 2019, from My Cuppa Jo: www.mycuppajo.com/language

Brand, J. (2021, 12 February). *I have been a care worker and know what the job involves – they deserve a real living wage.* Retrieved 31 October 2021, from The Independent: www.independent.co.uk/independentpremium/voices/care-workers-real-living-wage-covid-jo-brand-b1801521.html

Britannica Dictionary. (n.d.). *Resilience.* Retrieved 4 May 2024, from Britannica: www.britannica.com/dictionary/resilience

British Association of Social Workers. (2018, 17 September). *80-20 campaign final report.* Retrieved 20 August 2022, from BASW: www.basw.co.uk/resources/80-20-campaign-final-report-2018

British Association of Social Workers. (2021, 7 July). *BASW Code of Ethics for Social Work*. Retrieved 11 June 2023, from BASW: www.basw.co.uk/about-basw/code-ethics

British Association of Social Workers. (2023). *The BASW Social Work Journalism Awards*. Retrieved 28 December 2023, from BASW: https://new.basw.co.uk/about-basw/awards/basw-social-work-journalism-awards

British Medical Association. (2022, 8 June). *BMA warns of social care crisis as current system is 'deeply flawed' and in need of 'urgent reform'*. Retrieved 24 September 2022, from British Medical Association: www.bma.org.uk/bma-media-centre/bma-warns-of-social-care-crisis-as-current-system-is-deeply-flawed-and-in-need-of-urgent-reform

Broad, R. (2012). *Local Area Coordination: From Service Users to Citizens*. Retrieved 27 August 2022, from Centre for Welfare Reform: https://citizen-network.org/uploads/attachment/340/local-area-coordination.pdf

Brown, B. (2017, 17 May). *Dehumanizing always starts with language*. Retrieved 6 January 2024, from Brené Brown: https://brenebrown.com/articles/2018/05/17/dehumanizing-always-starts-with-language

Brown, B. (2022, 4 February). *Belonging vs fitting in – Brené Brown*. Retrieved 2 January 2023, from YouTube: www.youtube.com/watch?v=CkC6PeseGds

Bunting, M. (2020). *Labours of Love*. Granta.

Cahn, E. (2000). *No More Throw-Away People: The Co-Production Imperative*. Essential Books.

Cambridge Dictionary. (n.d.). *Care*. Retrieved 12 August 2023, from Cambridge Dictionary: https://dictionary.cambridge.org/dictionary/english/care

Cambridge Dictionary. (n.d.). *Challenge*. Retrieved 21 March 2025, from Cambridge Dictionary: https://dictionary.cambridge.org/dictionary/learner-english/challenge

Cambridge Dictionary. (n.d.). *Client*. Retrieved 21 September 2023, from Cambridge Dictionary: https://dictionary.cambridge.org/dictionary/english/client

Cambridge Dictionary. (n.d.). *Community*. Retrieved 3 December 2023, from Cambridge Dictionary: https://dictionary.cambridge.org/dictionary/english/community

Cambridge Dictionary. (n.d.). *Complex*. Retrieved 21 March 2025, from Cambridge Dictionary: https://dictionary.cambridge.org/dictionary/english/complex

Cambridge Dictionary. (n.d.). *Dependency*. Retrieved 24 March 2024, from Cambridge Dictionary: https://dictionary.cambridge.org/dictionary/english/dependency

Cambridge Dictionary. (n.d.). *Fear*. Retrieved 13 February 2024, from Cambridge Dictionary: https://dictionary.cambridge.org/dictionary/english/fear

Cambridge Dictionary. (n.d.). *Frontline*. Retrieved 29 May 2021, from Cambridge Dictionary: https://dictionary.cambridge.org/dictionary/english/front-line

Cambridge Dictionary. (n.d.). *Needs*. Retrieved 20 May 2023, from Cambridge Dictionary: https://dictionary.cambridge.org/dictionary/english/needs

Cambridge Dictionary. (n.d.). *Prevention*. Retrieved 11 March 2023, from Cambridge Dictionary: https://dictionary.cambridge.org/dictionary/english/prevention

Cambridge Dictionary. (n.d.). *Reablement*. Retrieved 1 April 2024, from Cambridge Dictionary: https://dictionary.cambridge.org/dictionary/english/reablement

Cambridge Dictionary. (n.d.). *Transformation*. Retrieved 25 March 2023, from Cambridge Dictionary: https://dictionary.cambridge.org/dictionary/english/transformation

Cambridge University Press. (n.d.). *Placement.* Retrieved 27 October 2024, from Cambridge Learner's Dictionary: https://dictionary.cambridge.org/dictionary/learner-english/placement

Cambridge University Press. (n.d.). *Someone.* Retrieved 27 October 2024, from Cambridge Advanced Learner's Dictionary & Thesaurus: https://dictionary.cambridge.org/dictionary/english/someone

Camerados. (n.d.). *Camerados.* Retrieved 3 March 2024, from Camerados: https://camerados.org

Care Act 2014, c. 23. (2014, 14 May). Retrieved 14 October 2023, from legislation.gov.uk: www.legislation.gov.uk/ukpga/2014/23/contents/enacted

Care Quality Commission. (2022a, 11 July). *Profad Care Agency Limited Inspection report.* Retrieved 20 August 2022, from Care Quality Commission: https://api.cqc.org.uk/public/v1/reports/90c763ba-7772-4ae0-b90f-446aeee64e83?20220709120000

Care Quality Commission. (2022b, 14 July). *Gables Care Home Inspection report.* Retrieved 20 August 2022, from Care Quality Commission: https://api.cqc.org.uk/public/v1/reports/ebb2f1ff-f7ef-4653-8f74-0b41ba9f9ee5?20220715120000

Care Quality Commission. (2023, 10 August). *Regulation 16: Notification of death of service user.* Retrieved 15 August 2023, from Care Quality Commission: www.cqc.org.uk/guidance-providers/regulations/regulation-16-notification-death-service-user

Careleaver123. (2022, 23 April). *Reading through my SW files a few years ago...* Retrieved 3 June 2022, from Twitter: https://twitter.com/careleaver123/status/1517868729618550784

Carers UK. (n.d.). *Key facts and figures about caring.* Retrieved 20 May 2023, from Carers UK: www.carersuk.org/policy-and-research/key-facts-and-figures

Carpani, J. & Kelly-Linden, J. (2020, 19 December). *Boris Johnson speaks of 'heavy heart' as Christmas is sacrificed to protect the vulnerable.* Retrieved 20 August 2021, from The Telegraph: www.telegraph.co.uk/global-health/science-and-disease/covid-coronavirus-news-vaccine-moderna-pfizer-christmas-lockdown

Catley, A. (2023a, 28 February). *'In the world of #socialcare...* Twitter. Retrieved 11 March 2023, from Twitter: https://twitter.com/angelacommcats/status/1626849858983194624?s=20

Catley, A. (2023b, 30 May). *Mavis and Meena – social care abundance or deficit?* Retrieved 11 June 2023, from Community Catalysts: www.communitycatalysts.co.uk/2023/05/30/mavis-and-meena-social-care-abundance-or-deficit

Changing Futures Northumbria. (n.d.). *Liberated method.* Retrieved 28 April 2024, from Changing Futures Northumbria: www.changingfuturesnorthumbria.co.uk/liberated-method

Chapple, E. (2019, July). *Diversity is the key to our survival: The Shoeness of a Shoe.* Retrieved 20 March 2025, from TED: www.ted.com/talks/elly_chapple_diversity_is_the_key_to_our_survival_the_shoeness_of_a_shoe

Chapple, E. (2021, 8 November). *#Flip the narrative.* Retrieved 29 August 2022, from Twitter: https://twitter.com/elly_chapple/status/1457824785627553793?

Chapple, E. (2023, 31 December). *The space in the middle is where we have a real chance to connect...* Retrieved 16 February 2024, from Twitter: https://twitter.com/elly_chapple/status/1741431422533906866

Chapple, E. (2024). *Elly Chapple Founder #FlipTheNarrative.* Retrieved 5 January 2024, from Twitter: https://twitter.com/elly_chapple

Clough, I. (2022, 28 April). *The power of co-creation in social change*. Retrieved 24 September 2022, from Act Build Change: https://actbuildchange.com/blog/the-power-of-co-creation-in-social-change

Collins. (n.d.). *Assessment*. Retrieved 6 September 2019, from Collins dictionary: www.collinsdictionary.com/dictionary/english/assessment

Collins. (n.d.). *Community*. Retrieved 3 December 2023, from Collins dictionary: www.collinsdictionary.com/dictionary/english/community

Collins. (n.d.). *Dependency*. Retrieved 23 March 2024, from Collins dictionary: www.collinsdictionary.com/dictionary/english/dependency

Collins. (n.d.). *Independence*. Retrieved 11 December 2021, from Collins dictionary: www.collinsdictionary.com/dictionary/english/independence

Collins. (n.d.). *Independent*. Retrieved 11 December 2021, from Collins dictionary: www.collinsdictionary.com/dictionary/english/independent

Collins. (n.d.). *Resilience*. Retrieved 11 December 2021, from Collins dictionary: www.collinsdictionary.com/dictionary/english/resilient

Collins. (n.d.). *Safe*. Retrieved 2 March 2024, from Collins dictionary: www.collinsdictionary.com/dictionary/english/safe

Collins. (n.d.). *Special*. Retrieved 13 August 2023, from Collins dictionary: www.collinsdictionary.com/dictionary/english/special

Collins. (n.d.). *Support*. Retrieved 12 August 2023, from Collins dictionary: www.collinsdictionary.com/dictionary/english/support

Collins. (n.d.). *What is the difference between customer and client?* Retrieved 12 August 2023, from Collins dictionary: https://grammar.collinsdictionary.com

Community Catalysts. (2023a, 31 May). *Narrow definitions of 'social care'...* Retrieved 29 December 2023, from Twitter: https://twitter.com/CommCats/status/1663817422803988482

Community Catalysts. (2023b, 1 November). *Worried about the sense that...* Retrieved 3 December 2023, from Twitter: https://x.com/CommCats/status/1719703656231039357?s=20

Cottam, H. (2018). *Radical Help: How We Can Remake the Relationships Between Us and Revolutionise the Welfare State*. Virago Press Ltd.

Cottam, H. (2020, September). *Welfare 5.0: Why we need a social revolution and how to make it happen*. Retrieved 14 February 2023, from UCL: www.ucl.ac.uk/bartlett/public-purpose/publications/2020/sep/welfare-50-why-we-need-social-revolution-and-how-make-it-happen

Cottam, H. (2021, November). *A radical new vision for social care: How to reimagine and redesign support systems for this century*. Retrieved 20 August 2022, from The Health Foundation: www.health.org.uk/publications/reports/a-radical-new-vision-for-social-care

Cox, C. (2022, 17 January). *Desperate, exhausted and poorly paid: Workers lift the lid on Greater Manchester's crumbling social care*. Retrieved 20 August 2022, from Manchester Evening News: www.manchestereveningnews.co.uk/news/greater-manchester-news/social-care-crisis-greater-manchester-22744992

Crowther, N. (2020a, 21 July). *Somewhere north of Preston*. Retrieved 10 October 2020, from Making Rights Make Sense: https://makingrightsmakesense.wordpress.com/2020/07/21/somewhere-north-of-preston

Crowther, N. (2020b, 18 September). *Custard*. Retrieved 3 March 2024, from Making Rights Make Sense: https://makingrightsmakesense.wordpress.com/2020/09/18/custard

Crowther, N. (2021a, 13 February). *Working in social care is boring, thankless & unenviable – sign up today!* Retrieved 29 May 2021, from Social Care Future.

Crowther, N. (2021b, 2 March). *A 'larger us' or 'them and us'*. Community Catalysts.

Crowther, N. (2021c, 23 March). *Anchored*. Retrieved 2 January 2023, from Making Rights Make Sense: https://makingrightsmakesense.wordpress.com/2021/03/26/anchored

Crowther, N. (2021d, 14 October). *Reframing dementia*. Retrieved 2 January 2023, from Making Rights Make Sense: https://makingrightsmakesense.wordpress.com/2021/10/14/reframing-dementia

Crowther, N. (2022a, 23 April). *With shared power comes shared responsibility*. Retrieved 11 June 2023, from Making Rights Make Sense: https://makingrightsmakesense.wordpress.com/2022/04/23/with-shared-power-comes-shared-responsibility

Crowther, N. (2022b, 4 November). *Prevention and intervention are both...* Retrieved 11 March 2023, from Twitter: https://twitter.com/neilmcrowther/status/1588481107997396992?s=20

Crowther, N. (2023a, 6 February). *The workforce being imagined is one for...* Retrieved 28 December 2023, from Twitter: https://twitter.com/neilmcrowther/status/1622568046995857413

Crowther, N. (2023b, 20 May). *@BryonyShannon nails it. We all have human needs...* Retrieved 4 February 2024, from Twitter: https://twitter.com/neilmcrowther/status/1659909697472716800?

Crowther, N. (2024, 18 February). *From closing down institutions to opening up communities*. Retrieved 22 February 2024, from Making Rights Make Sense: https://makingrightsmakesense.wordpress.com/2024/02/18/from-closing-down-institutions-to-opening-up-communities

Crowther, N. & Quinton, K. (2021, April). *How to build public support to transform social care: A practical guide for communicating about social care*. Retrieved 16 August 2023, from Social Care Future: https://socialcarefuture.org.uk/wp-content/uploads/2023/10/SCF-Building-Support-REPORT-h.pdf

Den Heijer, A. (n.d.). *Alexander Den Heijer > Quotes > Quotable Quote*. Retrieved 8 April 2023, from Good Reads: www.goodreads.com/quotes/8708203-when-a-flower-doesn-t-bloom-you-fix-the-environment-in

Department of Health. (1998). *Modernising Social Services*. Retrieved 22 February 2024, from The National Archives: https://webarchive.nationalarchives.gov.uk/ukgwa/20131205101158/http://www.archive.official-documents.co.uk/document/cm41/4169/4169.htm

Department of Health. (2007, 27 March). *Human Rights in Healthcare – A Framework for Local Action*. Retrieved 11 June 2023, from The National Archives: www.dh.gov.uk/en/Publicationsandstatistics/Publications/PublicationsPolicyAndGuidance/DH_073473

Department of Health and Social Care. (2000, 20 March). *No secrets*. Retrieved 20 August 2021, from GOV.UK: www.gov.uk/government/publications/no-secrets-guidance-on-protecting-vulnerable-adults-in-care

Department of Health and Social Care. (2017, 21 January). *Strengths-based social work practice with adults*. Retrieved 25 March 2023, from GOV.UK: www.gov.uk/government/publications/strengths-based-social-work-practice-with-adults

Department of Health and Social Care. (2018, 5 November). *Prevention is better than cure: our vision to help you live well for longer*. Retrieved 11 March 2023, from Department of Health and Social Care.

Department of Health and Social Care. (2019, 12 February). *Strengths-based social work: practice framework and handbook*. Retrieved 11 December 2021, from GOV.UK: www.gov.uk/government/publications/strengths-based-social-work-practice-framework-and-handbook

Department of Health and Social Care. (2020a, 27 April). *As of 9am 27 April, there have been 719,910 tests...* Retrieved 28 April 2020, from Twitter: https://twitter.com/DHSCgovuk/status/1254834459846811651?s=20

Department of Health and Social Care. (2020b, 9 June). *Health and Social Care Secretary's statement on coronavirus (COVID-19): 8 June 2020*. Retrieved 20 August 2021, from GOV.UK: www.gov.uk/government/speeches/health-and-social-care-secretarys-statement-on-coronavirus-covid-19-8-june-2020

Department of Health and Social Care. (2021, 9 February). *Public urged to consider work in adult social care*. Retrieved April 29, 2021, from GOV.UK: www.gov.uk/government/news/public-urged-to-consider-work-in-adult-social-care

Department of Health and Social Care. (2022, 18 March). *People at the Heart of Care: adult social care reform white paper*. Retrieved 11 March 2023, from Department of Health and Social Care: www.gov.uk/government/publications/people-at-the-heart-of-care-adult-social-care-reform-white-paper

Department of Health and Social Care. (2023, updated 19 January). *Care and support statutory guidance*. Retrieved from GOV.UK: www.gov.uk/government/publications/care-act-statutory-guidance/care-and-support-statutory-guidance

Duffy, S. (2010, 9 April). *The Future of Personalisation: Implications for welfare reform*. Retrieved 27 October 2024, from The Centre for Welfare Reform: https://citizen-network.org/library/future-of-personalisation.html

Duffy, S. (2015). *Customers or citizens*. Retrieved 27 September 2019, from Simon Duffy: https://simonduffy.info/blog/customers-or-citizens

Duffy, S. (2023, 6 June). *The path to community*. Retrieved 11 June 2023, from Citizen Network: https://citizen-network.org/library/the-path-to-community.html

Ellis Gray, H. (2023, 24 August). *Today in Stirling...* Retrieved 17 September 2023, from Twitter: https://x.com/hannah_ellis89/status/1694759638976065887?s=20

Equality and Human Rights Commission. (2009, 2 February). *From safety net to springboard: A new approach to care and support for all based on equality and human rights*. Retrieved 11 June 2023, from Equality and Human Rights Commission: www.equalityhumanrights.com/sites/default/files/from-safety-net-to-springboard-new-approach-to-care-and-support.pdf

Equality and Human Rights Commission. (2021, 12 May). *Strengthening the right to independent living*. Retrieved 29 April 2024, from Equality and Human Rights Commission: www.equalityhumanrights.com/human-rights/strengthening-right-independent-living

Etmanski, A. (2015, 23 June). *Slow change*. Retrieved 22 October 2022, from Al Etmanski: https://aletmanski.com/impact/slow-change

Farquharson, C. (2019, 10 May). *The care we want*. Retrieved 8 April 2023, from Think Local Act Personal: www.thinklocalactpersonal.org.uk/Blog/The-Care-We-Want

Fox, A. (2010, 6 December). *Social work chief talks about Shared Lives*. Retrieved 14 February 2020, from Escaping the invisible asylum: https://alexfoxblog.wordpress.com/2010/12/06/social-work-chief-talks-about-shared-lives

Fox, A. (2012, 15 March). *Ditch 'prevention'.* Retrieved 11 March 2023, from Escaping the Invisible Asylum: https://alexfoxblog.wordpress.com/2012/03/15/ditch-prevention

Fox, A. (2018). *A New Health and Care System: Escaping the Invisible Asylum.* Policy Press.

Fox, A. (2023, 23 June). *From strength to strength.* Retrieved 1 July 2023, from Escaping the Invisible Asylum: https://alexfoxblog.wordpress.com/2023/06/23/from-strength-to-strength

Goble, C. (2004). Dependence, Independence and Normality. In J. Swain, S. French, & C. Barnes (eds), *Disabling Barriers – Enabling Environments* (pp.41–46). Sage.

Grant, M. (2020, 28 March). *The PM can now say with conviction that we're all in this together.* Retrieved 18 December 2020, from The Telegraph: www.telegraph.co.uk/politics/2020/03/28/pm-can-now-say-conviction-together

Hammond, C. (2020, 22 January). *D for Diagnosis.* Retrieved 23 April 2022, from BBC: www.bbc.co.uk/programmes/m0007126

Hannan, R. (2019, October). *Radical home care: How self-management could save social care.* The RSA.

Hansard. (2021, 14 October). *Social Care in England – Volume 814.* Retrieved 24 September 2022, from UK Parliament: https://hansard.parliament.uk/Lords/2021-10-14/debates/DB7F5FAD-989B-4992-AA8F-DD5DEE049700/SocialCareInEngland

Hardy, R. (2017, 27 November). *Strengths-based questions for social work assessments.* Retrieved 11 December 2021, from Community Care: www.communitycare.co.uk/2017/11/27/strengths-based-questions-social-work-assessments-quick-tips

Harvey, M. (2020, 24 May). *Adult social work – 50 years young (and the Debate is only just starting).* Retrieved 31 May 2020, from Social Work, Cats and Rocket Science: https://socialworkcatsandrocketscience.com/2020/05/24/adult-social-work-50-years-young-and-the-debate-is-only-just-starting

Hasler, F. (2004). Disability, Care and Controlling Services. In J. Swain, S. French, & C. Barnes (eds), *Disabling Barriers – Enabling Environments.* Sage.

Hilton, E. (2023, 26 January). *On bumpy but exciting starts, relationships and complexity.* Retrieved 25 March 2023, from Platfform: https://platfform.org/blog/on-bumpy-but-exciting-starts-relationships-and-complexity

HM Government. (2014). *Children and Families Act 2014.* Retrieved 13 August 2023, from Legislation.gov.uk: www.legislation.gov.uk/ukpga/2014/6/contents

Holmes, P. (2023a, 20 May). *[I] believe it's also possible to flip our practice within the existing legal framework...* Retrieved 11 June 2023, from Twitter: https://twitter.com/PhilHolmesPPF/status/1659895114565550082?s=20.

Holmes, P. (2023b, 25 November). *'You've got to have a system'.* Retrieved 2 January 2024, from Public Service Blogcasting: https://publicserviceblogcasting.wordpress.com/2023/11/25/youve-got-to-have-a-system

hooks, b. (2016). *All About Love: New Visions – Love Song to the Nation 1.* Harper Collins.

Hosali, S. (2020, 2 April). *The fight against Covid-19: Whose life counts?* The British Institute of Human Rights.

House of Commons. (2020, 9 June). *Health and Social Care Committee Oral evidence: Management of the coronavirus outbreak, HC 206.* Retrieved 20

August 2022, from UK Parliament: https://committees.parliament.uk/oralevidence/482/html

House of Lords Adult Social Care Committee. (2022, 21 March). *Corrected oral evidence: Adult Social Care*. Retrieved 22 February 2024, from UK Parliament: https://committees.parliament.uk/oralevidence/9969/pdf

Humphries, R. (2022). *Ending the Social Care Crisis: A New Road to Reform*. Policy Press.

Hyatt, T. (2018). *What does the British public think when they hear the words 'social care'?* Social Care Future.

Independent Care Review. (2020, July). *Evidence Framework Feb 2017 – Feb 2020*. Retrieved 1 January 2023, from Independent Care Review: www.carereview.scot/wp-content/uploads/2020/07/ICR_Evidence_Framework_v2-1.pdf

International Federation of Social Workers. (2014, July). *Global definition of social work*. Retrieved 11 June 2023, from International Federation of Social Workers: www.ifsw.org/what-is-social-work/global-definition-of-social-work

ITV (Producer). (2024). *Kate Garraway: Derek's Story* [Motion Picture]. Retrieved 29 March 2024, from www.itv.com/watch/kate-garraway-dereks-story/10a1610/10a4482a0001

ITV News. (2019, 25 December). *Small steps can bring lasting change in the world, the Queen says in her Christmas Day message*. Retrieved 22 October 2022, from ITV News: www.itv.com/news/2019-12-25/small-steps-can-bring-lasting-change-in-the-world-the-queen-says-in-her-christmas-day-message

ITV News. (2020, 22 April). *Coronavirus will affect everyday life for 'really quite a long time' Professor Whitty says*. Retrieved 20 August 2021, from ITV News: www.itv.com/news/2020-04-22/government-daily-coronavirus-update-dominic-raab

Jackson, J. et al. (2020, April). *The lockdown and social norms: why the UK is complying by consent rather than compulsion*. Retrieved 18 December 2020, from LSE Blogs: https://blogs.lse.ac.uk/politicsandpolicy/lockdown-social-norms

James, E., Mitchell, R., & Morgan, H. (2019). *Social Work, Cats and Rocket Science: Stories of Making a Difference in Social Work with Adults*. Jessica Kingsley Publishers.

Leedham, M. (2023, 12 October). *How negative perceptions of social workers are reinforced in the media*. Retrieved 28 December 2023, from Community Care: www.communitycare.co.uk/2023/10/12/how-negative-perceptions-of-social-workers-are-reinforced-in-the-media

Local Authority X v MM & Anor (No. 1) [2007] EWHC 2003 (Fam). (2007, 21 August). Retrieved 11 June 2023, from Bailii: www.bailii.org/ew/cases/EWHC/Fam/2007/2003.html

Loomes-Quinn, G. (2018, 9 April). *What you can't know...* Retrieved 20 December 2019, from Twitter: https://twitter.com/GillLoomesQuinn/status/983424200596709382

Lowe, T. (2021, 24 February). *What is 'community' and why is it important?* Retrieved 26 November 2023, from Centre for Public Impact: https://medium.com/centre-for-public-impact/what-is-community-2e895219a205

Maguire, S. (2020, 7 April). *When is your home not a home?* Retrieved 10 October 2020, from Choice Support: www.choicesupport.org.uk/about-us/blog/when-is-your-home-not-a-home

Maitlis, E. (2020, 9 April). *Coronavirus: They tell us it's a great leveller... it's not*. Retrieved 18 December 2020, from YouTube: www.youtube.com/watch?v=L6wlcpdJyCI

Marriott, A. (2019, 17 June). *Supporting people with learning disabilities to have positive sexual relationships*. Retrieved 14 February 2020, from RiPfA: www.researchinpractice.org.uk/adults/news-views/2019/june/supporting-people-with-learning-disabilities-to-have-positive-sexual-relationships

McGarvey, D. (2018, 22 December). *Many rough sleepers...* Retrieved 10 October 2020, from Twitter: https://twitter.com/lokiscottishrap/status/10765 69147272818688?

McLaughlin, H. (2009). What's in a Name: 'Client', 'Patient', 'Customer', 'Consumer', 'Expert by Experience', 'Service User' – What's Next? *The British Journal of Social Work*, 39(6). Retrieved 22 February 2024, from https://academic.oup.com/bjsw/article/39/6/1101/1677129

McPherson, J. (2020). Now Is the Time for a Rights-Based Approach to Social Work Practice. *Journal of Human Rights and Social Work* (3 June 2020).

Mental Deficiency Act 1913. (1913). Retrieved 14 February 2023, from Education in the UK: https://education-uk.org/documents/acts/1913-mental-deficiency-act.html

Merriam-Webster. (n.d.). *Can 'other' be used as a verb?* Retrieved 2 January 2023, from Merriam-Webster: www.merriam-webster.com/wordplay/other-as-a-verb

Merriam-Webster. (n.d.). *Care*. Retrieved 12 August 2023, from Merriam-Webster: www.merriam-webster.com/dictionary/care

Merriam-Webster. (n.d.). *Challenge*. Retrieved 21 March 2025, from Merriam-Webster: www.merriam-webster.com/dictionary/challenge

Merriam-Webster. (n.d.). *Client*. Retrieved 23 September 2023, from Merriam-Webster: www.merriam-webster.com/dictionary/client

Merriam-Webster. (n.d.). *Engagement*. Retrieved 1 July 2023, from Merriam-Webster: www.merriam-webster.com/dictionary/engagement

Merriam-Webster. (n.d.). *Frontline*. Retrieved 29 May 2021, from Merriam-Webster: www.merriam-webster.com/dictionary/frontline

Mind. (n.d.). *Mental health facts and statistics*. Retrieved 20 May 2023, from Mind: Mental health facts and statistics: www.mind.org.uk/information-support/types-of-mental-health-problems/statistics-and-facts-about-mental-health/how-common-are-mental-health-problems

Mitchell, R. (2016, 24 September). *Someone to Safeguard*. Retrieved 15 March 2025, from Social Work, Cats and Rocket Science: https://socialworkcatsandrocketscience.com/2016/09/24/someone-to-safeguard

Mitchell, R. (2018, 10 February). *For the Valentines I never knew*. Retrieved 14 February 2020, from Social Work, Cats and Rocket Science: https://lastquangoinhalifax.wordpress.com/2018/02/10/for-the-valentines-i-never-knew

Mitchell, R. (2021, 12 May). *It isn't patient, or service user, or client or customer...* Retrieved 27 April 2024, from Twitter: https://twitter.com/RobMitch92/status/1392347844129050624

Mitchell, R. (2022, 30 April). *Here's a social work trap...* Retrieved 3 March 2024, from Twitter: https://twitter.com/RobMitch92/status/1520349506319040514?

Mitchell, R. (2023, 4 August). *A few years old now is the Munby quote...* Retrieved 3 March 2024, from Twitter: https://twitter.com/RobMitch92/status/1687362694674894848

Mitchell, W. (2018). *Somebody I Used to Know*. Bloomsbury..

Mitchell, W. (2020, September). *The changing conversations around social care*. Retrieved 18 December 2020, from Which Me Am I today?: https://

whichmeamitoday.wordpress.com/2020/09/09/the-changing-conversations-around-social-care

Mitchell, W. (n.d.). *Which me am I today?* Retrieved 17 March 2024, from Which Me Am I today?: https://whichmeamitoday.wordpress.com

Money Advice Service. (n.d.). *How a local authority care needs assessment works.* Retrieved 6 September 2019, from Money Advice Service: www.moneyadviceservice.org.uk/en/articles/how-a-local-authority-care-needs-assessment-works

Moore, C. (2022, 16 December). *Inclusion should accept and celebrate differences...* Retrieved 2 January 2023, from Twitter: https://twitter.com/DrChrisMooreEP/status/1603822652229025801

Morris, J. (1993). *Independent Lives? Community Care and Disabled People.* Macmillan.

Morris, J. (2013, 12 September). *Welfare reform and the social model of disability.* Retrieved 1 September 2023, from Jenny Morris: https://jennymorrisnet.blogspot.com/2013/09/welfare-reform-and-social-model-of.html

Morris, J. (2014, 22 September). *'Independence.'* Retrieved 1 April 2024, from Jenny Morris: https://jennymorrisnet.blogspot.com/2014/09/independence.html

Morris, J. (2018, June). *Communication: Everyone's human right.* Retrieved 23 April 2022, from The Rightfullives Exhibition: https://rightfullives.net/Stories/Communication-and-rights.html

National Assistance Act, 1948. (1948). Retrieved 3 January 2024, from Legislation. gov.uk: www.legislation.gov.uk/ukpga/1948/29/pdfs/ukpga_19480029_en.pdf

National Development Team for Inclusion. (2017, 11 July). *Round Table Discussion Notes: Care Act (2014) – Assessments and Effective Conversations.* Retrieved 27 July 2019, from NDTI: www.ndti.org.uk/assets/files/Round_Table_Discussion_Notes_-_Effective_Conversations_and_the_Care_Act.pdf

Naylor, C. *et al.* (2012, 9 February). *Long-term conditions and mental health: the cost of co-morbidities.* Retrieved 2 March 2025, from The King's Fund. www.kingsfund.org.uk/insight-and-analysis/reports/long-term-conditions-mental-health

Naysmith, S. (2018, 28 April). *Children in care singled out for speaking social work jargon, review chief warns.* Retrieved 2 January 2023, from The Herald: www.heraldscotland.com/news/16190390.children-care-singled-speaking-social-work-jargon-review-chief-warns

Neary, M. (2014, 13 April). *Carespeak & care plans.* Retrieved 19 November 2023, from Love, Belief and Balls: https://markneary1dotcom1.wordpress.com/2014/04/13/carespeak-care-plans

Neary, M. (2015, 25 February). *Paraphrasing Princess Di.* Retrieved 20 December 2019, from Love, Belief and Balls: https://markneary1dotcom1.wordpress.com/2015/02/24/paraphrasing-princess-di

Neary, M. (2016a, 1 January). *Measurable outcomes.* Retrieved 11 December 2021, from Love, Belief and Balls: https://markneary1dotcom1.wordpress.com/2016/01/01/measurable-outcomes

Neary, M. (2016b, 5 August). *The cliff edge.* Retrieved 6 September 2019, from Love, Belief and Balls: https://markneary1dotcom1.wordpress.com/2016/08/05/the-cliff-edge

Neary, M. (2017, 12 July). *A new conversation.* Retrieved 20 May 2023, from Love, Belief and Balls: https://markneary1dotcom1.wordpress.com/2017/07/12/a-new-conversation

Neary, M. (2018, 2 December). *The words on the tin*. Retrieved 14 February 2023, from Love, Belief and Balls: https://marknearyɪdotcomɪ.wordpress. com/2018/12/02/the-words-on-the-tin

Neary, M. (n.d.). *Parley Vouz Health & Social Care? (An A to Z of Carespeak)*. Retrieved 20 May 2023, from Love, Belief and Balls: https://marknearyɪdotcomɪ.wordpress.com/parley-vouz-health-social-care-an-a-to-z-of-carespeak

New York Times. (2008, 5 February). *Barack Obama's Feb. 5 Speech*. Retrieved 22 October 2022, from New York Times: www.nytimes.com/2008/02/05/us/ politics/05text-obama.html

NHS. (n.d.). *Care after illness or hospital discharge (reablement)*. Retrieved 26 April 2024, from NHS: www.nhs.uk/conditions/social-care-and-support-guide/care-after-a-hospital-stay/care-after-illness-or-hospital-discharge-reablement

NHS Digital. (2022, 8 March). *Short and Long Term (SALT) Data Return 2021-22 guidance*. Retrieved 20 August 2022, from NHS Digital: https://digital.nhs. uk/data-and-information/data-collections-and-data-sets/data-collections/ social-care-collection-materials-2022/salt-data-return-2021-2022-guidance

Nicoll, T. (2021, 31 May). Tricia Nicoll – Workforce. In Control Partnerships. Retrieved 29 December 2023, from YouTube: www.youtube.com/ watch?v=rATuP6nq8BU

Nicoll, T. (2023). *Why it matters*. Retrieved 27 April 2024, from Gloriously Ordinary Lives: www.gloriouslyordinarylives.co.uk/why-it-matters

Nicoll, T. (2024). *The five tests*. Retrieved 21 September 2024, from Gloriously Ordinary Lives: www.gloriouslyordinarylives.co.uk/the-five-tests

Office for Health Improvement & Disparities. (2022, 29 March). *Vulnerabilities: applying All Our Health*. Retrieved 13 August 2023, from GOV.UK: www. gov.uk/government/publications/vulnerabilities-applying-all-our-health/ vulnerabilities-applying-all-our-health

Office for National Statistics. (2022, 2 November). *Voices of our ageing population: Living longer lives*. Retrieved 20 May 2023, from Office for National Statistics: www.ons.gov.uk/peoplepopulationandcommunity/ birthsdeathsandmarriages/ageing/articles/voicesofourageingpopulation/ livinglongerlives

Office for National Statistics. (2023, 19 January). *Disability, England and Wales: Census 2021, Office for National Statistics, 19 January 2023*. Retrieved 20 May 2023, from Office for National Statistics: www.ons.gov.uk/peoplepopula-tionandcommunity/healthandsocialcare/healthandwellbeing/bulletins/ disabilityenglandandwales/census2021

Oliffe, D. (2021, November). *Safe waiting*. Retrieved 27 August 2022, from Local Area Coordination Network: www.communitycatalysts.co.uk/lacnetwork/ safe-waiting

Oliver, M. (1990). *The Politics of Disablement*. Macmillan.

Open Future Learning. (2023, 22 October). *Is this an institution?* Retrieved 19 April 2024, from Open Future Learning: www.openfuturelearning.org/blog/index. php/is-it-an-institution

Open Future Learning. (2024). *Man w/ developmental disability will not bathe*. Retrieved 15 March 2025, from https://youtu.be/oARSsYr32Y0?si=_ VsUɪ9YCTrtVvHUL

O'Shea, P., Cohen, E., Hestres, E., & Miller, T. (2023, 1 August). *Communicating about Disability in Australia*. Retrieved 7 January 2024, from

Frameworks Institute: www.frameworksinstitute.org/publication/communicating-about-disability-in-australia

Oxford Languages. (n.d.). *Caring*. Retrieved 4 February 2024, from Google: www.google.com/search?q=define+caring

Oxford Languages. (n.d.). *Front line*. Retrieved 29 May 2021, from Google: www.google.com/search?q=define:frontline

Oxford Languages. (n.d.). *Practice*. Retrieved 4 November 2023, from Google: www.google.com/search?q=practice

Oxford Languages. (n.d.). *Respite*. Retrieved 21 March 2025, from Google: www.google.co.uk/search?q=define+respite

Oxford Languages. (n.d.). *Vulnerable*. Retrieved 21 March 2025, from Google: www.google.co.uk/search?q=define+vulnerable

Oxford Learner's Dictionaries. (n.d.). *Individual*. Retrieved 3 February 2024, from Oxford Learner's Dictionaries: www.oxfordlearnersdictionaries.com/definition/english/individual_1

Oxford Reference. (n.d.). *Othering*. Retrieved 23 January 2023, from Oxford Reference: www.oxfordreference.com/display/10.1093/acref/9780191834837.001.0001/acref-9780191834837-e-283

Parker, S. (2019, 5 December). *Love in action: a force for social justice*. Retrieved 21 February 2020, from Sophia Parker: https://medium.com/@sophiaparker_241/love-in-action-a-force-for-social-justice-416cf27ee28a

Passing the Message Stick. (2021). *Full guide – Passing the Message Stick: A guide for changing the story on self-determination and justice*. Retrieved 22 October 2022, from Passing the Message Stick: https://indd.adobe.com/embed/2dee7279-22dc-41e3-99c7-c5fe016f32fb

Patel, l. (2022, 7 September). *I don't feel the emphasis on fixing is right...* Retrieved 24 September 2022, from Twitter: https://twitter.com/Haloabletec/status/1567470749685784576?s

Pierre, R. (2023, 2 February). *You can't raise children on the cheap, so why is this government set on doing so?* Retrieved 14 February 2023, from The Guardian: www.theguardian.com/commentisfree/2023/feb/02/children-care-leaver-social-worker-tories

Pierre, R. (ed.). (2024). *Free loaves on Fridays: the care system as told by people who actually get it*. Unbound.

Pitts, J. (2018, 15 March). *Release social workers to do what they do best*. Retrieved 6 September 2019, from Social Care Future.

Potts, M. (2020, 21 May). *Bad kindness*. Retrieved 21 January 2024, from YouTube: www.youtube.com/watch?v=BAk6R4P5mOc&t=208s

Potts, M. (2021a, 4 May). *Why we dread Mental Health Awareness Week every year*. Retrieved 2 January 2023, from Camerados: https://camerados.medium.com/why-we-dread-mental-health-awareness-week-every-year-efd2f4e94484

Potts, M. (2021b, 7 September). *Been hearing stories of what real world changing work looks like...* Retrieved 2 March 2024, from Twitter: https://twitter.com/MaffPotts/status/1435187078510391306?

Potts, M. (2025). *Friends and Purpose: Stories From Sofas on Streets and Some Confounding Ideas for Tough Times*. Gometra Press.

powell, j. a. (2017, 8 November). *Us vs them: the sinister techniques of 'Othering' – and how to avoid them*. Retrieved 2 January 2023, from The Guardian: www.theguardian.com/inequality/2017/nov/08/us-vs-them-the-sinister-techniques-of-othering-and-how-to-avoid-them

Prime Minister's Office, 10 Downing Street and The Rt Hon Boris Johnson. (2019, 24 July). *Boris Johnson's first speech as Prime Minister: 24 July 2019*. Retrieved 16 August 2019, from GOV.UK: www.gov.uk/government/speeches/boris-johnsons-first-speech-as-prime-minister-24-july-2019

Prime Minister's Office, 10 Downing Street and The Rt Hon Boris Johnson MP. (2020a, 17 March). *Prime Minister's statement on coronavirus (COVID-19): 17 March 2020*. Retrieved 28 April 2020, from GOV.UK: www.gov.uk/government/speeches/pm-statement-on-coronavirus-17-march-2020

Prime Minister's Office, 10 Downing Street and The Rt Hon Boris Johnson MP. (2020b, 22 March). *PM Mother's Day words: 22 March 2020*. Retrieved 18 December 2020, from GOV.UK: www.gov.uk/government/speeches/pm-mothers-day-words-22-march-2020

Prime Minister's Office, 10 Downing Street and The Rt Hon Boris Johnson MP. (2020c, 23 March). *Prime Minister's statement on coronavirus (COVID-19): 23 March 2020*. Retrieved 18 December 2020, from GOV.UK: www.gov.uk/government/speeches/pm-address-to-the-nation-on-coronavirus-23-march-2020

Prime Minister's Office, 10 Downing Street and The Rt Hon Boris Johnson MP. (2022, 6 September). *Boris Johnson's final speech as Prime Minister: 6 September 2022*. Retrieved 24 September 2022, from GOV.UK: www.gov.uk/government/speeches/boris-johnsons-final-speech-as-prime-minister-6-september-2022

Public Health England. (2020, 12 November). *People with learning disabilities had higher death rate from COVID-19*. Retrieved 15 November 2020, from GOV.UK: www.gov.uk/government/news/people-with-learning-disabilities-had-higher-death-rate-from-covid-19

Quinn, A. (2022, 14 April). *The problem with behaviour support – Alexis Quinn*. Retrieved 23 April 2022, from YouTube: www.youtube.com/watch?v=I5iywkTlPmQ

Rapoport, L. (1961). The concept of prevention in social work. *Social Work*, 6(1). Retrieved 11 March 2023, from www.jstor.org/stable/23708392

Reclaiming Our Futures Alliance. (2019, June). *Independent Living for the Future*. Retrieved 2 April 2024, from Inclusion London: www.inclusionlondon.org.uk/wp-content/uploads/2019/06/NILSS_final.pdf

Renke, S. (2021, 2 February). *I don't want to be your inspiration porn*. Retrieved 15 January 2024, from Metro: https://metro.co.uk/2021/02/02/i-dont-want-to-be-your-inspiration-porn-13991239

Rewilding Britain. (n.d.). *Rewilding Britain*. Retrieved 8 April 2023, from Rewilding Britain: www.rewildingbritain.org.uk

Roberts, L. *et al.* (2020, 8 April). *Boris Johnson 'is a fighter' and will be back at the helm to lead us through coronavirus crisis, Dominic Raab says*. Retrieved 28 April 2020, from The Telegraph: www.telegraph.co.uk/global-health/science-and-disease/coronavirus-news-latest-uk-cases-covid-19-boris-johnson-updates

Robins, S. (2020a, 21 September). *People are not numbers*. Retrieved 15 November 2020, from Sue Robins: www.suerobins.com/post/people-are-not-numbers

Robins, S. (2020b). *Ducks in a Row*. Bird Communications.

Routledge, M. (2022, 25 July). *Social care and the leadership contest: what next?* Retrieved 22 October 2022, from The MJ: www.themj.co.uk/Social-care-and-the-leadership-contest-what-next/223779

Runswick-Cole, K. (2019, 8 November). *If you don't use their language...* Retrieved 20 December 2019, from Twitter: https://twitter.com/k_runswick_cole/status/1192803008150683649?s=20

Russell, C. (2020). *Rekindling Democracy: The Professional's Guide to Working in Citizen Space*. Cascade Books.

Russell, C. (2022, 16 April). *Again look at the question: 'how do we get people to engage?'...* Retrieved 23 April 2022, from Twitter: https://twitter.com/CormacRussell/status/1515378190998515714

Ryan, F. (2020, 11 March). *Coronavirus hits ill and disabled people hardest, so why is society writing us off?* Retrieved 15 November 2020, from The Guardian: www.theguardian.com/commentisfree/2020/mar/11/coronavirus-ill-disabled-people

Ryan, S. (2018). *Justice for Laughing Boy: Connor Sparrowhawk – A Death by Indifference*. Jessica Kingsley Publishers.

Ryan, S. (2021). *Love, Learning Disabilities and Pockets of Brilliance*. Jessica Kingsley Publishers.

Salman, S. (2019a, 30 October). *'It's a human right': the campaign for learning disabled people's love lives*. Retrieved 14 February 2020, from The Guardian: www.theguardian.com/society/2019/oct/30/campaign-for-learning-disabled-peoples-love-lives

Salman, S. (2019b, 4 June). *Sheila Hollins: 'People with learning disabilities must be put at the centre of their care'*. Retrieved 3 December 2023, from The Guardian: www.theguardian.com/society/2019/jun/04/sheila-hollins-learning-disability-care

Saltmarshe, E. (2018, 20 February). *Using Story to Change Systems*. Retrieved 22 October 2022, from Stanford Social Innovation Review: https://doi.org/10.48558/4FVN-0333

Schnall, M. (2009, 17 February). *An Interview With Maya Angelou*. Retrieved 20 January 2024, from Psychology Today: www.psychologytoday.com/intl/blog/the-guest-room/200902/interview-maya-angelou

Schraer, R. (2013, 23 July). *'Social work is a human rights discipline': IFSW president speaks up for the profession*. Retrieved 11 June 2023, from Community Care: www.communitycare.co.uk/2014/07/23/social-work-human-rights-discipline-ifsw-president-speaks-profession

SEIN. (2024, 8 April). *Disability Awareness Training: Addressing attitudinal barriers*. Retrieved 4 May 2024, from SEIN: www.seinglasgow.org.uk/blog/disability-awareness-training-addressing-attitudinal-barriers

Series, L. (2015, 18 February). *A stupid question about supported living*. Retrieved 3 April 2024, from The Small Places: https://thesmallplaces.wordpress.com/2015/02/18/a-stupid-question-about-supported-living

Severwright, A. (2021). *Opinion: We are so much more*. Community Catalysts.

Shafak, E. (2022). *The Island of Missing Trees*. Penguin.

Sharp, J. (2024, 25 April). *When I say I want independence...* Retrieved 26 April 2024, from Twitter: https://twitter.com/juliesharp86/status/1783440801193775309

Shetty, S. (2017, 22 February). *'Politics of demonization' breeding division and fear*. Retrieved 11 June 2023, from Amnesty International: www.amnesty.org/en/latest/press-release/2017/02/amnesty-international-annual-report-201617

Sibthorp, K. (2019, 8 February). *What does Making it Real have to say about Valentine's Day?* Retrieved 14 February 2020, from Think Local Act Personal: www.thinklocalactpersonal.org.uk/Blog/What-does-Making-it-Real-have-to-say-about-Valentines-day-

Sinek, S. (2020, 2 September). *Trust is built on telling the truth...* Retrieved 26 January 2024, from Twitter: https://twitter.com/simonsinek/status/1301217570687799296

Skills for Care. (2018). *Using conversations to assess and plan people's care and support: The principles of conversational assessment.* Retrieved 6 September 2019, from Skills for Care: www.skillsforcare.org.uk/resources/documents/Support-for-leaders-and-managers/Managing-a-service/Community-Asset-and-strength-based-approaches/Using-conversations-to-assess-and-plan-peoples-care-and-support.pdf

Skills for Care. (2023, October). *The state of the adult social care sector and workforce in England.* Retrieved 21 May 2024, from Skills for Care: www.skillsforcare.org.uk/Adult-Social-Care-Workforce-Data/Workforce-intelligence/publications/national-information/The-state-of-the-adult-social-care-sector-and-work force-in-England.aspx

Skills for Care. (n.d.). *Person-centred and community based working (strength-based approach).* Retrieved 11 December 2021, from Skills for Care: www.skillsforcare.org.uk/resources/documents/Support-for-leaders-and-managers/Workforce-commissioning-planning/Quality-of-care/Community-asset-and-strength-based-working/Person-centred-and-community-based-working-strength-based-approach-guide.pdf

Sky News. (2020, 27 March). *Coronavirus: 'Virus does not discriminate' – Gove.* Retrieved 18 December 2020, from Sky News: https://news.sky.com/video/coronavirus-virus-does-not-discriminate-gove-11964771

Smith, M. A. (2022a, 10 July). *So someone with over 300 offences in his life story...* Retrieved 27 August 2022, from Twitter: https://twitter.com/MarkAdamSmith/status/1545912478558715906?s=20

Smith, M. A. (2022b, 10 August). *Eligibility criteria – what if we just turned them off?* Retrieved 27 August 2022, from Changing Futures Northumbria: www.changingfuturesnorthumbria.co.uk/eligibility-criteria-what-if-we-just-turned-them-off

Social Care Future. (2019, 31 October). *Talking about a brighter social care future.* Retrieved 27 October 2024, from Social Care Future: https://socialcarefuture.org.uk/talking-about-a-brighter-social-care-future

Social Care Future. (2023, October). *Building public support for a brighter social care future in 5 easy reframes – quick read.* Retrieved 23 December 2023, from Social Care Future: https://socialcarefuture.org.uk/noticeboard/building-public-support-for-a-brighter-social-care-future-in-5-easy-reframes-quick-read

Social Care Future. (2023, October). *The #SocialCareFuture gathering 2023.* Retrieved 3 January 2024, from Social Care Future: https://socialcarefuture.org.uk/noticeboard/the-socialcarefuture-gathering-2023

Social Care Future. (2024, February). *Living good lives in the place we call home – An outline programme for the next government.* Retrieved 3 March 2024, from Social Care Future: https://socialcarefuture.org.uk/noticeboard/living-good-lives-in-the-place-we-call-home-an-outline-programme-for-the-next-government

Social Care Future. (n.d.). *Social Care Future.* Retrieved November 2023, from Social Care Future: https://socialcarefuture.org.uk

Social Care Institute for Excellence. (2015, March). *Care Act guidance on strengths-based approaches.* Retrieved 11 December 2021, from Social Care Institute for Excellence: www.scie.org.uk/strengths-based-approaches/guidance

Social Care Institute for Excellence. (2021a, May). *Prevention in social care.* Retrieved 11 March 2023, from Social Care Institute for Excellence: www.scie.org.uk/integrated-care/prevention-in-social-care

Social Care Institute for Excellence. (2021b, 15 June). *Webinar: Developing strengths-based places – the next steps for strengths-based practice*. Retrieved 11 December 2021, from Social Care Institute for Excellence: www.scie.org.uk/strengths-based-approaches/webinar20210615

Social Care Institute for Excellence. (2022, September). *Strengths-based approach training course*. Retrieved 29 October 2023, from Social Care Institute for Excellence: www.scie.org.uk/training/culture-change/strengths-based-approach

Social Work England. (2024, 18 March). *The social work workforce*. Retrieved 18 March 2024, from Social Work England: www.socialworkengland.org.uk/about/publications/the-social-work-workforce

Social Workers Union. (2022). *Media reporting guidelines for cases involving social workers*. Retrieved 28 December 2023, from Social Workers Union: www.impress.press/wp-content/uploads/2022/12/media-guidelines-for-reporting-on-social-workers.pdf

Stillman, D. (2022, 6 June). *Minimum Viable Transformation: How many people does it take to change a culture?* Retrieved 25 March 2023, from Daniel Stillman: https://daniel-stillman.medium.com/minimum-viable-transformation-6016919f6700

Surviving Safeguarding. (2018, 10 May). *Divisive, demeaning and devoid of feeling: How social work jargon causes problems for families*. Retrieved 2 January 2023, from Community Care: www.communitycare.co.uk/2018/05/10/divisive-demeaning-devoid-feeling-social-work-jargon-causes-problems-families

Sutton, J. (2014, 19 February). *Striving: A right, a responsibility and a risk*. Retrieved 11 December 2021, from Authors of Our Lives: https://theindependentlivingdebate.wordpress.com/2014/02/19/striving-a-right-a-responsibility-and-a-risk

Taylor, P. (2019, 12 December). *The problem with seeing people as vulnerable*. Retrieved 14 August 2023, from Paul Taylor: https://paulitaylor.com/2019/12/20/the-problem-with-seeing-people-as-vulnerable

Taylor, P. (2020, 25 June). *The regressive power of labelling people as vulnerable*. Retrieved 14 August 2023, from Paul Taylor: https://paulitaylor.com/2020/06/25/the-regressive-power-of-labelling-people-as-vulnerable

The Guardian. (2020, 28 April). *Care home fatalities to be included in daily coronavirus death tolls*. Retrieved 14 August 2023, from The Guardian: www.theguardian.com/world/2020/apr/28/uk-records-4343-care-home-coronavirus-deaths-in-a-fortnight

The King's Fund. (1980, February). *An ordinary life: Comprehensive locally-based residential services for mentally handicapped people*. Retrieved 22 February 2024, from The King's Fund Digital Archive: https://archive.kingsfund.org.uk/concern/published_works/000001408?locale=pt-BR#

Think Local Act Personal. (2016). *Developing a wellbeing and strengths-based approach to social work practice: Changing culture*. Retrieved 11 December 2021, from Think Local Act Personal: www.thinklocalactpersonal.org.uk/Latest/Developing-a-Wellbeing-and-Strengths-based-Approach-to-Social-Work-Practice-Changing-Culture

Think Local Act Personal. (2018). *Making It Real: How to do personalised care and support*. Retrieved 8 April 2023, from Think Local Act Personal: https://thinklocalactpersonal.org.uk/our-hubs/making-it-real

Trump, D. (2020, 6 April). *President @realDonaldTrump on British Prime Minister...* Retrieved 28 April 2020, from Twitter: https://twitter.com/realDailyWire/status/1246952092037574656

TUC. (2020, 7 September). *Fixing social care*. Retrieved 29 April 2021, from TUC: www.tuc.org.uk/research-analysis/reports/fixing-social-care

Tulloch, G., & Schulman, S. (2020). *The Trampoline Effect: Redesigning Our Social Safety Nets*. Reach Press.

Tutu, D. (1999). *No Future Without Forgiveness*. Rider.

Unison. (2020, 24 June). *A national care service is the only way to prevent more deaths*. Retrieved 29 April 2021, from Unison: www.unison.org.uk/news/2020/06/national-care-service-way-prevent-deaths

United Nations. (2006). *Convention on the Rights of Persons with Disabilities (CRPD)*. Retrieved 29 December 2023, from United Nations: https://social.desa.un.org/issues/disability/crpd/convention-on-the-rights-of-persons-with-disabilities-crpd

United Nations. (n.d.). *Building on the Legacy of Nelson Mandela*. Retrieved 11 June 2023, from United Nations: www.un.org/en/exhibits/page/building-legacy-nelson-mandela

Unwin, J. (2018). *Kindness, emotions and human relationships: The blind spot in public policy*. Retrieved 21 January 2024, from Carnegie UK Trust: https://carnegieuktrust.org.uk/publications/kindness-emotions-and-human-relationships-the-blind-spot-in-public-policy

Unwin, S. (2022, 2 July). *Need, not diagnosis: Towards a more realistic language and understanding*. Retrieved 14 February 2023, from Stephen Unwin: www.stephenunwin.uk/thoughts-and-provocations/2022/7/2/need-not-diagnosis-towards-a-more-realistic-language-and-understanding

Viki. (2020, 19 April). *Met with a yr10 boy last week*. Retrieved 13 August 2023, from Twitter: https://twitter.com/viki9801588/status/1251840683780046848

Vocabulary.com. (n.d.). *Transformation*. Retrieved 25 March 2023, from Vocabulary.com: www.vocabulary.com/dictionary/transformation

Warren, S. (2019, 31 July). *Social care funding reform: More haste, less speed*. Retrieved 16 August 2019, from The King's Fund: www.kingsfund.org.uk/blog/2019/07/social-care-funding-reform

White, A. (2020, 23 March). *Coronavirus: Madonna calls pandemic 'the great equaliser' in bizarre nude bathtub video*. Retrieved 18 December 2020, from Independent: www.independent.co.uk/arts-entertainment/music/news/madonna-coronavirus-nude-bathtub-covid-19-instagram-fried-fish-a9417441.html

Williams, R. (n.d.). *To be truly radical...* Retrieved 24 September 2022, from Goodreads: www.goodreads.com/quotes/221182-to-be-truly-radical-is-to-make-hope-possible-rather

Winman, S. (2017). *A Year of Marvellous Ways*. Headline.

World Health Organization. (2020, 23 April). *Statement – Invest in the overlooked and unsung: Build sustainable people-centred long-term care in the wake of COVID-19*. Retrieved 14 August 2023, from World Health Organization: www.who.int/europe/news/item/23-04-2020-statement-invest-in-the-overlooked-and-unsung-build-sustainable-people-centred-long-term-care-in-the-wake-of-covid-19

Wren. (2021, 22 August). *Mental Health Clinical Notes: The Curse of the Paper-Self*. Retrieved 23 April 2022, from Psychiatry Is Driving Me Mad: www.psychiatryisdrivingmemad.co.uk/post/mental-health-clinical-notes-the-curse-of-the-paper-self

Young, S. (2012, 2 July). *We're not here for your inspiration*. Retrieved 15 January 2024, from ABC: www.abc.net.au/rampup/articles/2012/07/02/3537035.htm

Index

RAISING READERS
Books Build Bright Futures

Dear Reader,

We'd love your attention for one more page to tell you about the crisis in children's reading, and what we can all do.

Studies have shown that reading for fun is the **single biggest predictor of a child's future life chances** – more than family circumstance, parents' educational background or income. It improves academic results, mental health, wealth, communication skills, ambition and happiness.[1]

The number of children reading for fun is in rapid decline. Young people have a lot of competition for their time. In 2024, 1 in 10 children and young people in the UK aged 5 to 18 did not own a single book at home.[2]

Hachette works extensively with schools, libraries and literacy charities, but here are some ways we can all raise more readers:

- Reading to children for just 10 minutes a day makes a difference
- Don't give up if children aren't regular readers – there will be books for them!
- Visit bookshops and libraries to get recommendations
- Encourage them to listen to audiobooks
- Support school libraries
- Give books as gifts

There's a lot more information about how to encourage children to read on our website: **www.RaisingReaders.co.uk**

Thank you for reading.

hachette
UK

---

1   National Literacy Trust, 'Book Ownership in 2024', November 2024, https://literacytrust.org.uk/research-services/research-reports/book-ownership-in-2024
2   OECD, '21st-Century Readers: Developing Literacy Skills in a Digital World', OECD Publishing, Paris, 2021, https://www.oecd.org/en/publications/21st-century-readers_a83d84cb-en.html